sushi

taste and technique

sushi
taste and technique

Kimiko Barber and Hiroki Takemura

Photography by Ian O'Leary

A Dorling Kindersley Book

LONDON, NEW YORK, MUNICH,
MELBOURNE, and DELHI

Project Editor Hugh Thompson
Project Art Editor Sara Robin
Book Editor Nasim Mawji
Designer Colin Goody
Managing Editor Gillian Roberts
Category Publisher Mary-Clare Jerram
Art Director Tracy Killick
DTP Designers Sonia Charbonnier, Louise Waller
Production Controller Louise Daly

First edition published in Great Britain in 2002
This paperback edition published in 2011
by Dorling Kindersley Limited
80 Strand, London WC2R 0RL
A Penguin Company

A CIP catalogue record for this book
is available from The British Library

ISBN 9781405373388

Colour reproduction by GRB, Italy
Printed and bound in China by Leo

See our complete catalogue at
www.dk.com

Contents

What is sushi?
a history of sushi

The simple definition of sushi is 'vinegared rice with a filling or topping of raw, cooked or marinated fish, shellfish, vegetables, or egg'. It is eaten as a snack, a starter or as a main course and comes in many different forms, from bowls of rice scattered with fish and vegetables to rolled, pressed and hand-formed sushi. Apart from its appeal as a delicious healthfood, sushi is exquisitely and often artistically presented.

In Japan, sushi is an everyday food. It began as a way of preserving fish and grew in popularity to become the nation's most famous food, not only in sushi bars, but also at home where it is prepared and eaten by the whole family. A Japanese ambassador once joked that sushi had done as much to raise the profile of Japan as the country's official efforts.

Sushi's arrival in Japan

No one knows exactly when sushi was invented, but fish was being pickled with rice in Southeast Asia as early as the 5th century BC. Some say that sushi came to Japan with the introduction of rice cultivation in the 4th century BC, while others believe that the practice was brought back by Buddhist priests returning from China after their training in the 7th century AD. The two Chinese characters for sushi, meaning 'preserved

< Rice soon became a staple food of Japan after its introduction in the 4th century BC

< Buddhist priests may have brought sushi back from China in the 7th century AD

Changes in culinary culture

By the middle of the 15th century, rice was being boiled rather than steamed and lunch had been introduced. The Japanese were now eating three meals a day.

Then, at the beginning of the 17th century, the new government moved from the ancient imperial capital city of Kyoto to Edo [now Tokyo]. With the establishment of a powerful political and social structure came increased food production and more rice was grown. The increased rice production led to the wider use of other rice products such

fish' and 'fish fermented in rice and salt', first appeared in Japan at the beginning of the 8th century AD.

Fish preserved in rice was sent to the land-bound capital of Kyoto as a form of tax payment. This early form of sushi, *nare zushi*, made from carp and rice packed into layers and fermented for up to a year, can still be found today. Something of an acquired taste, it is best described as a mixture of very mature Camembert cheese and Thai fish sauce.

∨ Meaning 'sushi' in Japanese, this Chinese symbol first appeared in the 8th century AD

or hand-formed sushi, that we know today. He was the first chef to squeeze vinegared rice into a ball and top it with a slice of raw fish. Although the addition of rice vinegar had reduced preparation time, sushi chefs still made traditional pressed sushi, which took some time to prepare. The residents of Edo were notoriously impatient, so Yohei's newly invented *nigiri zushi*, which took only a few minutes to prepare, soon caught on.

World War Two further boosted the popularity of *nigiri zushi*. Food rationing prevented sushi shops from operating normally. When the Allied Occupation authorities issued a directive allowing the exchange of one cup of rice for 10 pieces of *nigiri zushi* and a sushi roll, they did not include any other type of sushi. To keep his shop open, the sushi chef was forced to make hand-formed sushi.

Sushi stalls disappear

It was at about this time that sushi stalls began to disappear completely. Shops served mainly take-away customers during the day while stalls were familiar

as rice vinegar. Instead of letting rice ferment naturally and produce lactic acid, rice vinegar was added to it, which reduced the time it took to prepare sushi from several days to just a few hours. However, sushi was still pressed in a box and the fish was marinated and boiled or grilled, not eaten raw.

Nigiri zushi – the first fast food

Yohei Hanaya, who set up a sushi stall in Edo in the early 1800s, is widely credited with being the inventor of the *nigiri zushi*,

∧ Pressed sushi is the oldest form of sushi but almost disappeared after World War II

Today it is winning recognition as the world's healthiest fast food. Although I am happy to see sushi gaining in popularity, I am filled with a mixture of delight and sadness when I see it in a supermarket – refrigerated and prepared by machines in factories, it is a far cry from what sushi is meant to be.

I am not dismissing take-away boxes or conveyer-belt sushi, but with fresh ingredients and a little care, you can make your own sushi at home and it will taste far better than anything you could buy ready-prepared.

features on Tokyo street corners in the evening. They were hauled into their alloted place where they were often strategically positioned to catch hungry men on their way back from public bath houses. Customers shared communal bowls of pickled ginger and soy sauce and wiped their hands on a curtain hung behind them. A sure sign of a good sushi stall was a filthy curtain as this showed that more hungry diners had eaten there.

Sushi today

Sushi has come a long way since its origin as a means of preserving fish.

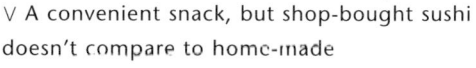

∨ A convenient snack, but shop-bought sushi doesn't compare to home-made

The sushi chef's training
mastering the art of sushi

I have often thought that if I could turn back time and start my life over again, I would like to have trained to be a master sushi chef. It probably wouldn't have been possible – apart from the fact that I am a woman and all sushi chefs are men, the hard training can often take over 10 years to complete. This is my co-author chef Takemura's story.

Starting young

Chef Takemura left school at the age of 15 to work in a sushi bar in his local town of Matsuyama in Shikoku Island. He was lucky to get an apprenticeship in his home-town as many young aspiring sushi chefs have to leave home to work in faraway cities. He knew that many years of hard work lay ahead of him.

Menial tasks

His day started in the early hours of the morning when he would accompany the master or his senior chef to the local fish market as a bag carrier. Here, by carefully watching his master buying the fish for that day, he learned invaluable lessons about selecting only the freshest fish.

Once back in the shop, his job was to clean it until it was spotless. His duties were to deliver platters of sushi around the town, to collect dirty dishes and to do the washing up. He was not allowed anywhere near the fish, let alone the counter where the sushi was prepared – that would take a few more years. He learnt how to prepare sushi rice by quietly watching his master from a distance. When he was finally allowed to stand beside his master, it was to fan the steaming rice in order to cool it.

The counter

It was nearly ten years before Takemura was finally allowed to stand at the counter at the front of the shop. The counter is the most important part of every sushi bar, the stage where sushi chefs perform their art. By then he had moved on to a bigger sushi bar in Osaka, the second biggest city in Japan and the culinary capital. Here he quickly had to discard his regional accent so as not to offend the customers. Now an assistant, or *wakiita*, which literally means 'side chopping board', he was allowed to prepare fish for more senior chefs and to roll sushi for delivery. It took a few more years before he was finally allowed to stand at the counter as an *itamae*, which means 'in front of the chopping board'.

He was now a fully-fledged sushi chef and could prepare his own sushi for customers, but his training did not end there. He had to proactively contribute to the success of the shop, which meant that he had to cultivate his own loyal customers who would return regularly.

The master sushi chef

I first met Takemura in a top Japanese restaurant in London where he was head chef. We had a memorable meal that night, but it wasn't until we returned a few weeks later that I really understood what it takes to be a top sushi chef. Somehow he remembered us, what we ate and our likes and dislikes. He therefore adjusted the menu and the food he prepared for us accordingly.

I urge you to make your own sushi at home, but there is no better way to perfect your technique than to watch a master sushi chef at work.

Health benefits
sushi as a health food

Sushi is not only delicious, it's also very good for you. It is a wonderful bonus to be able to eat the food you love without paying the price for your indulgence. Great claims have been made for the health benefits of the typical Japanese diet of fish and rice. For example, average life expectancy for both women and men in Japan is one of the highest in the world.

Fish and seafood

Sushi is low in calories. White fish such as sea bass and red snapper have less than 100 calories per 100g [3½ oz]. Even richer fish such as mackerel, eel and the fattier cut of tuna, *toro*, have less than 200 calories per 100g [3½ oz]. Oily fish such as mackerel, sardines and herring are high in omega-3 fatty acids, which can be effective in preventing heart disease, strokes and arthritis.

Rice

More than half of the world's population lives on rice. An excellent source of carbohydrate and protein, it is gluten-free so suitable for those with wheat allergies.

Ginger

Like rice vinegar, ginger is an effective natural antiseptic. It aids digestion as well as boosting the immune system and helping the body to fight colds and flu.

Vinegar

Rice vinegar has amazing antibacterial properties, which have long been used to preserve food. It gently aids digestion

∨ Ginger root is pickled and served as a palate cleanser with sushi

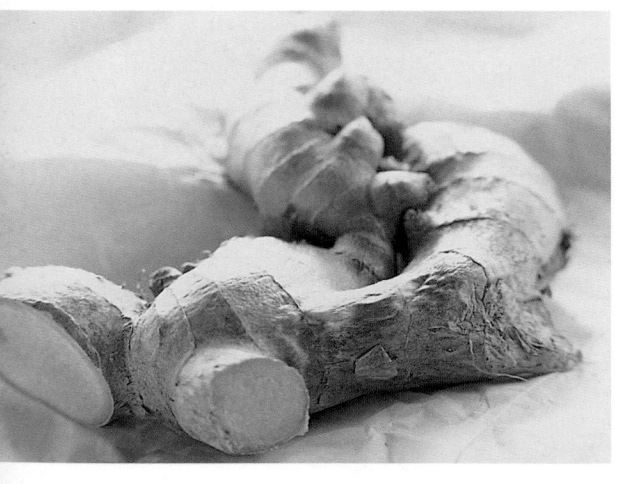

< Shredded nori adds a decorative touch to scattered sushi and soups

Nori

Seaweed may be considered an unusual food by some, but it is highly nutritious. It contains protein, minerals – especially iodine – and is rich in vitamins A, B1, B2, B6, niacin and C. It helps prevent cholesterol deposits from building up in the blood vessels. The darker the nori, the higher the quality.

Wasabi

Rich in vitamin C, wasabi stimulates the production of saliva and aids digestion. It has powerful anti-bacterial properties and is mildly antiseptic.

while also lowering the risk of high blood pressure and working as a mild pick-me-up. In its diluted form it also works as an effective skin conditioner.

Soy sauce

This is made from fermented soybeans, which are high in protein, magnesium, potassium and iron. Soy products contain phytoestrogens, which have been successfully used to treat problems associated with the menopause. A reduced sodium variety is now available. Tamari, which contains no wheat, is a good alternative for those with wheat allergies.

> Soybeans are crushed with salt, wheat and yeast and left to ferment to make soy sauce

Basics

Utensils
dōgu

Although you may have to hunt for the more obscure items, thanks to the ever increasing popularity of sushi, most of the equipment you need to prepare it can be found in the kitchen sections of large department stores or in Japanese or Asian supermarkets. It's always preferable to have the right equipment, but in most cases you can improvise – a springform cake tin or a plastic box lined with clingfilm are good substitutes for a pressed sushi mould, for example.

A set of good knives is a sound investment for any kitchen, but the only essential piece of equipment for which there is no substitute is a bamboo rolling mat for making rolled sushi. For a keen cook, it's always a pleasure adding to your kitchen equipment and most of the traditional equipment is inexpensive and has the advantage of having been designed specifically for sushi preparation.

< In most cases you don't need specialized equipment to make sushi

> A sushi chef's knives are a treasured possession; he regularly cleans and sharpens them, and he wraps them up carefully when not in use

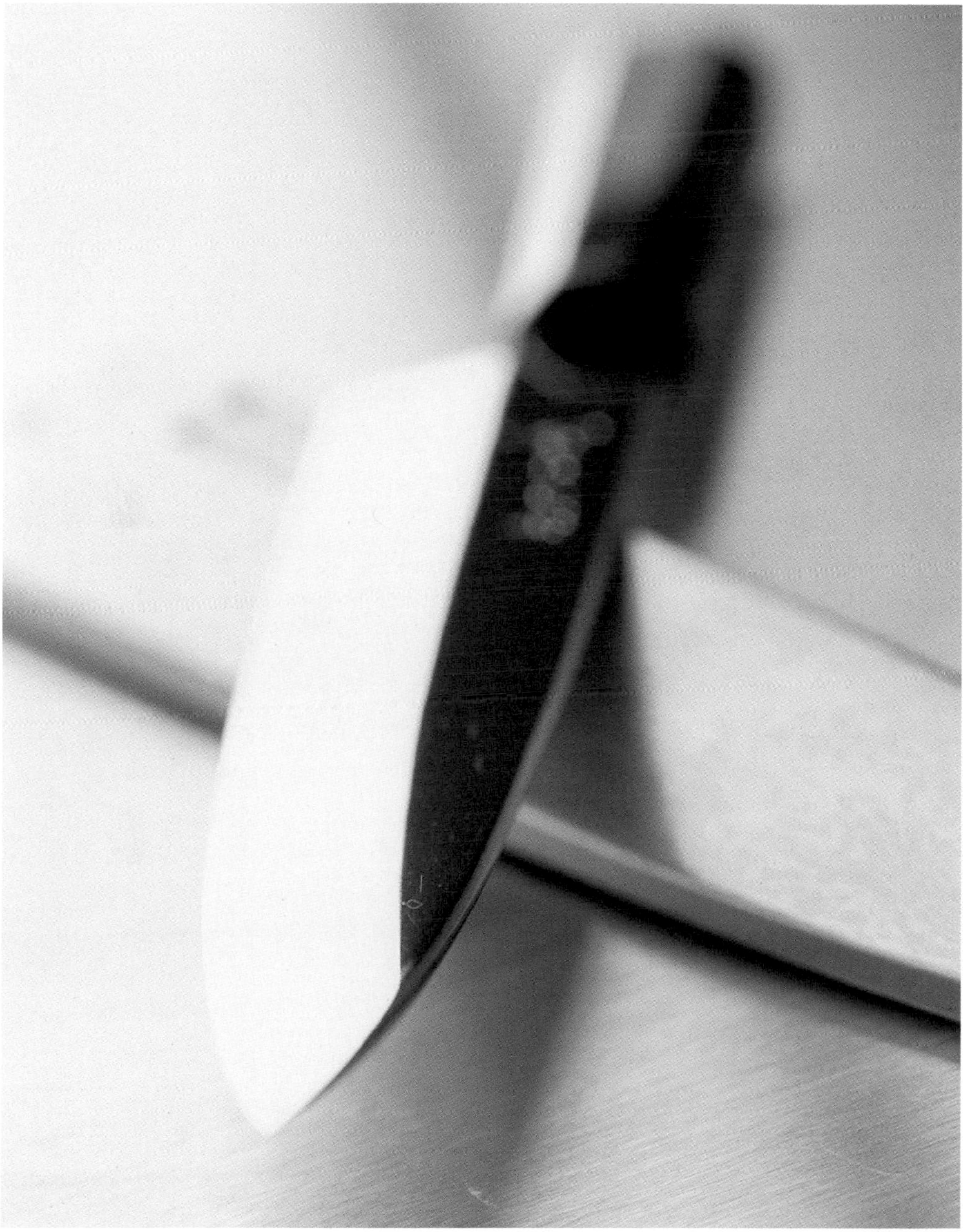

Utensils
specialized equipment

These utensils will make sushi preparation easier and most are available from kitchen sections in large department stores. It is always preferable to have the best tool for the job, but wherever possible, I have suggested good substitutes that can be found in any well-equipped kitchen. The only essential is a bamboo rolling mat for making rolled sushi.

∨ Wooden rice tub [hangiri]

Made of cypress wood and bound with copper wire, this broad low-sided tub is specially designed for preparing sushi rice. Its shape speeds the cooling process and makes it easier to fold in the vinegar

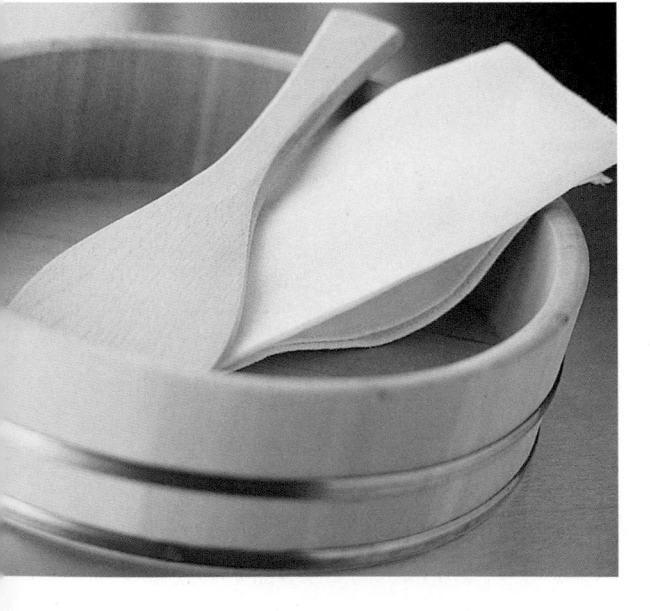

mixture. The wood absorbs the excess moisture and helps give the rice its characteristic glossiness. The tub should be soaked in cold water and then wiped dry before use. After use, wash it in cold water and don't use washing-up liquid. Dry it well to prevent it from going mouldy, and store it upside-down in a cool dark place. A non-metallic salad bowl makes a good alternative.

< Cloth [fukin]

Simple but very useful – damp cotton or linen cloths are used to clean fish, utensils or to wipe the chef's hands.

< Rice paddle [shamoji]

A flat round shaped paddle is traditionally used to serve rice and is made of bamboo or wood. Soak it in cold water before use to prevent rice from sticking to it.

> **Bamboo strainer** [zaru]

This traditional bamboo strainer is indispensable in the Japanese kitchen. It is used in many different cooking processes, from draining water from cooked foods to tenderizing fish skin and marinating mackerel. It must be dried thoroughly and aired well after use, or it will quickly turn musty and mouldy. A plastic or metal colander does the same job, but a real bamboo one is inexpensive and more pleasing to handle.

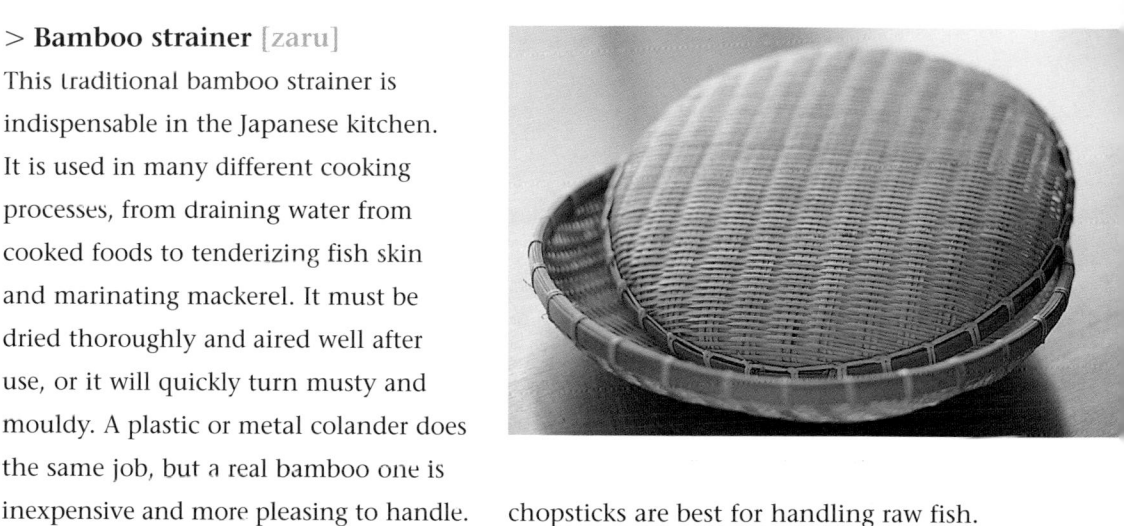

∨ **Cooking chopsticks** [sai bashi]

The chopsticks used for cooking are two or three times the length of ordinary chopsticks. They are long to protect your hands from the heat of cooking. Metal chopsticks are best for handling raw fish. Once you have mastered the technique, chopsticks become the most useful and versatile kitchen implements – an extension of your fingers, they enable you to manipulate food with just one hand. I can't cook without them.

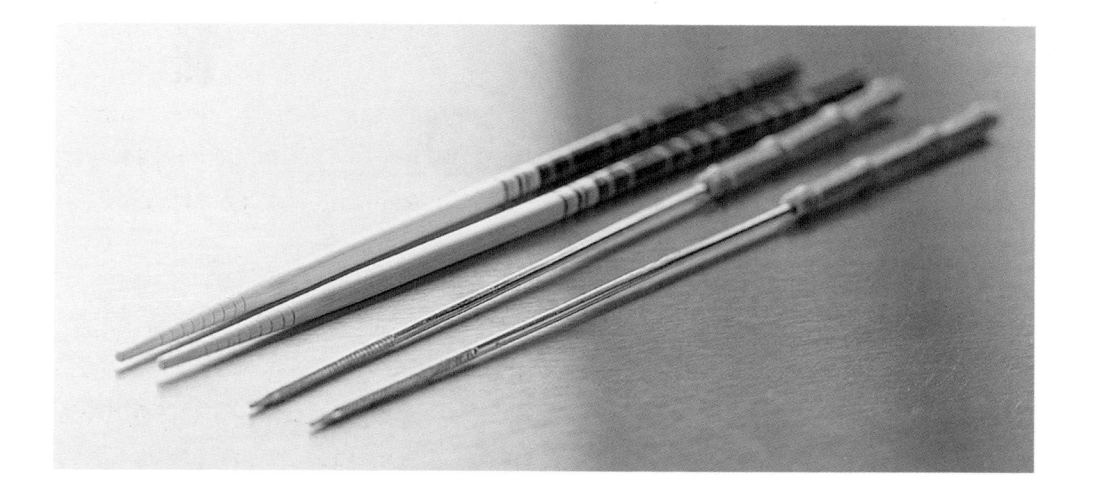

You are more likely to injure yourself with a blunt knife, so look after your knife and it will serve you well. Don't put it in the dishwasher, wash it by hand. Don't store it in a drawer with other kitchen tools that might chip the blade. If you have a knife block, slide the knife into a slot on its back, not on the sharp blade. If you cannot sharpen it yourself, have it done professionally; good kitchen shops should offer the service.

Japanese knives are sharpened on one side of the blade, the cutting edge, which is always on the right side. A sushi chef normally has at least three different types of knife [pictured from left to right]:

Cleaver [deba bōchō]
This knife's heavy, curved blade is ideal for cutting through fish bones.

Vegetable knife [usuba bōchō]
In the hands of a sushi chef, this knife peels, cuts and chops faster and finer than a food processor.

Fish knife [yanagi bōchō]
This long, slender blade is used for slicing fish fillets, cutting sushi rolls and making decorative garnishes.

∧ **Knives** [hōchō]
A sushi chef's knife is as precious to him as a sword to a samurai warrior. The ancient craft of Japanese sword making is still practised today, only it is used to forge kitchen knives made of superior quality carbon steel. These knives need to be properly looked after to maintain their hair-splitting sharpness. They should be sharpened by hand with a whetstone, never with a steel knife sharpener or grinding wheel.

> Shellfish tools

Shellfish and crustaceans such as crab and lobster are popular sushi ingredients, but often it is difficult to get to their meat. The specialized utensils below are not traditional sushi tools, but you'll find them indispensable.

Claw cracker

Crabs and lobsters have hard outer shells and some of their meat is found in their even harder claws. Although you can use a hammer or even the blade of a heavy kitchen knife to crack the shells open and get at the meat, it is easier to control the force – and also avoid unnecessary damage to the meat – if you use a claw cracker. If you haven't got a claw cracker, a nut cracker is just as effective.

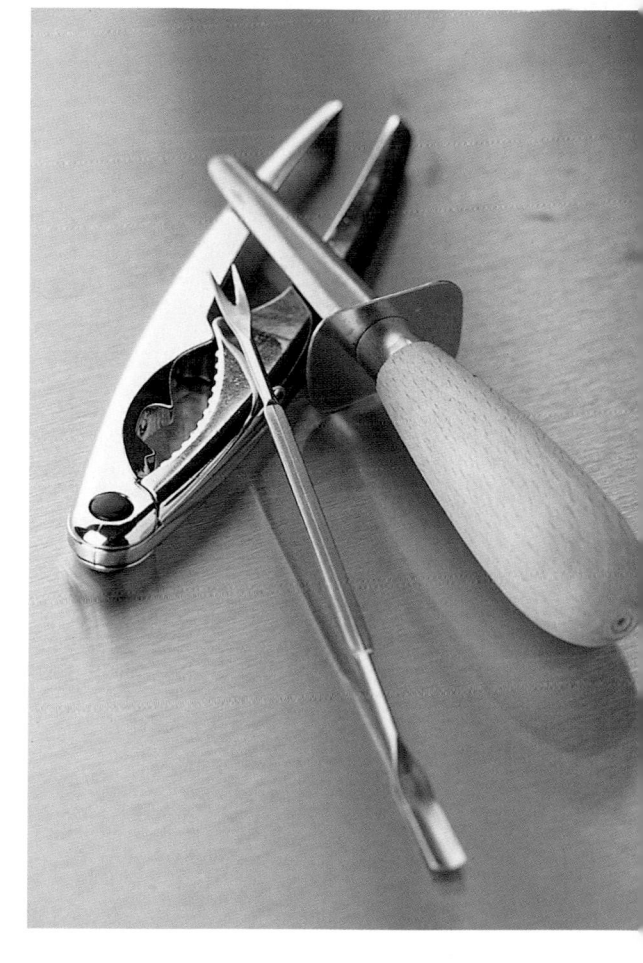

Crab pick

This is for reaching the more inaccessible meat in the recesses of the crab shell. A cocktail fork or a skewer is a good substitute, but the correct tool will make your work much easier.

Oyster knife

This is for opening oyster and scallop shells. You can use a screwdriver or the blade of small kitchen knife instead, but they are more likely to damage the oyster inside or worse still cut your hands. To open an oyster, hold it steady with a tea towel wrapped around it, then insert the tip of the oyster knife blade and twist [see p122].

> Fish scaler

A fish scaler simply removes the scales of the fish without damaging the flesh. The back of a kitchen knife or even a scallop shell make effective substitutes, but again, having the right tool will make the job much easier. When scaling fish, a useful tip is to place it inside a large plastic bag to catch flying fish scales.

< Japanese square omelette pan

The thick Japanese omelette [see p40–42] is traditionally made in a square pan with a depth of 2cm [1in]. This type of omelette pan is usually made from thick, heat-retaining metal and has a good solid feel to it. It is possible to use a conventional round skillet or frying pan of about 20cm [10in] in diameter instead; simply trim off the round edges of the finished omelette to make it square.

< Bamboo rolling mat [makisu]
Essential for making any type of rolled sushi, the bamboo rolling mat is made of bamboo sticks woven together with cotton string. There is no real substitute for it, but the mats are not expensive and are easily available from any good kitchen shop. Choose a large tightly woven one. Wash and clean it with cold water and wipe dry immediately after use otherwise water will soak into the bamboo slats and attract mould.

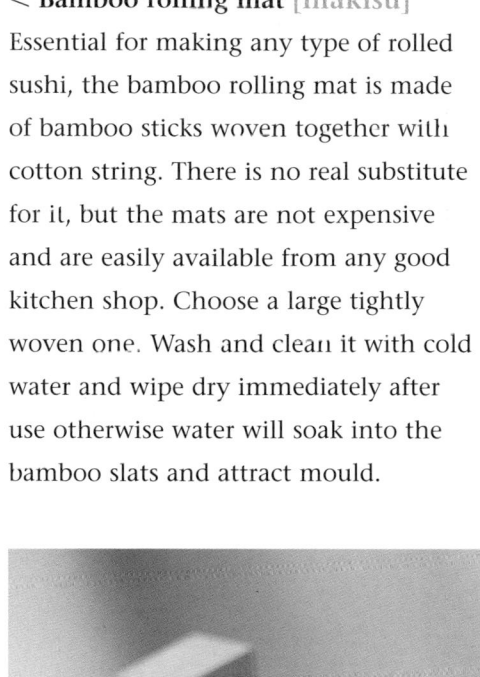

> Pressed sushi mould [oshibako]
Traditionally made from cypress wood, which is the same wood usually used for the sushi counter, pressed sushi moulds have removable bottoms and lids. They come in various sizes and may be square or rectangular in shape. To prevent the rice from sticking they need to be soaked in cold water before use and the excess water wiped away with a damp cloth. Care for it in the same way as the rice tub [see p18]. A rectangular springform cake tin or a plastic box lined with cling film are good substitutes.

Ingredients
zairyō

Sushi's ever-increasing popularity has made it much easier to find the essentials
in large supermarkets – staple ingredients such as Japanese-style short grain rice,
nori seaweed, wasabi, rice vinegar and Japanese soy sauce are readily available.
Wherever possible, I have suggested substitutes, but for best results try to use the
real thing. More unusual ingredients are available from specialist Japanese food
shops or by mail order [see p250–51].

Ingredients such as dried gourd [*kampyō*] and shiitake mushrooms need to be
reconstituted and flavoured in a seasoned broth before use. You need to set aside
time to do this, but they can be prepared in advance and kept in an airtight
container in the refrigerator for up to three days. Most of the ingedients in the
pages that follow have long shelf-lives if kept in the right conditions, so stock up
and all you'll need to shop for when making sushi are the fish and vegetables.

< Sake, Japanese rice wine, is used to tenderize
meat and fish and to enhance flavour; inexpensive
cooking varieties are available

> Fresh wasabi root is very difficult to find, even
in Japan; it is normally sold in powdered form or
ready made up in tubes

Ingredients
storecupboard essentials

Many of the essential ingredients needed for making sushi at home, Japanese-style rice, soy sauce and wasabi, for example, are available in large supermarkets these days. More specialist sushi ingredients are easy to find in Japanese food shops and most have long shelf-lives. I have suggested alternatives wherever possible.

> Japanese-style rice [kome]

Japanese short grain rice is essential for sushi. It is high in starch, which gives it its characteristic stickiness when cooked. Store it in a cool dark place in an airtight container. Long grain rice such as basmati is not suitable for sushi as it is too hard and dry and does not possess the necessary absorbency. The US, Spain and China grow short grain rice.

< Dried seaweed sheets [nori]

Sheets of nori are used for rolled sushi; shredded, it makes an attractive garnish for other types of sushi. It is made from different types of Porphyra algae that are washed and spread thinly to dry on mesh sheets. Choose nori that is dark and tightly grained; the thinner and greener, the more inferior the quality. Store it in an airtight bag or container in a dark place.

Japanese horseradish [wasabi]

This green horseradish is also known as *namida*, meaning tears, as it is fiercely pungent. Wasabi should not be used to prove one's bravery, but eaten in very small quantities, it will enhance the flavour of the sushi. It is readily available as a powder and ready-mixed in tubes.

∧ **Fresh wasabi roots**
The fresh root is native to Japan and grows there in clear mountain streams. It is expensive in its fresh form and usually difficult to obtain outside of Japan.

∨ **Ready-mixed tubes of wasabi**
Although convenient to use, once opened, the wasabi quickly loses its pungency and flavour.

∧ **Powdered wasabi**
Widely available from supermarkets and Japanese shops, powdered wasabi has a long shelf-life and retains its flavour well. Make a stiff paste by mixing 1 tsp wasabi powder with 1 tsp water. Leave to stand for 5–10 minutes before use to allow the flavours to develop. The paste can be moulded into decorative shapes and used as a garnish [see p51].

light soy sauce   dark soy sauce   tamari

∧ **Soy sauce** [shōyu]

This is probably the most important seasoning in Japanese cooking. Made from fermented soybeans, wheat and salt, both light and dark varieties are available. Light sauce is saltier than the dark variety and not as thick. Dark soy sauce is used both as an ingredient and as a dipping sauce for sushi. Tamari is a wheat-free alternative that is more fragrant than soy sauce.

> **Pickled ginger** [gari]

Usually served on the corner of a sushi tray to accompany sushi, pink pickled ginger should be eaten a slice at a time. It cleanses the palate between mouthfuls and aids digestion. Although you can make your own, ready-prepared is normally of good quality. Once opened, it should be kept in the refrigerator.

> **Rice vinegar** [su]
Pale gold in colour, Japanese rice vinegar has a mild slightly tart flavour and leaves a subtle aftertaste. It is an essential ingredient in sushi, not least because it is used to flavour the rice. Rice vinegar is a preservative and also has antibacterial properties. It is available in Japanese food shops and supermarkets but cider or red wine vinegar diluted with a little water make adequate substitutes.

∧ **Japanese rice wine** [sake]
The national alcoholic drink of Japan, sake is one of the best accompaniments to sushi and can be drunk hot or cold. It is an important ingredient in cooking, where it is used to tenderize meat and fish, and to enhance flavour. Dry sherry is a good substitute. For cooking purposes, buy sake labelled as *ryori* sake, or inexpensive drinking sake.

> **Sweet rice wine** [mirin]
Also known as sweet sake, mirin is used strictly for cooking. If unavailable, use 1 tsp sugar for 1 tbsp mirin. Store in a cool, dark place after opening.

∨ **Dried gourd** [kampyō]

Kampyo is sold dried in long, thin strips.
It is traditionally used as a filling for
rolled sushi, chopped up as a topping for
scattered sushi and also makes a useful
ribbon to tie parcels of stuffed sushi.
It has a firm almost chewy texture. It
is available from Japanese food shops.
Before use, it needs to be reconstituted
in a lightly seasoned broth [see right].
Prepared kampyo will keep refrigerated
in a sealed container for three days.

∧ **Preparing kampyo**

Wash 30g [1oz] kampyo in cold water
with a scrubbing action. Add 2 tbsp salt
and rub in the water until soft [see above].
Rinse and soak in water for two hours
or overnight [check packet instructions].
Drain, place in a saucepan with enough
fresh water to cover and simmer for
10–15 minutes. Add 500ml [17floz]
dashi [see p39], 2 tbsp sugar and 2 tbsp
soy sauce, bring to the boil, then simmer
for 10 minutes or until the kampyo is
golden [see below]. Allow to cool in the
stock before cutting to desired lengths.

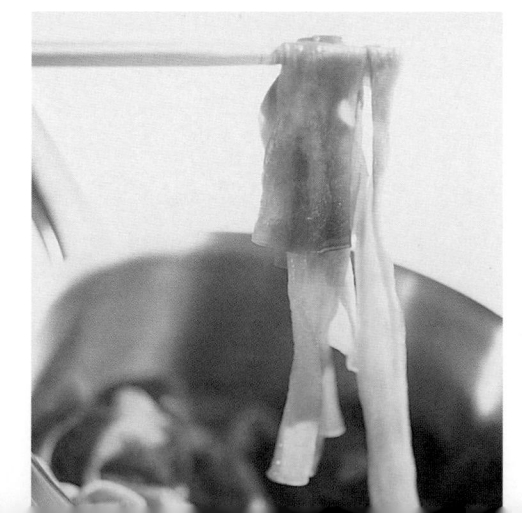

∧ Dried shiitake mushrooms

These intensely flavoured mushrooms
are used as a filling in thick roll sushi
and as a versatile topping for scattered,
pressed and hand-formed sushi. They
will keep for up to six months in a cool,
dry place. They need to be reconstituted
and seasoned before use [see right], but
when soaked, good-quality shiitake are
fleshy, plump and meaty tasting and
stronger in flavour than fresh ones.

∧ Seasoning shiitake mushrooms

Soak 30g [1oz] dried shiitake mushrooms
in 250ml [8floz] hot water for about
20 minutes. Drain, reserving the soaking
liquid, and cut off and discard the stems.
Add the mushrooms to 250ml [8floz]
dashi [see p39] and the reserved liquid
in a saucepan, and cook over a gentle
heat for about 30 minutes or until the
liquid has reduced by half. Add 1 tbsp
mirin, then remove from heat and let
cool in the liquid before using.

< Perilla leaves [shiso]

This aromatic Japanese herb belongs to
the mint family. It resembles the stinging
nettle, with its fringed leaves, but has no
sting. It has a distinctive, pungent flavour
and is often used as an edible garnish for
sushi platters and sashimi arrangements.

∨ **Bonito flakes** [katsuo bushi]

The pink flakes are traditionally shaved from blocks of the dried, smoked and cured bonito fish [see p58]. They are essential for flavouring dashi, the classic Japanese stock [see p39]. Packets of shaved bonito flakes are available from Japanese food shops.

∧ **Kelp** [konbu]

This seaweed grows near Hokkaido island, north Japan and is cooked, pickled and then dried. Before use, wipe it with a damp cloth – do not wash it, as this will destroy its flavour and nutrients. It keeps indefinitely in an airtight container. Choose dark – almost black – thick sheets, not thin green wrinkled ones.

< **Toasted sesame seeds** [iri goma]

Both black and white sesame seeds are available ready-toasted from Japanese food shops, but their nutty flavour tends to fade. To revive their flavour, dry toast them in a pan over gentle heat for 1–2 minutes; keep them moving to prevent burning, which makes them bitter.

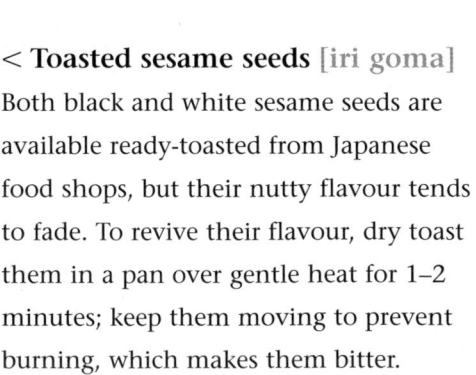

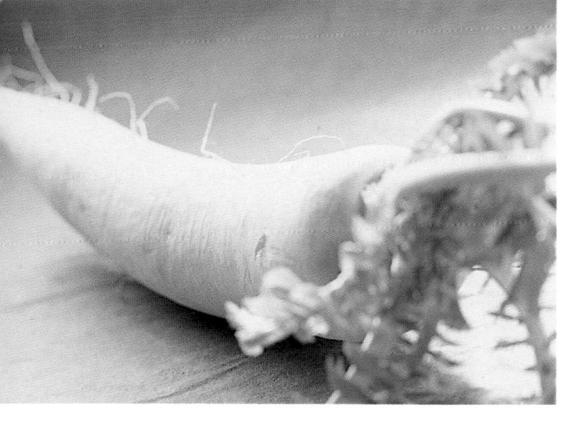

∧ **Mouli** [daikon]

This large white radish is available from Asian supermarkets. Its subtle yet pungent flavour makes it an ideal accompaniment to sushi and sashimi. It can be cut into decorative shapes or shredded [see p48] and used as a garnish. It should be peeled and soaked in cold water before use.

∧ **Making chilli daikon relish**

This mildly spicy fresh-tasting relish is the ideal accompaniment to Seared Beef Fillet and Red Onion Sushi [see p146]. Peel 250g [8oz] daikon, soak briefly, then grate it into a bowl. Deseed and finely chop a small red chilli [or use a teaspoon of chilli paste] and mix with the daikon.

< **Lotus root** [renkon]

The crunchy white root of the water lily, lotus root is white and honeycombed with holes. Highly seasonal, it is not always available fresh, even in Japan. Fresh lotus root is peeled and boiled in a mixture of water, sugar and rice vinegar until soft. It is usually available tinned or pickled in vinegar from Japanese shops – this needs no further cooking.

Basic recipes
kihon

Preparing sushi does not have to be time-consuming and complicated. Some of the ingredients may be new to you, but the basic recipes are straightforward and easy for any moderately confident cook to master. The key to quick and effortless sushi is good organization. If you prepare your ingredients beforehand, making sushi is simply a matter of assembly.

At the base of it all is the vinegared sushi rice, *sushi meshi*. Apprentice sushi chefs can spend several years just watching the master chef before being allowed to prepare the sushi rice, but here you'll find a simple step-by-step recipe that, with a little practice, will ensure success. Remember that you can make rice in the morning, store it at room temperature covered with a clean damp cloth and use it the same day.

Most cooks will be familiar with techniques such as making thin Japanese omelettes and scrambled eggs, but new recipes only require a little practice. Your first attempts at making sushi may lack the perfection of the master sushi chef's, but they will still look impressive enough and they will certainly taste delicious.

< Perfect sushi rice is firm, slightly sticky and flavoured with a delicate balance of sugar and vinegar, which gives it its characteristic gloss

> Dried bonito flakes are added to the pot to make *dashi*, the basic Japanese stock

Preparing sushi rice
sushi meshi

Good sushi begins with good quality rice. Choose
Japanese-style short grain rice, which is available from
large supermarkets and Japanese food shops. The rice
is first cooked, then it is flavoured with a mixture of
vinegar, sugar and salt. The general rule is the stronger
the filling or topping served with it, the more salty and
less sweet the vinegar mixture. In Japan, every sushi bar
has its own closely guarded vinegar mixture recipe. Once
prepared, cover the rice with a clean damp cloth until
needed; use it on the same day and don't refrigerate it.
Soak the rice tub beforehand to prevent sticking.

Ingredients

*300g [10 oz] Japanese
short grain rice*

330ml [11 fl oz] water

*1 postcard size piece of
kombu [optional]*

for vinegar mixture:

4 tbsp Japanese rice vinegar

2 tbsp sugar

½ tsp salt

Preparation time
1 hour 30 minutes

1 Put the rice in a sieve and
submerge in a large bowl
of water. Wash it thoroughly
and discard the milky water.
Keep washing and changing
the water until it is clear.
Drain the water and leave
the rice to stand in the sieve
for 30 minutes.

2 If using kombu, make a few cuts in it to help release its flavour as it cooks.

3 Put the washed rice and water in a heavy-bottomed saucepan. Add the kombu, if using, and cover with a close-fitting lid. Bring to the boil over a medium heat. Resist the temptation to lift the lid, and listen for the sound of boiling instead. Adjust the heat, if necessary, to prevent the water boiling over and cook for a further 3–5 minutes.

4 Reduce the heat to its lowest setting and simmer for a further 8–10 minutes, then remove from the heat and leave to stand for 10 minutes. Lift the lid and discard the kombu.

5 Heat the ingredients for the vinegar mixture in a non-aluminium saucepan, stirring until the sugar and salt have dissolved. Don't allow it to boil. Remove from the heat and set aside to cool. Transfer the cooked rice to a pre-soaked wooden rice tub or salad bowl. Pour a little of the vinegar mixture over a spatula into the rice.

6 Spread the rice evenly in the tub. Slowly add a little more of the vinegar mixture, using a slicing action to coat the grains of rice and separate them.

7 Fan the rice gently to cool it. Continue to fold the vinegar mixture into the rice with the spatula until it begins to look glossy and has cooled to room temperature.

Making Japanese stock
dashi

Dashi is the basic stock used to flavour many Japanese dishes. For a vegetarian version, omit the bonito flakes and double the quantity of kombu. If you prefer a stronger flavoured stock, once strained, return the dashi to the heat and simmer gently for a further 10 minutes.

Ingredients

1 postcard-size piece of kombu

1 litre [1¾ pints] water

10g [⅓ oz] bonito fish flakes

Preparation time
20 minutes

1 Prepare the kombu [see p37]. Put the water in a saucepan, add the kombu and bring to the boil over a medium heat. Just before boiling point, remove the kombu and discard. Add the bonito flakes and bring back to the boil. Do not stir.

2 Remove from the heat when the dashi begins to boil. When the bonito flakes have settled, strain the dashi through a muslin-lined sieve.

Thick Japanese omelette
dashi maki tamago

Some sushi connoisseurs suggest that you begin your meal with a piece of hand-formed sushi topped with thick Japanese omelette in order to test a sushi shop's rice and vinegar mix. The omelette is slightly sweet in flavour and succulently moist. It's best to use a square Japanese omelette pan, but you can use a round pan and trim the round ends off the omelette. Once prepared, it keeps for a day wrapped in clingfilm and refrigerated.

Ingredients
6 eggs, beaten

125ml [4floz] dashi stock [p39]

2 tbsp sugar

1 tsp salt

1 tbsp sake [optional]

1 tbsp mirin [optional]

1 tbsp vegetable oil for frying

Preparation time
20 minutes

1 Combine the eggs and all the remaining ingredients except the oil in a mixing bowl. Heat the oil in a square omelette pan; wipe away excess oil with a piece of folded kitchen paper.

2 Drop a small amount of egg mixture into the pan to test the temperature. If it sizzles, the pan is hot enough. Ladle a third of the mixture into the pan, so that the base is thinly covered.

3 Cook over a medium heat until the surface begins to set and the edges begin to crisp.

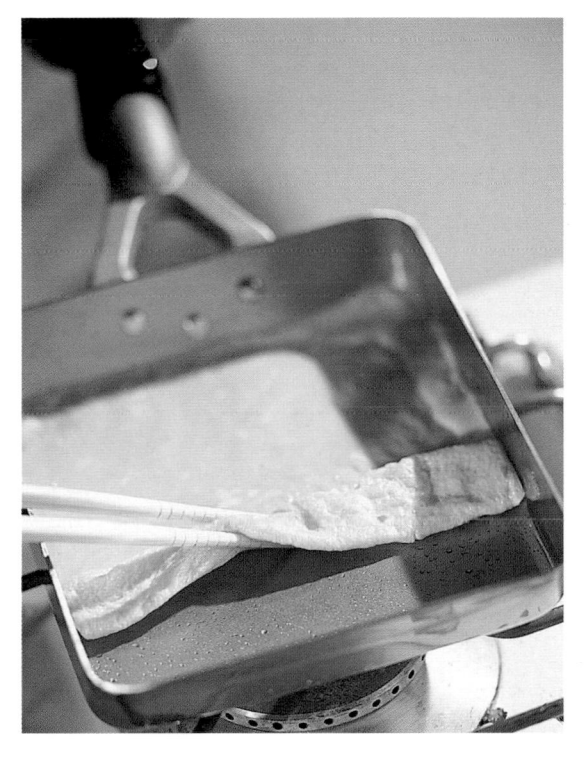

4 Fold the omelette towards you in quarter sections using either chopsticks or a fork.

5 Push the folded omelette to the far end of the pan.

7 When the egg begins to set, fold it towards you in quarters with the first roll at the centre.

8 Shape the omelette roll by gently pushing it against the side of the pan. Repeat the process until all the egg mixture is finished. Remove from the heat, and set aside to cool before cutting.

6 Add a little more oil to the exposed surface of the pan. Ladle in enough egg mixture to coat the base of the pan. Gently lift the folded omelette to allow the egg mixture to cover the entire base of the pan.

Scrambled eggs
tamago soboro

The key to preparing Japanese scrambled eggs is to use cooking chopsticks to stir them. This action gives them their stringy appearance and keeps the pieces separate. Try them as a colourful topping for scattered sushi.

Ingredients

2 eggs, beaten

1 tsp sugar

1 tsp salt

1 tsp vegetable oil

Preparation time
10 minutes

1 Combine the eggs, sugar and salt in a mixing bowl. Heat the oil in a frying pan over a medium heat. Pour the egg mixture into the pan, and cook stirring continuously with either chopsticks or a whisk.

2 When the egg begins to set, remove the pan from the heat but continue to stir to get a fluffy consistency.

Thin Japanese omelette
usuyaki tamago

This thin omelette is folded and stuffed with sushi rice or thinly sliced, known as *kinshi tamago* or 'golden shreds', and used as a topping for scattered sushi. This should make two to three omelettes, using an omelette pan about 18cm [7in] in size.

Ingredients

1 tsp cornflour

1 egg

1 egg yolk

1 tsp salt

1 tbsp vegetable oil

Makes 2–3 omelettes

Preparation time
5 minutes per omelette

1 Dissolve the cornflour in a tablespoon of water. Add to a mixing bowl with all the remaining ingredients except the oil and mix well. Heat the oil in a pan over a medium heat [wipe away excess oil with a piece of folded kitchen paper], then pour in enough egg mixture to coat the base of the pan thinly.

2 When the omelette begins to set, pick it up and turn it over with a chopstick or fork to cook the other side. Don't allow the omelette to crisp or overcook – it should remain a golden yellow colour.

3 Remove from the pan and transfer to an upturned bamboo strainer or a plate lined with kitchen paper while you repeat the process to make more omelettes.

4 Either cut the round edges off the omelettes for omelette parcels or roll up and cut into fine shreds.

Seasoning deep-fried tofu
abura age

Deep-fried tofu, or *abura age*, can be eaten without any further preparation but its flavour is much improved by seasoning. The pieces are cut in half and stuffed with sushi rice or chopped for scattered sushi. Available from Japanese shops, deep-fried tofu can be bought seasoned or unseasoned. Once seasoned, they will keep for up to three days in an airtight container in the refrigerator.

Ingredients

3 pieces deep-fried tofu

½ quantity dashi stock [p39]

3 tbsp sugar

4–5 tbsp soy sauce

2 tbsp sake

2 tbsp mirin

Makes 6 pouches

Preparation time
30 minutes

1 Roll a chopstick over each piece of tofu to make it easier to open. Cut each one in half and then gently open it to make a pouch. Place in a bamboo strainer or colander and pour boiling water over both sides to remove oil.

2 Heat the remaining ingredients in a saucepan and add the tofu pouches. Simmer over a low heat until most of the liquid has reduced, about 15–20 minutes. Remove from the heat and drain in a bamboo strainer or colander.

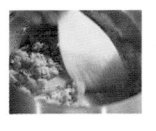

Making ground fish
soboro

This seasoned ground fish is often dyed pale pink with beetroot powder or vegetable dye. It makes a colourful filling for rolled sushi, brightens up scattered sushi and can be a cheerful topping for children's pressed sushi. It is available in bottles from Japanese shops, but is easy to prepare at home and will keep for up to four weeks in the freezer.

Ingredients

200g [7oz] white fish such as cod or plaice, skinned and bones removed

½ tsp beetroot powder or red food colouring

1 tbsp sugar

1 tbsp sake or water

½ tsp salt

Preparation time
45 minutes

1 Bring a saucepan of water to the boil, add the fish and boil for 10 minutes, then drain. Heat the fish in a saucepan over a low heat for about 5–10 minutes, stirring continuously to break it up. Don't let the fish burn.

2 Dissolve the beetroot powder or food colouring and sugar in the sake or water. Add to the fish, stirring continuously to mix and fluff it up. Season with salt.

Garnishes and decorations
tsuma / kazari

It's not enough for sushi simply to taste delicious –
take care over presentation as well. Carrot, daikon
and cucumber can be cut into flowers or shredded, and
clever knife work can transform a cucumber into a pine
branch to decorate sushi and soups. Wasabi leaves add
an artistic touch to sushi and sashimi arrangements.

> **Specialized equipment**
> *flower-shaped vegetable cutter*
>
> **Preparation time**
> about 5 minutes per decoration

making carrot flowers

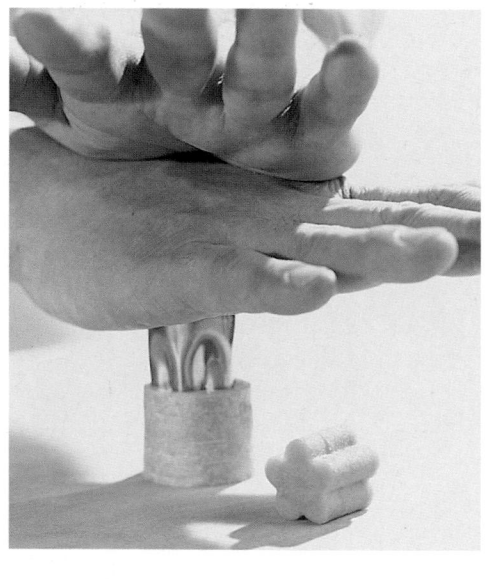

1 Peel a small to medium-sized carrot and cut
into 4 cm [1¾ in] lengths. Place a piece of
carrot on its end on a stable chopping board and
use a vegetable cutter to cut it into flower-shaped
pieces. Repeat with the remaining pieces.

2 Slice the carrot pieces as thinly as possible
to make small flowers.

shredding cucumber

1 Take a 6 cm [2½ in] piece of cucumber and slice about 1 cm [½ in] off lengthways to give a flat edge. Cut several very thin slices, stopping when you reach the seeded core. Rotate the cucumber and do the same on the other side.

2 Place the slices on top of each other and slice thinly to give a shredded effect. Soak in water for 10 minutes, then use as a garnish.

making an expert cucumber garnish

1 Insert a knife blade under the skin of a 10 cm [4 in] length of cucumber. Turn the cucumber against the knife to produce a long thin sheet.

2 Cut the cucumber sheet into several equal sized pieces, pile on top of each other and slice carefully into fine strands. Soak in water for 10 minutes, then use as a garnish.

making a cucumber pine branch

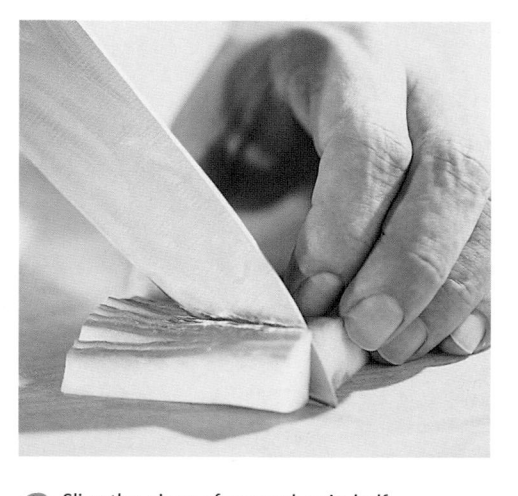

1 Cut a 6cm [2½ in] long piece of cucumber in half and cut off the skin on the sides. Make a series of lengthways cuts about 2–3mm [⅛ in] apart, leaving a 1cm [½ in] base at the end.

2 Slice the piece of cucumber in half lengthways.

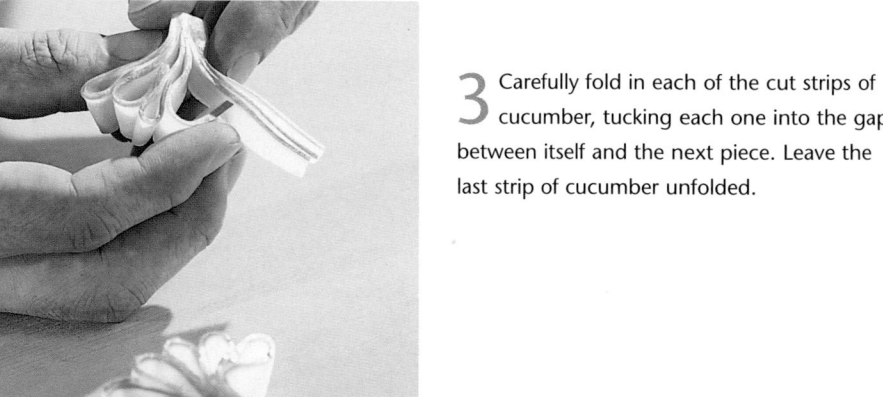

3 Carefully fold in each of the cut strips of cucumber, tucking each one into the gap between itself and the next piece. Leave the last strip of cucumber unfolded.

making a wasabi leaf

1 To make 4 leaves, mix 8 tbsp wasabi powder to a smooth paste with a little water. Take a quarter of the mixture and work it into a cylindrical shape by rolling it in the palm of your hand.

2 Place the cylinder on a chopping board and pinch one end to make a stem. Flatten the cylinder with the flat part of a knife blade and mould into a leaf shape with your fingers. Smooth over any cracks with a damp knife blade, if necessary.

3 Use a knife to score a stem and the veins of a leaf on to the wasabi. Repeat the process to make the remaining leaves.

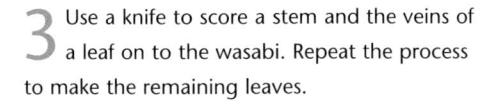

Round and flat fish
sakana

The pages that follow will help you to identify fish that are suitable for sushi and sashimi and help you to buy them in their freshest state and in season – not only because their flavour and texture are better, but because they cost less. You will also learn which cuts of fish to choose and the correct way to prepare them.

I cannot stress enough the importance of buying the freshest fish possible for sushi and sashimi. A whole fish offers more clues to its freshness than a small cut piece, and although it is not always practical to buy a whole fish, it is often possible to see it before it is filleted. Check the following when buying fish:

• The eyes – should be clear, bright and plump, not cloudy and sunken.

• The gills – should be a bright pink or red colour, not a dark, murky red.

• The body – press it gently; it should feel firm and springy, not spongy and sticky.

• The smell – fresh fish smells clean and fresh from the sea, not unpleasantly fishy. You will become more confident in your judgement with a little experience. Make friends with your fishmonger – he or she should be happy to answer your questions.

< Fresh fish fillets should be moist but not watery, almost translucent and firm enough to slice easily with a sharp knife

> Whole specimens often give a better idea of the freshness of the fish. A well-looked after fish should look like it has just come out of the sea

Horse mackerel
aji

For the Japanese, horse mackerel are one of the most popular *hikari mono*, or 'shiny things', a term that refers to oily fish with shiny silver/blue skin. It is inexpensive, available throughout the year and has a simple yet satisfying taste. However, outside Japan, its bony skeleton, sharp spines and strong flavour make it something of an acquired taste – indeed it is often discarded when caught on mackerel lines. Like all oily fish, horse mackerel can lower blood cholesterol levels, which can help prevent heart disease and strokes.

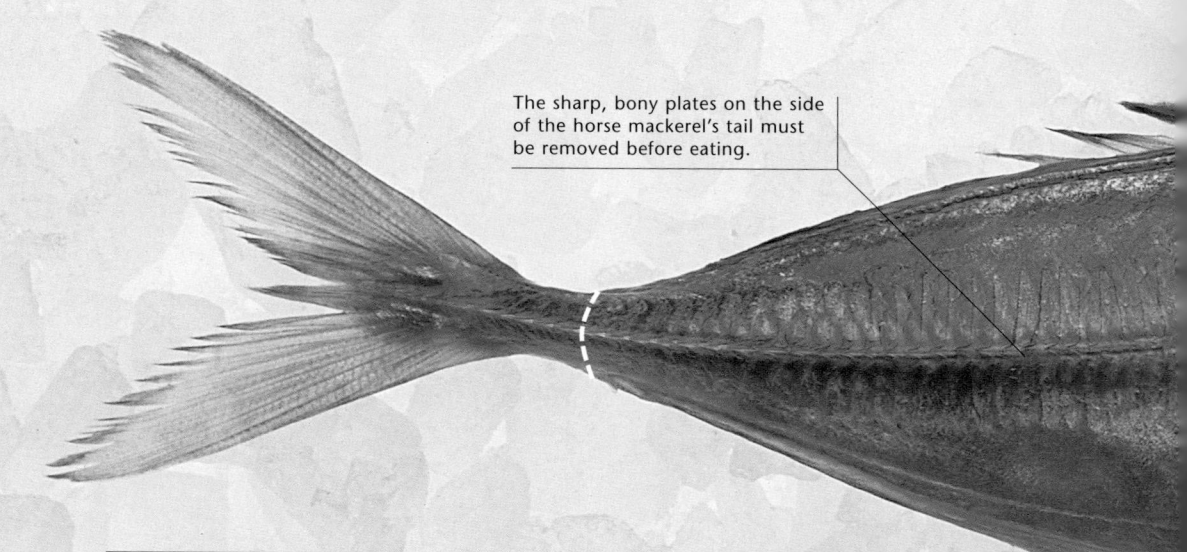

The sharp, bony plates on the side of the horse mackerel's tail must be removed before eating.

Availability

There are 13 varieties of horse mackerel widely distributed in shallow waters around the world. Although available all year round, horse mackerel are at their best at certain times of the year: in Australia and Japan they are best in winter; in North America, along the east coast, they reach their prime during spring and summer, and in Europe during summer and autumn.

fillets are usually sold with the skin left on

Horse mackerel fillets

As for all oily fish used in sushi, horse mackerel are served with the skin intact. They are milder in flavour than mackerel.

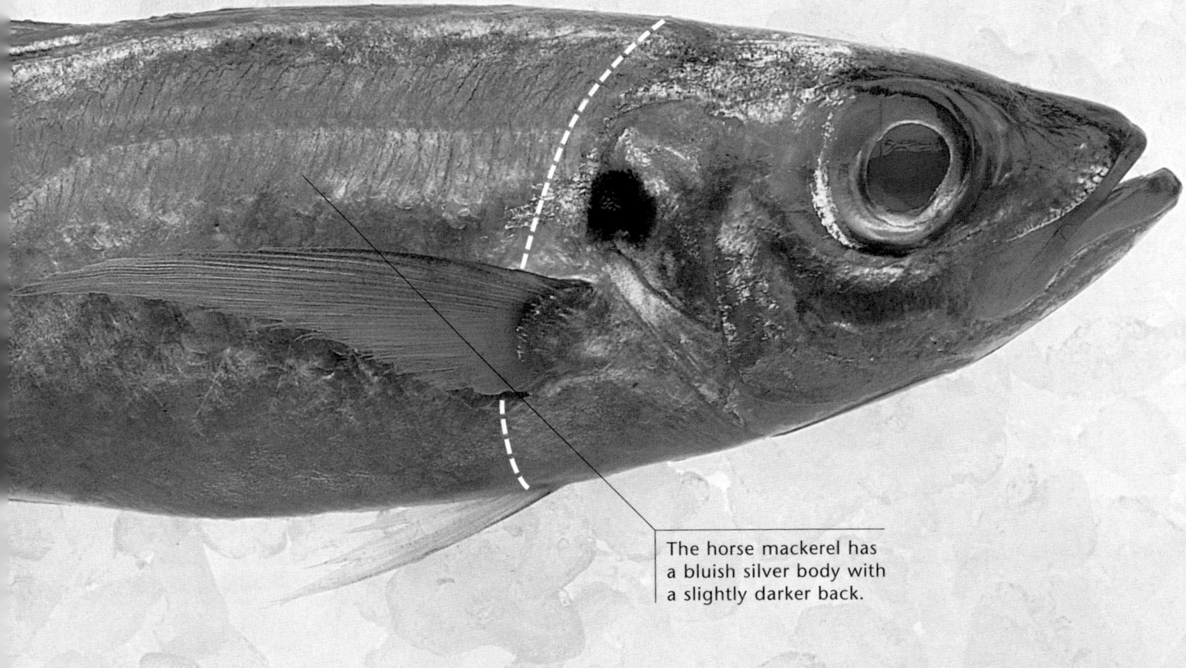

distinctive firm, red flesh

The horse mackerel has a bluish silver body with a slightly darker back.

Herring and sardine
nishin / iwashi

Herring and sardines are closely related; there are some 180 varieties found across the world. Both of these distinctively flavoured fish are classified as *hikari mono*, or 'shiny things' by the Japanese. Herring and sardines are rich in beneficial oils and have recently been reappraised as a healthfood. However, like *aji*, they are rarely seen on sushi menus, mainly because they spoil very quickly once caught. In Japan, herring are highly valued for their roes, which are known as *kazunoko*, or 'yellow diamonds'.

Herring and sardine fillets
Herring and sardines need to have their scales removed, but the fillets are served with the skin intact.

scales are easily removed

sardine fillets can still contain lots of feathery bones

Availability

Sardines are commercially important in North America and are available all year round, but are not at their best during summer. Herring are available all year round in Europe, but are best from May to September. They are in season between December and February on the Pacific coast of North America, when they produce herring roe, and between winter and spring on the Atlantic coast.

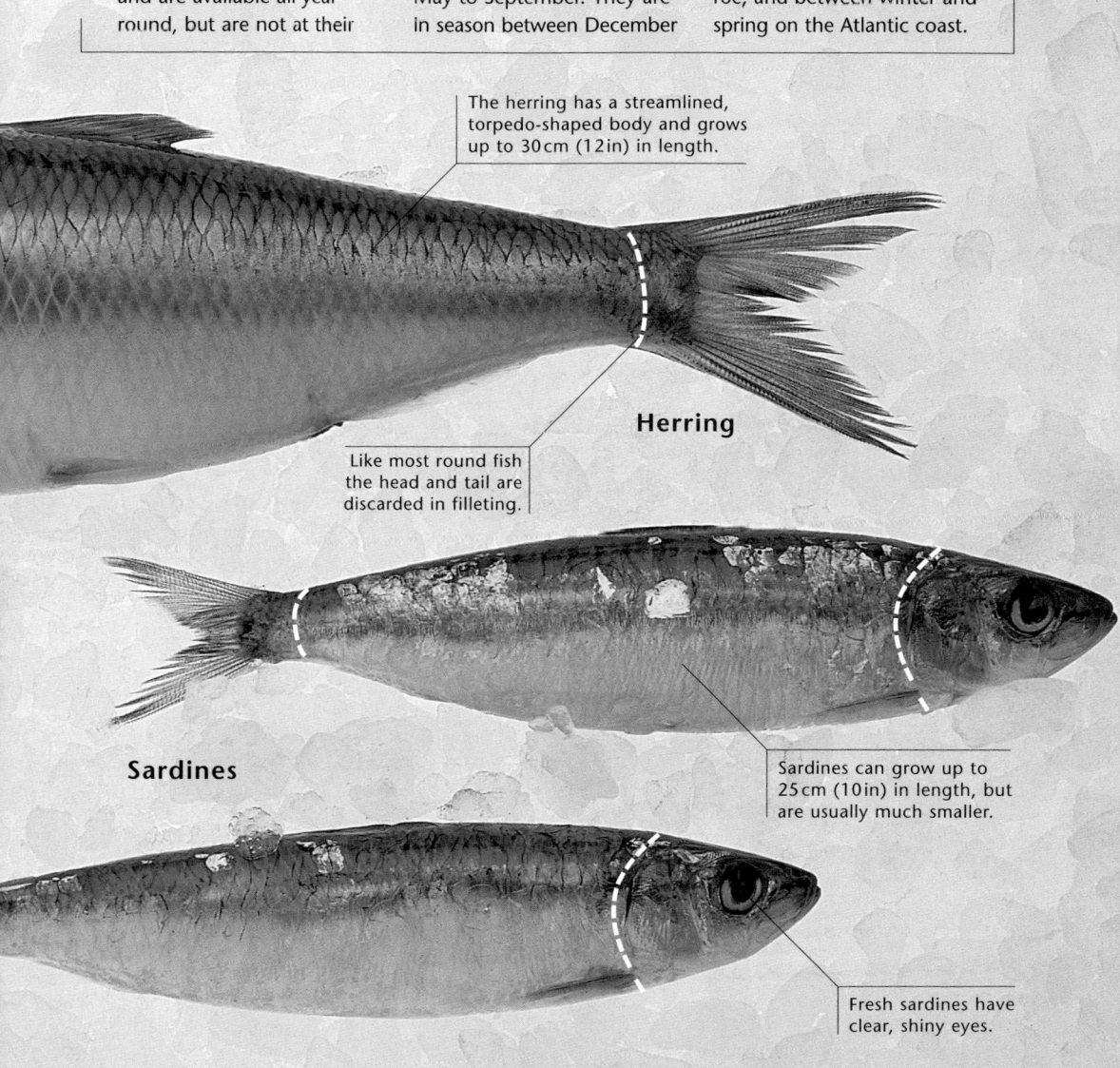

The herring has a streamlined, torpedo-shaped body and grows up to 30 cm (12 in) in length.

Herring

Like most round fish the head and tail are discarded in filleting.

Sardines

Sardines can grow up to 25 cm (10 in) in length, but are usually much smaller.

Fresh sardines have clear, shiny eyes.

Bonito
katsuo

Sometimes confused with the skipjack tuna, bonito is related to tuna but actually belongs to the mackerel family. Traditionally, it is fished with a single rod rather than a large trawling net, which might damage its flesh, and is one of the fastest swimmers in the sea. Bonito features in nearly every aspect of Japanese cuisine. It is eaten in sushi and marinated or lightly grilled as sashimi. Dried and shaved, it is used to make dashi, the basic Japanese stock. Bonito is often served with grated ginger, which complements its distinctive full, rich flavour.

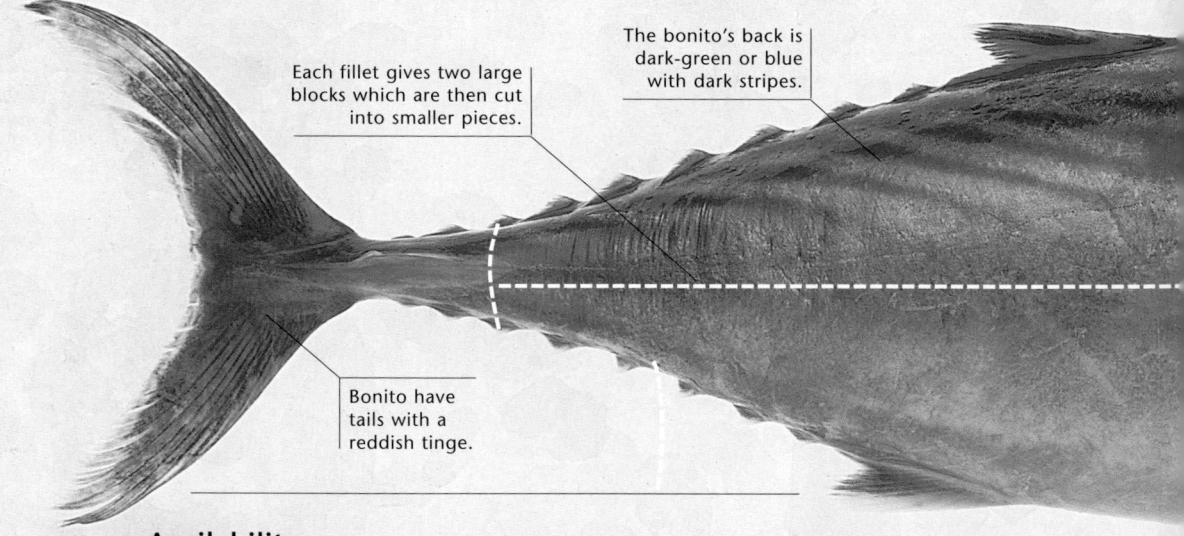

Each fillet gives two large blocks which are then cut into smaller pieces.

The bonito's back is dark-green or blue with dark stripes.

Bonito have tails with a reddish tinge.

Availability

A medium-sized migratory fish, bonito are prevalent in the warm waters of the Pacific. They migrate northwards along the Japanese coast, starting in February and appear on the menu of Tokyo sushi bars in early May, signalling the beginning of summer. They come into season in North America in spring to summer; outside Japan, the rest of the world relies on this supply.

Bonito fillets
For sushi and sashimi, the skin is left on. Bonito is lightly grilled, then submerged in cold water.

rosy coloured flesh

Cuts from the back are more meaty than from the belly [see above].

Unlike the skipjack tuna the bonito has no dark stripes on its belly.

Bluefin tuna
maguro

Although related to the mackerel, a fully grown bluefin tuna can weigh up to 250kg [600lb]. The Japanese classify the tuna as a red meat fish and divide each huge fillet into two blocks – upper and belly. These are then graded and priced according to their fat content – the fattiest part of the fish, the belly, being the most prized and the most expensive. Even in busy sushi bars in Japan, tuna is bought by different cuts: the pale, fatty belly part, the oily back fillet and the lean, dark tail end. Tuna has a soft texture and a clean taste.

Availability

Other varieties of tuna include *mebachi* [big-eye tuna], *binnaga* [albacore] and *kiwada* [yellowfin tuna]. Tuna are available all year in sushi shops world-wide, but are best from autumn to winter in Japan, Australasia and Europe, while summer is the best season in North America. Tuna has become a classic ingredient in hand-formed sushi [see p208–17] and rolled sushi [see p184–207].

Tuna steaks are usually cut from the back or tail.

The meat around the spine, *akami*, is very low in fat and dark red in colour; it is the least valued by the Japanese.

Tuna steaks

Avoid tuna that has become discoloured, grey or is leaking moisture, as this is an indication that it is not fresh. Ask your fishmonger to cut a fresh steak for you rather than buying a ready-cut piece.

distinctive red meat from the tail [see below]

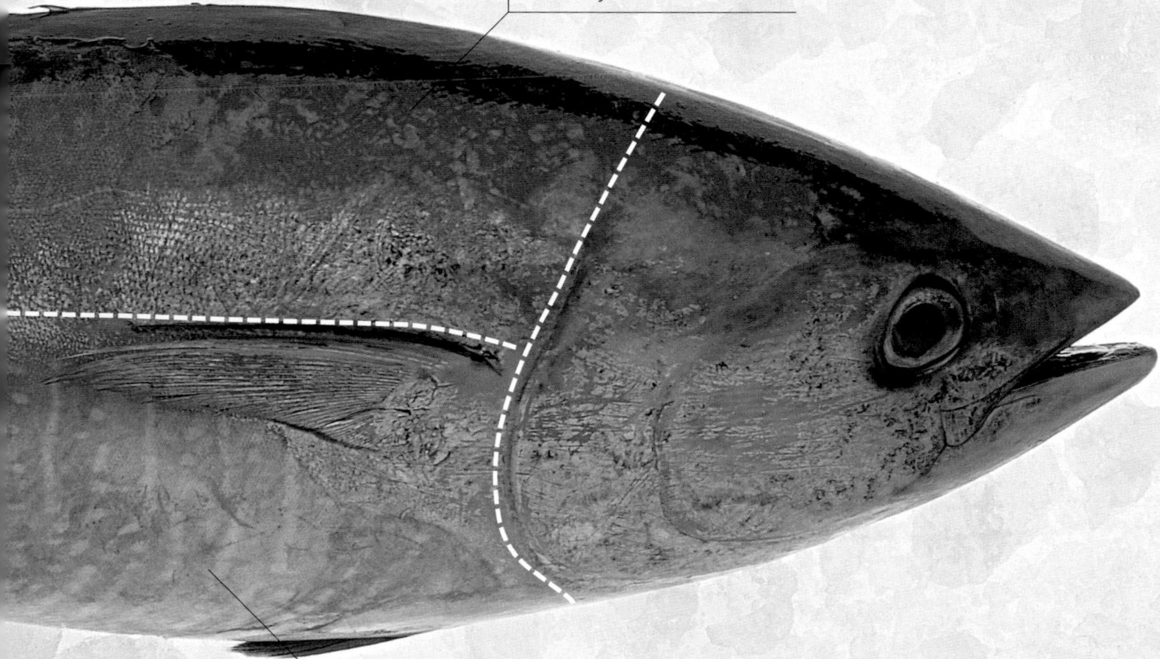

Chu toro comes mainly from the upper part of the tuna and has a very full and rich flavour.

The most prized cut of tuna comes from the belly; *oho toro* is light pink, marbled with fat and melts in the mouth.

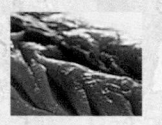

Mackerel
saba

One of the tastiest oily fish available, mackerel must be put on ice as soon as it is caught, otherwise its flavour is lost; Japanese fishermen go to great lengths to protect its freshness and quality. Before modern transportation, the land-bound former capital city, Kyoto, was too far inland to enjoy fresh mackerel, so pressed sushi, or *battera*, was invented as a method of preserving it. This type of pressed sushi is still popular in the region to this day. For hand-formed sushi, mackerel is first salted and marinated in a vinegar mixture [see p92–3]. It is often served with grated ginger, which balances its strong flavour.

Look for clear eyes with no traces of blood in them.

Less fresh mackerel develop a yellowish tinge in this region.

Its silvery white belly should be plump and firm to the touch.

Mackerel fillets

Intensely flavoured, mackerel is high in protein and rich in beneficial oils.

thin, parchment-like skin must be removed [see p93] as it can harbour bacteria

The mackerel has a shiny, blue-green back with distinctive dark tabby markings.

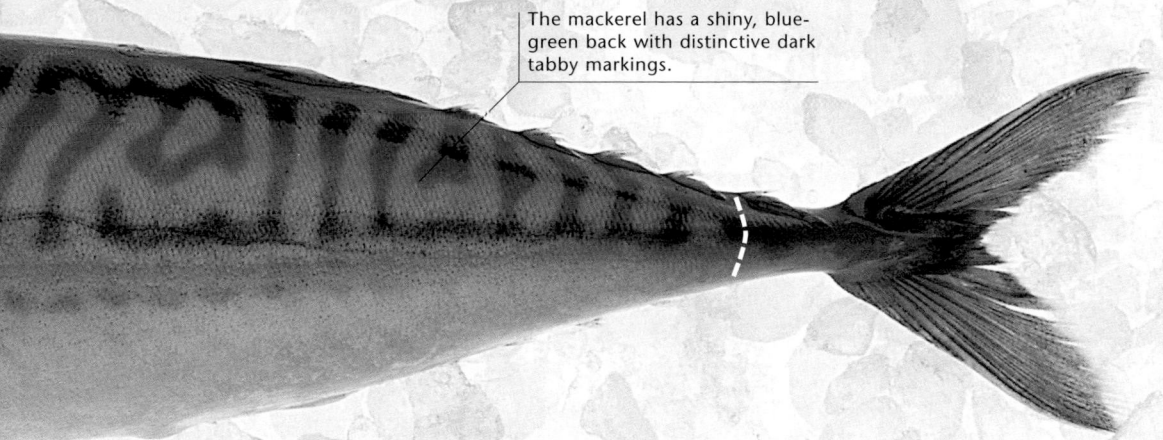

Availability

There are three varieties of mackerel widely distributed all over the world: Pacific mackerel, Atlantic mackerel and spotted mackerel, which are found in Australia, New Zealand and the Hawaiian Islands. Available throughout the year, mackerel are in season from February to June in Europe, from summer to autumn in North America and in the winter in Australia and New Zealand.

Salmon
sake

With its bright orange flesh, salmon is probably the most easily recognizable fish in sushi bars outside Japan. However, in Japan it is almost never eaten raw, but usually grilled or salted. There are two types of salmon, the Atlantic and the Pacific – of which there are six varieties. Wild salmon grow to maturity in the open sea, feeding on the fish and crustaceans that give the flesh its distinctive colour. Commercially farmed salmon, although noticeably inferior in taste and texture to wild salmon, is a far cheaper option and the quality is gradually improving. Look for 'tagged' salmon, which comes from farms where the fish are raised in better conditions.

The fillet is cut from the side of the whole fish.

Wild salmon have ragged tails.

Availability
Both the Pacific and the Atlantic salmon are widely farmed, resulting in cheap salmon that is available all year round. However, the pollution from intensive salmon farming threatens wild fish stocks already reduced by overfishing. Wild salmon are in season in spring in Australasia, from February to August in Europe and from summer to autumn in North America.

the fattier part
of the steak

Steaks and fillets

These are readily available at most
fishmongers. Fillets may be more
expensive but they are a better
shape for sushi [see p88].

firm, pink meat
with no gaps
appearing

When in season,
salmon have fat,
plump bellies.

Steaks are cut
from the middle
of the fish.

The inside of the gill
should be bright red;
avoid salmon with
very dark red gills.

John dory
matō dai

This fish has a distinctive spot behind its gills, which gives it its other name – St. Peter's fish. The spot is said to denote the place where St. Peter put his thumb when picking it up. John dory are rarely found in Japanese waters so are less common on Japanese sushi bar menus, but their firm, delicate tasting white meat makes them suitable for any type of sushi and a very popular sushi ingredient in Australia.

John dory fillets
John dory has a heavy bone, which makes it easier to fillet; it is not very fleshy.

relatively small and expensive fillets

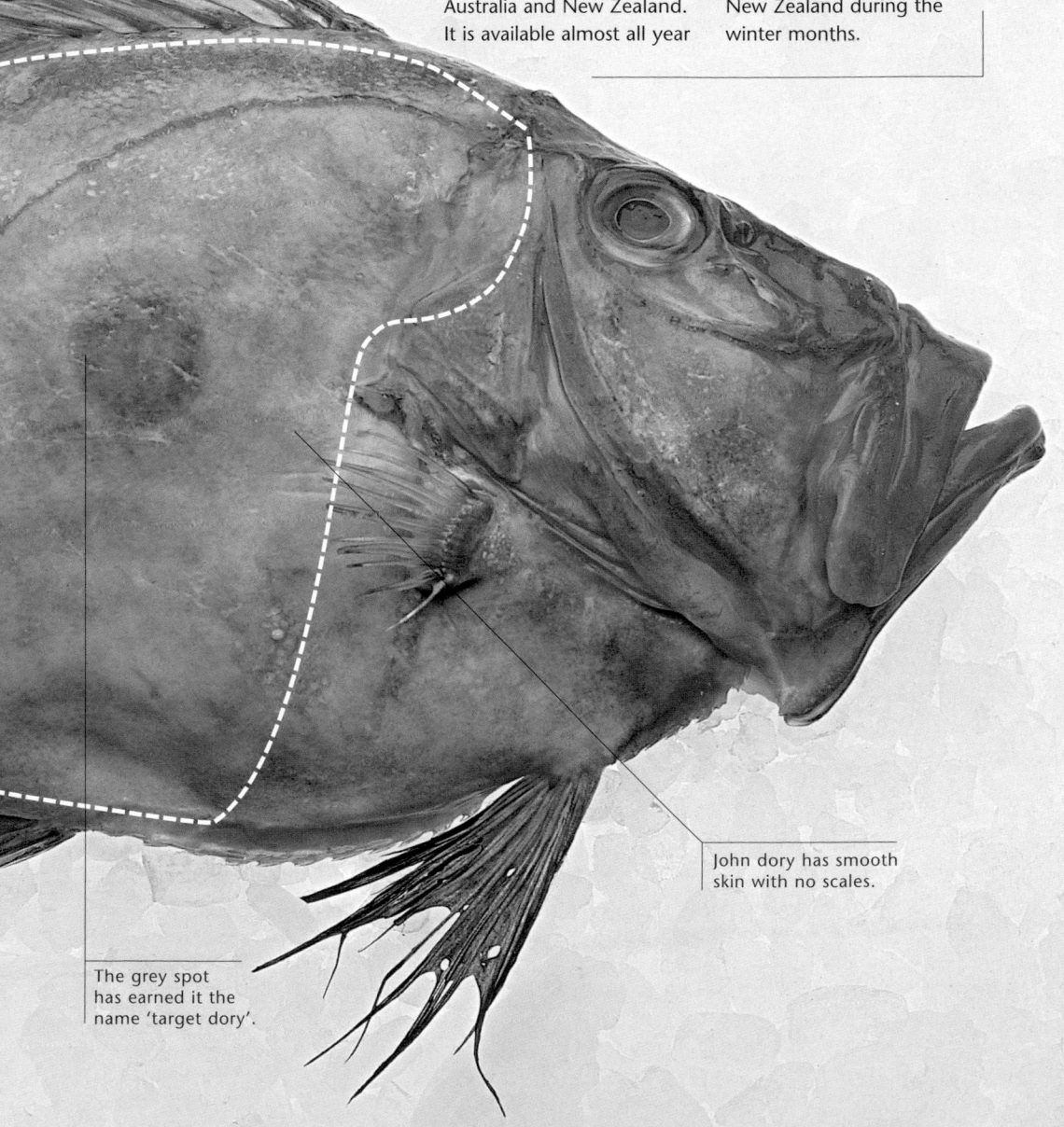

Availability
John dory live in the East China Sea, the Atlantic and also in the waters near Australia and New Zealand. It is available almost all year round in Europe, but is less good between June and August. It comes into season in Australia and New Zealand during the winter months.

John dory has smooth skin with no scales.

The grey spot has earned it the name 'target dory'.

Sea bass
s u z u k i

The Japanese regard the white flesh of the sea bass nearly as highly as
they do *tai* [red snapper] and associate the fish with success in life –
another name for it is *shusse uo*, meaning 'advancement in life' or
'promotion' fish. This is because, as it grows, the sea bass develops
through a series of stages, starting off in fresh water and ending up in
the sea. It is known by a different name at each stage and only when
the sea bass has lived in the sea and grown to a particular size does
it earn the name *suzuki*. The fish has firm white meat with a delicate
flavour and is a good topping for hand-formed sushi.
Cut paper thin, it makes elegant sashimi.

Look for clear
unsunken eyes.

Sea bass scales are
tough and need to
be removed before
filleting [see p72].

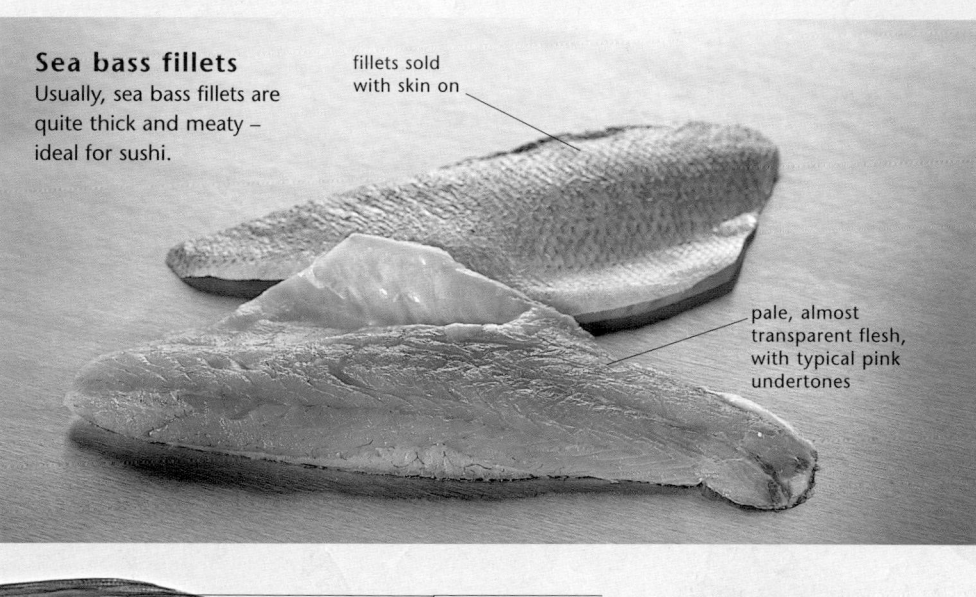

Sea bass fillets

Usually, sea bass fillets are quite thick and meaty – ideal for sushi.

fillets sold with skin on

pale, almost transparent flesh, with typical pink undertones

Spines and fins are usually intact on wild sea bass.

Availability

Wild sea bass are in season in early summer in Japan, all year round in North America, late summer in Australia and winter in Europe. Farmed bass are widely available and reasonably priced. However, flavour and texture bear little comparison to those of the wild fish. Sea bass should not be confused with the Patagonian Toothfish, a very endangered species, often sold as Chilean sea bass.

Red snapper
tai

Wild red snapper have unbroken, spiny fins.

The Japanese consider *tai* to be the best and most noble fish in the sea and the 'true' *tai* (*ma dai*), from the Seto Inland Sea, to be the finest of all. Its firm pink and white, broad-flaked flesh is delicately flavoured. A whole handsome grilled *tai* with its tail pointing up on the New Year's Day celebration table is as important as a roast turkey at Thanksgiving or Christmas in the West. Its demand far exceeds its supply, so it's no wonder that the name *tai* has been added to many non-related species. Real *tai* is only available in Japan, but red snapper, sea bream and porgy, which are often translated as *tai*, are close substitutes.

Availability

Ma dai are at their best in spring in Japan, while the North American substitute, porgy, come into season during September and May. In Europe, red snapper and sea bream are available between June and December; in Australia and New Zealand, red snapper, better known as broadbill snapper or just plain 'snapper', are at their best in the autumn months.

skin is often left on for sushi [p94]

Red snapper fillets
Its delicately flavoured pink and white flesh make red snapper a popular ingredient in sushi.

characteristic pink and white flesh

Look for clear, shiny eyes.

The red snapper's thick scales need to be removed before filleting [see p72–75].

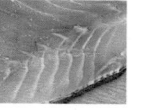

Filleting round fish
for sushi

It is more economical to buy a whole fish; it's also easier to assess its freshness. The Japanese call this method of filleting *sanmai oroshi*, or 'three-piece filleting', as the end result is two fillets and the skeleton. Use a sharp knife, and work within easy access of running water.

Specialized equipment

fish scaler

large plastic bag

pair of small tweezers or pliers

Preparation time
about 15 minutes

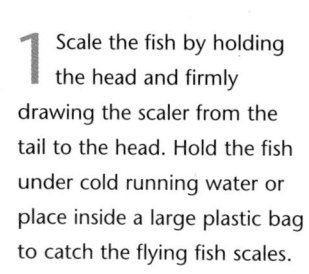

1 Scale the fish by holding the head and firmly drawing the scaler from the tail to the head. Hold the fish under cold running water or place inside a large plastic bag to catch the flying fish scales.

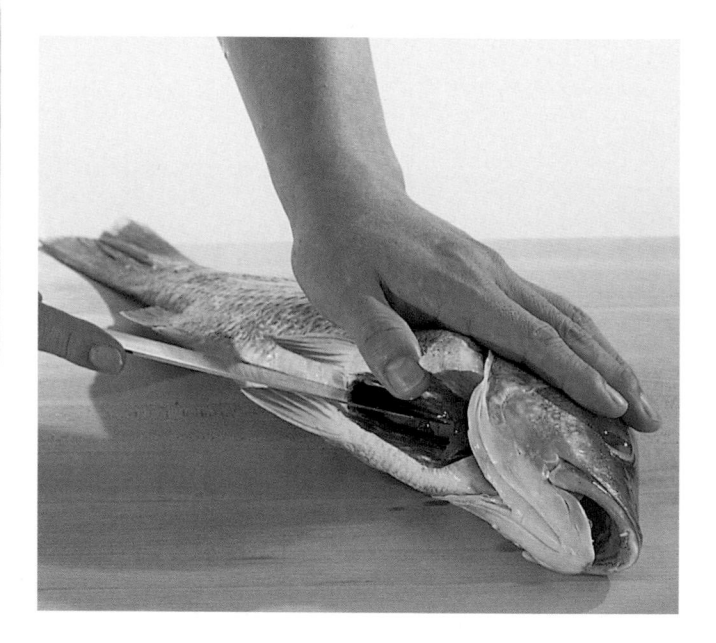

2 Insert the tip of a sharp knife into the belly and cut open the underside of the fish from the gills to the fin near the tail. Take care not to damage any internal organs.

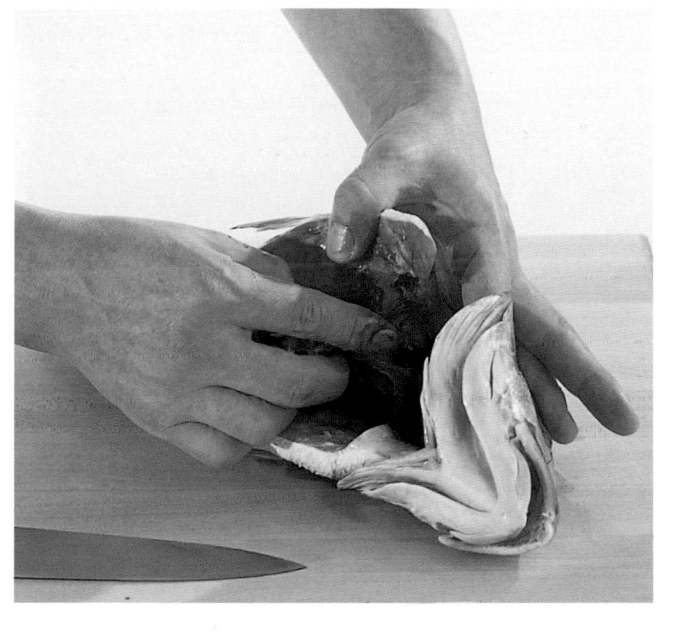

3 Cut from the tail fin to the tail. Open up the slit and remove the innards by pulling them firmly towards the tail. Discard the innards, and wash the cavity and the knife.

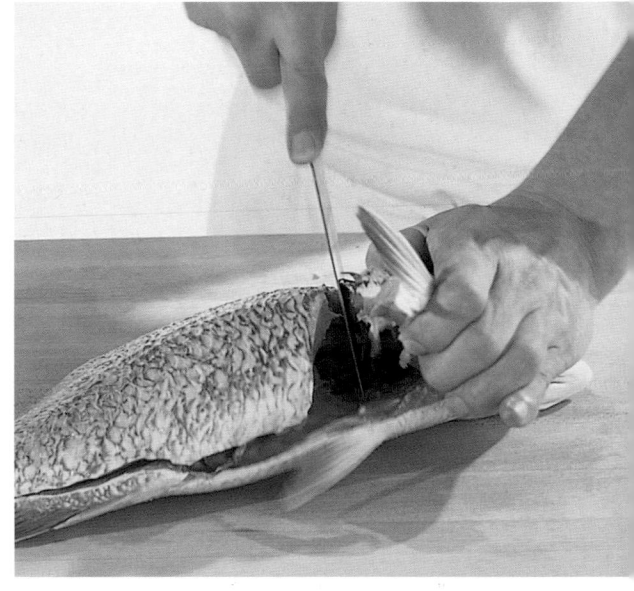

4 With the head facing you, carefully insert the knife into the back of the fish at the tail. Cut along towards the head with the knife blade resting on the backbone.

5 Hold the fish by its gills on one side and cut through the body to the spine. Turn the fish over and cut through the other side. Finally, cut through the spine to remove the head.

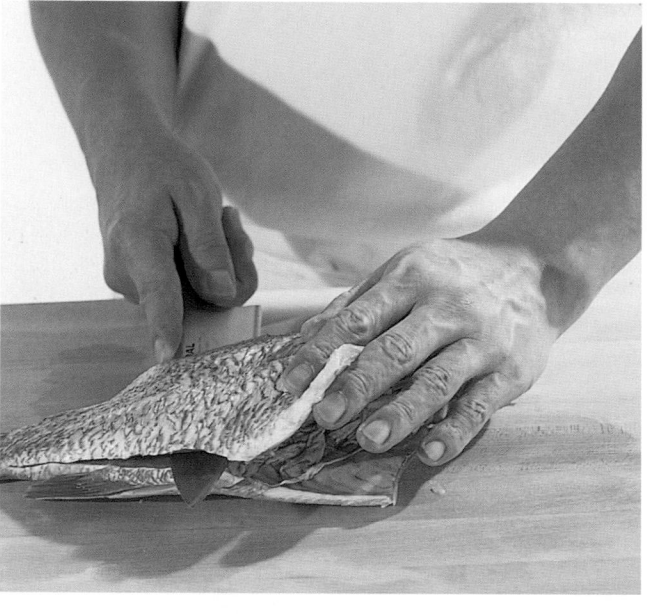

6 At the tail, insert the knife through the slit made on its back to the slit made in its underside so that the blade passes just over the skeleton. Keeping the blade flat and working away from the tail, cut the fillet loose with a firm sawing action. Use the ribs and backbone to guide the blade. Slice through the skin that attaches the fillet at the tail.

7 Turn the fish over and repeat steps 4 and 6, then cut away the second fillet.

8 You should have two large equally sized and shaped fillets and the skeleton.

9 With the knife almost horizontal, carefully cut the stomach cavity lining and any rib bones away. Run your hands lightly over the surface of the fillets to feel for any pin bones and remove with tweezers or small pliers. Trim the edges of the fillets.

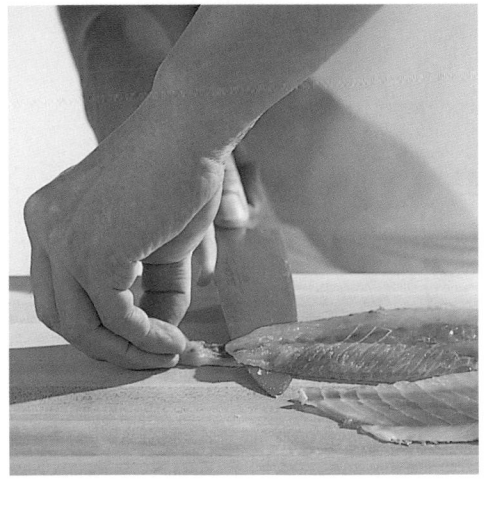

10 To skin the fillets, rub some salt on your fingers to provide a better grip. Grasp the tail and cut at a shallow angle as far as the skin, taking care not to cut through it.

11 Keeping the blade still and almost parallel with the chopping board, pull carefully on the fish skin, working it from side to side so that the skin comes away from the fillet.

Turbot
hirame

There is no direct translation for turbot, but the Japanese classify all flat fish with eyes on the left of the head as *hirame*. Similar looking but smaller fish from the Indian Ocean, the South China Sea and off the coast of Queensland, Australia are often exported to Japan as *hirame*. Of all *hirame*, the white flesh of the turbot is considered to have the most exquisite flavour and a meaty, succulent texture. It is excellent eaten raw in sushi and as sashimi.

Fresh fish do not have sunken eyes.

Turbot have a natural camouflage; colour can vary from grey-brown to dark chocolate brown.

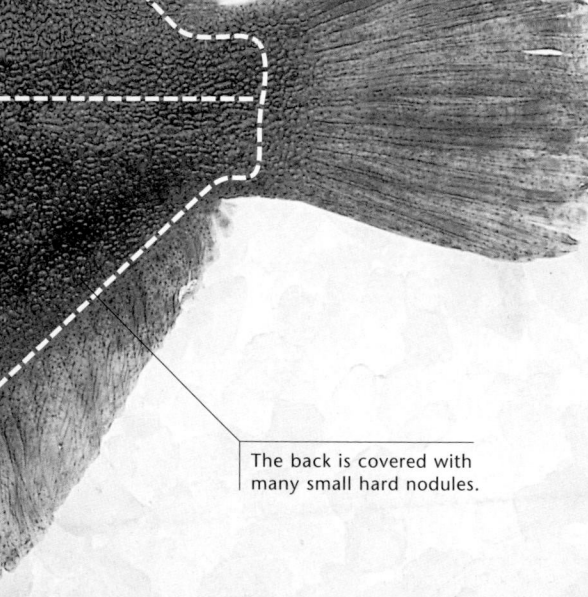

Ask your fishmonger
not to remove the
edges

Turbot fillets
The outer edges of the fillets
are considered to be a delicacy
as they are slightly crunchy and
each fish yields only small strips.

The back is covered with
many small hard nodules.

Availability
Wild turbot are widely
available in Canada,
Northern Europe and
the Mediterranean.
Although they are
caught all year round,
they come into season
in Japan and in the
rest of the northern
hemisphere in autumn
and winter. Farmed
turbot is becoming
increasingly available.
The spiny flatfish and
the Indian spiny turbot,
often exported to Japan
as *hirame*, come into
season between June
and December.

Brill
hirame

Another member of the *hirame* family [fish with eyes on the left side of the head], brill is slightly smaller than turbot [see p76–7] and is a popular ingredient in sushi. It should not be confused with megrim, which is similar in appearance but has a slightly watery, bland flavour and is the least popular of the *hirame*. If in doubt in a sushi bar, ask the sushi chef what the fish is called in English as it is probably served under the blanket Japanese term of *hirame*.

A fresh brill has a full, plump head.

Brill fillets

If buying a fillet of brill, insist on a back fillet as it has more meat.

firm, meaty flesh with a yellow tinge

Skin is olive to brown and should not feel slimy.

Availability

The name brill is given to several different types of flat fish around the world, but they are all very similar and can be used for sushi in the same way. In Europe, brill comes into season from June to February, but like most flat fish, it is at its tastiest during the autumn and winter months. The North American brill is in season all year round. Brill is also comercially fished in New Zealand and Australia.

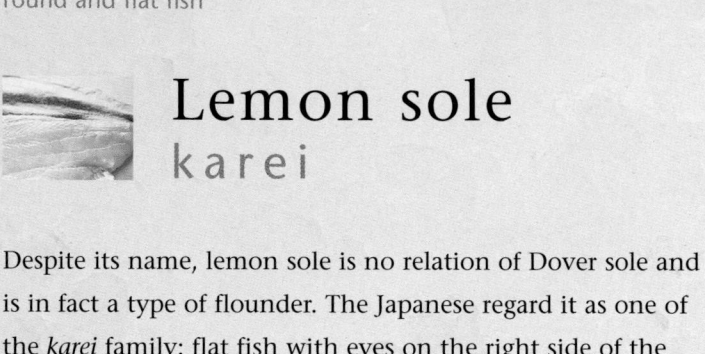

Lemon sole
karei

Despite its name, lemon sole is no relation of Dover sole and is in fact a type of flounder. The Japanese regard it as one of the *karei* family: flat fish with eyes on the right side of the head. Among the *karei* group, lemon sole is often overshadowed by the other more highly-prized flat fish such as halibut, flounder and plaice. However, its succulent white flesh makes it suitable for all types of sushi and sashimi.

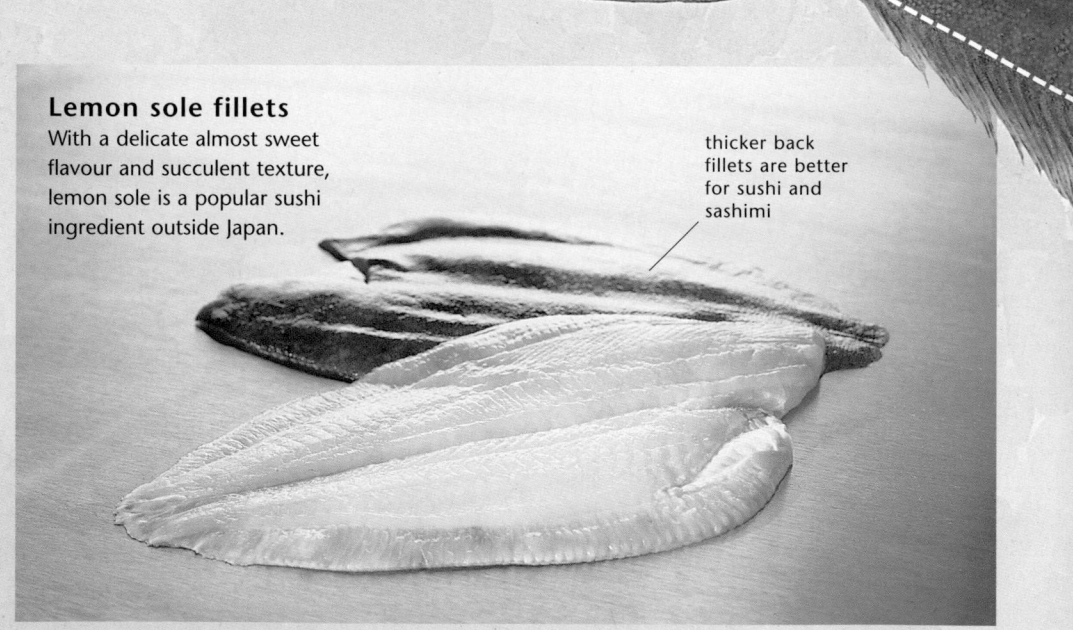

Lemon sole fillets
With a delicate almost sweet flavour and succulent texture, lemon sole is a popular sushi ingredient outside Japan.

thicker back fillets are better for sushi and sashimi

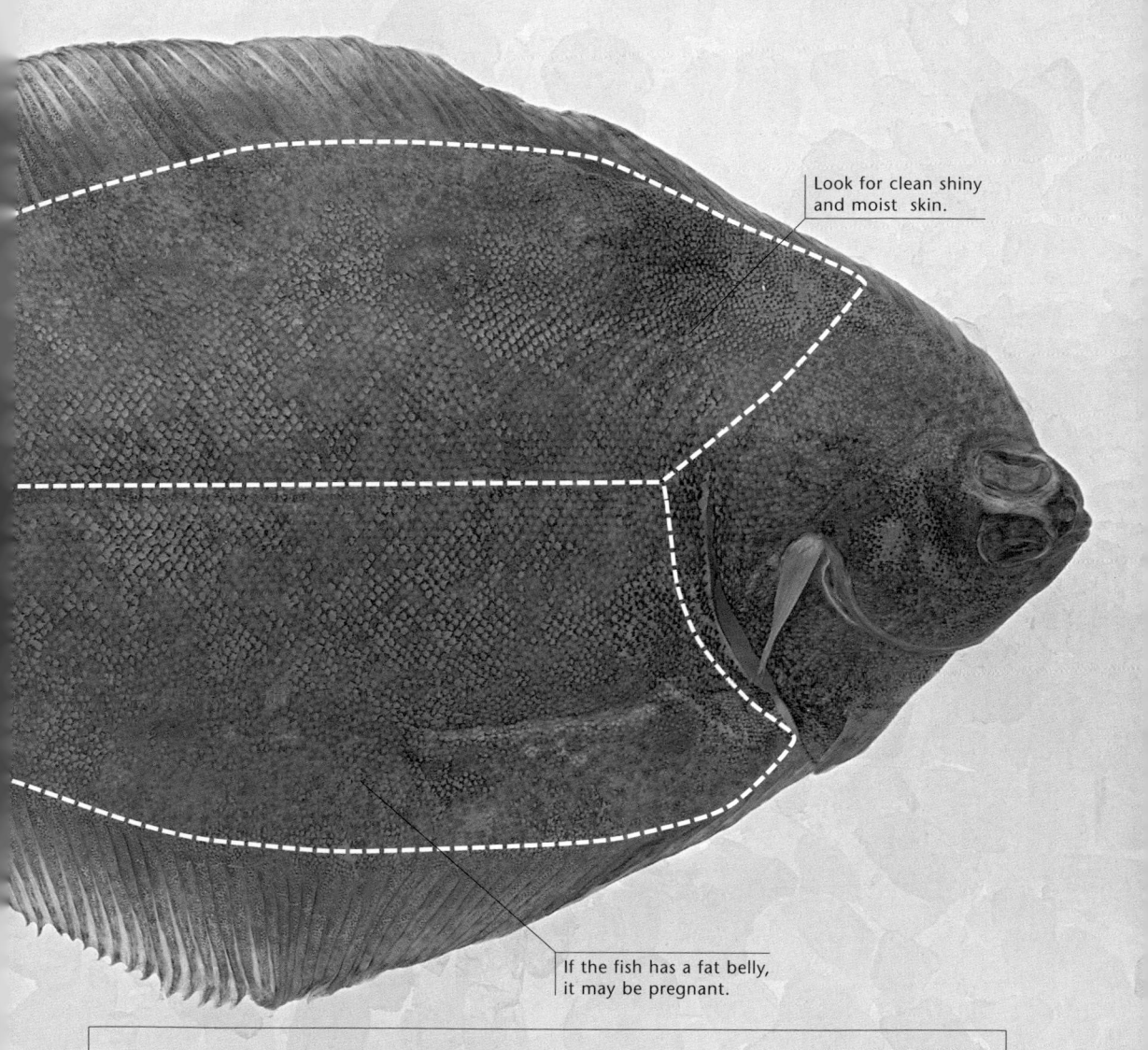

Look for clean shiny and moist skin.

If the fish has a fat belly, it may be pregnant.

Availability

Lemon sole are widely available in the North Atlantic, the North Sea and the Norwegian Sea.

In Europe, they are caught throughout the year, but are at their best between May and March. They are available throughout the year in North America, but should be avoided from April to September as this is when they breed and the flesh tends to be less flavoursome.

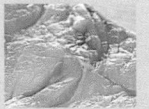

Halibut
ohyō garei

A member of the *karei* family [flat fish with eyes on the right of the head], halibut is the largest of the flat fish and often measures anything up to 2m [6½ft], but can grow to as long as 4m [13ft]. It has large, powerful jaws and is known for putting up a good fight when caught in the fishermen's net. To really appreciate its dense, meaty flesh, which has an excellent flavour, it is best to choose younger, smaller fish, sometimes called chicken halibut; the bigger the fish, the drier and blander it tends to be.

Availability

Halibut are plentiful both in the Atlantic and in the Pacific. They come into season in the US between May and September and between June and March in Europe. Like other flat fish from the northern hemisphere, they become oilier and more succulent during the winter.

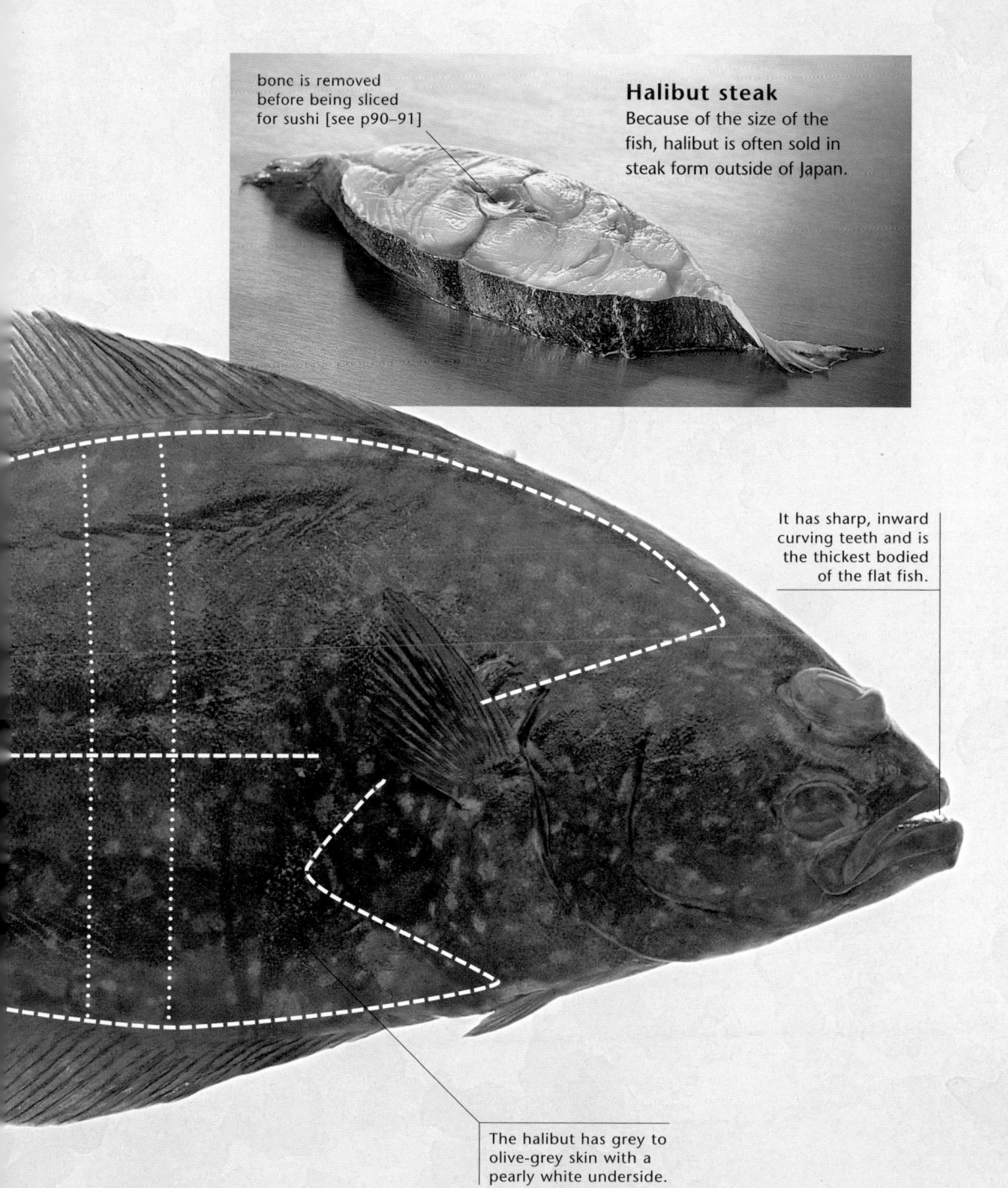

bone is removed before being sliced for sushi [see p90–91]

Halibut steak
Because of the size of the fish, halibut is often sold in steak form outside of Japan.

It has sharp, inward curving teeth and is the thickest bodied of the flat fish.

The halibut has grey to olive-grey skin with a pearly white underside.

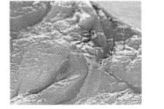

Filleting flat fish
for sushi

Japanese sushi chefs traditionally fillet flat fish using the 'five-piece filleting' method, so called because the end result is four equally sized fillets and the skeleton. Although flat fish don't have scales like round fish do, they are nearly always skinned for sushi.

Specialized equipment
pair of small tweezers or pliers

Preparation time
About 15 minutes

1 Insert the blade at a 45° angle just behind the central fin, and cut off the head. The innards should come away as you pull off the head.

The tiny fin on its back shows where the head ends

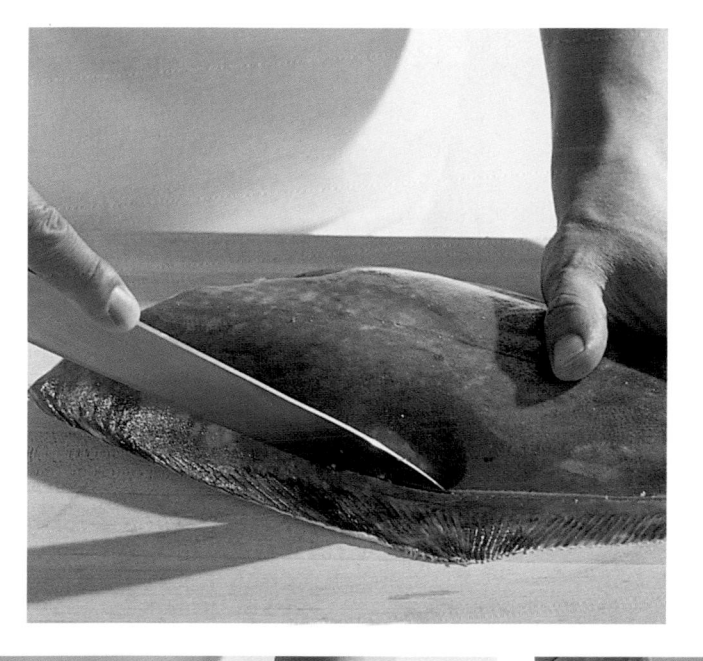

2 Place the fish on its lighter coloured belly and cut around one side of the fish just inside the outer fin.

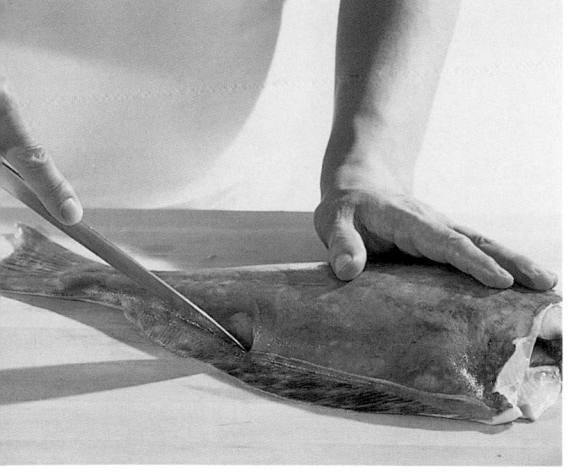

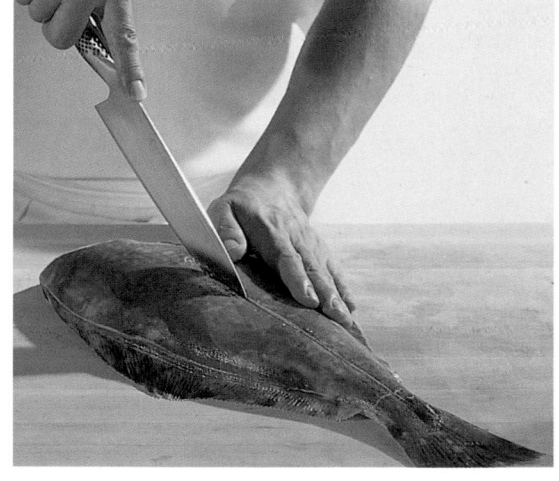

3 Turn the fish round and cut around the other side.

4 Starting at the tail, cut into the fish as far as the back bone. Cut down the middle of the fish, working towards the front of it.

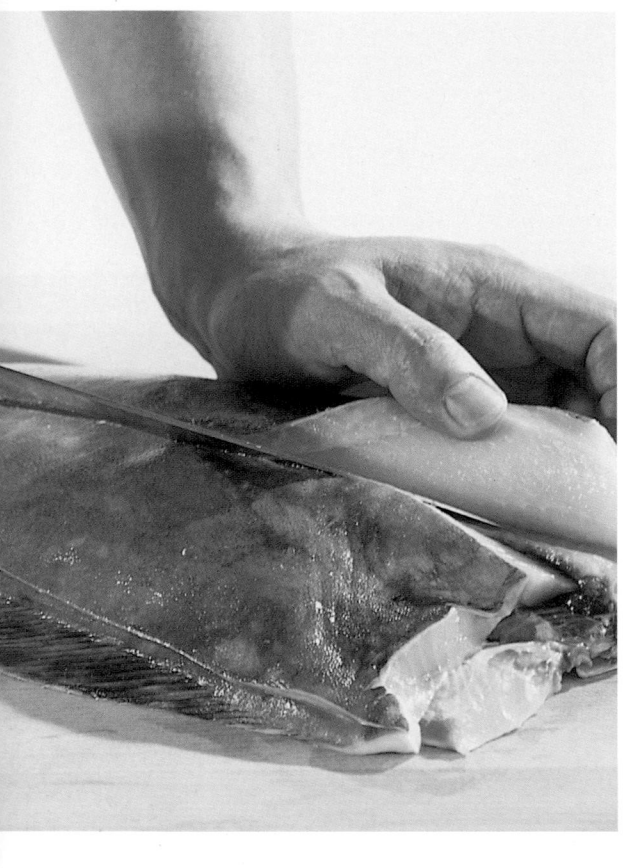

6 Turn the fish around and do the same to the fillet on the other side of the fish, this time starting at the tail end.

5 Turn the fish around so the tail is facing you. With the knife at a slight angle, ease the blade into the central cut, feeling for when it reaches the bones. Using the bones to guide the knife, work down the length of the fish cutting the fillet away from the skeleton. Long smooth strokes will give a cleaner, less jagged cut.

7 Flat fish are nearly symmetrical, so simply turn the fish over and repeat steps 4 to 6 to cut the fillets from the other side of the fish.

8 Cutting at an angle, carefully remove the stomach cavity lining and pull out any little bones with small tweezers or pliers. Trim the fillets to an even shape.

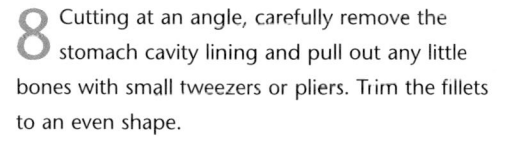

9 You are left with four equally sized fillets. To skin them, see p75, steps 10 and 11.

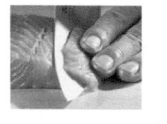

Slicing fish fillets
for sushi

Depending on the type of sushi, fish fillets can be sliced in four different ways. For hand-formed sushi, the fillet is cut diagonally into thin slices; for hand-rolled and thick roll sushi, it is then cut into 1cm [½ in] square sticks. Pressed sushi works best with large, flat pieces of fish, and scattered sushi requires uniform-size strips. Choose a skinless fish fillet that is roughly hand-sized and as even a shape as you can find.

Ingredients
300g [10oz] skinless fish fillet about 2.5–4cm [1–2in] thick

Preparation time
About 15 minutes

For Hand-formed Sushi [see p208–17], cut diagonal slices about 5mm [¼ in] thick. Hold the knife at a 45° angle to the fish. Resting your fingertips lightly on the fish, gently work the knife through the fish to produce even slices. The first slice may not be suitable for hand-formed sushi, but it can be used for thin roll sushi.

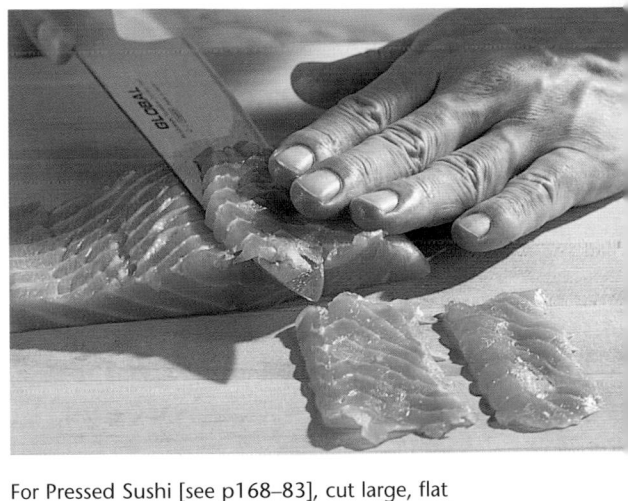

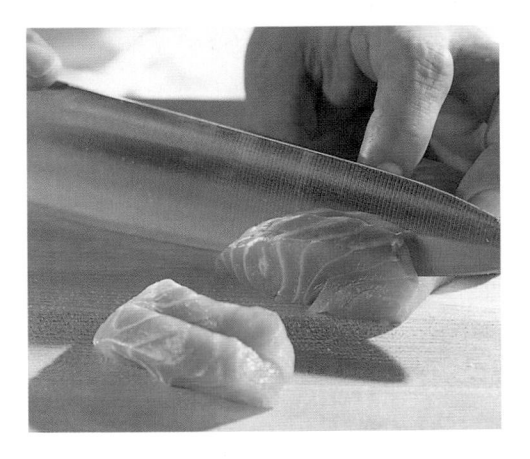

For Pressed Sushi [see p168–83], cut large, flat pieces of fish. Resting one hand lightly on the fillet and keeping the blade parallel to it, carefully cut as thin a slice as you can – about 3mm [⅛ in] thick – from the top of the fillet. Repeat as needed.

For Hand-rolled Sushi and Thick Roll Sushi [see p192–5 and p204–7], slice the fillet as for hand-formed sushi [see left] but cut the pieces slightly thicker. Next slice the pieces lengthways into 1cm [½ in] square sticks. For hand-rolled sushi, each stick should be about 6cm [2¾ in] long.

For Scattered Sushi [see p132–9] or Sashimi [see p240–3], cut slices 1cm [½ in] thick – these can also be cut into strips for rolled sushi.

Slicing fish steaks
for sushi

Many large fish are often sold as steaks and need some preparation before they can be sliced for sushi. Once the bones and skin have been removed and the fish shaped into blocks, it can be sliced for scattered, rolled and hand-formed sushi and sashimi.

Ingredients

1 fish steak about 250g [8oz] from any large fish such as salmon or halibut

Preparation time
About 15 minutes

1 Place the steak on the chopping board skin side down. Hold it securely in position and cut the steak in half, working a sharp knife carefully under the central bone.

2 Position the half of the steak with the bone skin side down. Holding it steady, repeat step 1 and carefully cut out the bone.

3 Remove any bones that might still be in the flesh [see p93] and, using a sharp knife, trim any fatty tissue from the fillet.

4 Position the fish with the skin side down. Holding the blade parallel to the chopping board, carefully cut off the skin.

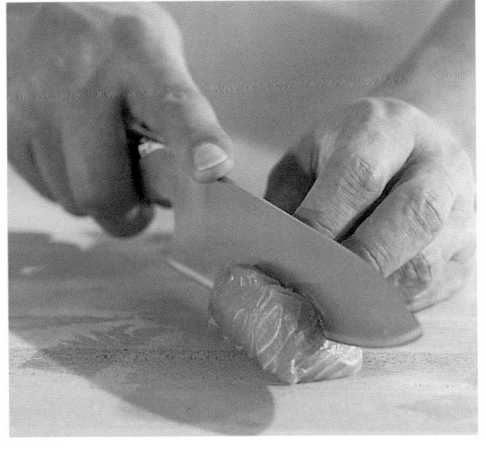

5 Cut the resulting evenly shaped pieces of fish into 1cm [½ in] strips for scattered sushi, hand-formed sushi or sashimi.

6 Alternatively, cut the slices in half lengthways into strips of about pencil-thickness, and use for rolled sushi.

Marinating mackerel
shime saba

Mackerel is inexpensive, available all year round and yet it is not as popular as it should be. Only the freshest mackerel is eaten raw as it deteriorates rapidly if not handled properly once caught. Marinating mackerel in vinegar enhances the flavour and also helps to preserve and tighten its oily flesh, making it easier to slice. It can be prepared up to six hours in advance.

Ingredients

4 mackerel fillets,
about 150g [5oz] each

about 8 tbsp sea salt

500ml [16floz] rice vinegar

2 tbsp mirin or
3 tbsp caster sugar

2 tsp salt

Preparation time
2–3 hours

1 Place the mackerel fillets in a large bowl, and pour over the salt. Gently rub the mackerel fillets with the salt, ensuring they are evenly covered.

2 Place the fillets on a bamboo strainer or in a colander. Leave for at least 30 minutes, preferably an hour, to allow juices drawn out by the salt to drain off. Rinse under cold running water, and pat dry with kitchen paper.

3 Mix together the vinegar, mirin or sugar, and salt in a plastic or glass bowl large enough to hold the fillets. Add the mackerel to the bowl and set aside to marinate for 1–2 hours.

4 Take the fillets out of the vinegar mixture, and pat dry with kitchen paper. The flesh should have whitened. Slowly peel off the papery thin outer skin, starting at the head. Don't worry if some of the iridescent underskin also comes off.

5 Place the fillets on a chopping board, and run the tips of your fingers lightly up and down them to feel for any small bones. Use tweezers to remove any that you find, and a sharp knife to trim and shape the fillets, if necessary.

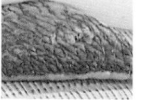

Tenderizing fish skin
for sushi

Medium-sized scaly fish such as red snapper, sea bass and silver bream have quite tough skin that needs to be blanched in order to tenderize it. The technique is called *matsukawa zukuri*, or the 'pine bark method', as the fish skin shrinks a little when blanched and is said to resemble the bark of pine trees. Blanching the skin also gives the fish a sweeter flavour. Use any size of fish fillet but it must be scaled first [see p72].

Specialized equipment
bamboo strainer or colander
fukin or tea towel
Preparation time
10 minutes

1 Place the scaled fillet skin side upwards on a bamboo strainer set over a shallow dish, and cover with a clean *fukin* or tea towel. Alternatively, place the fillet in a colander in the sink and cover.

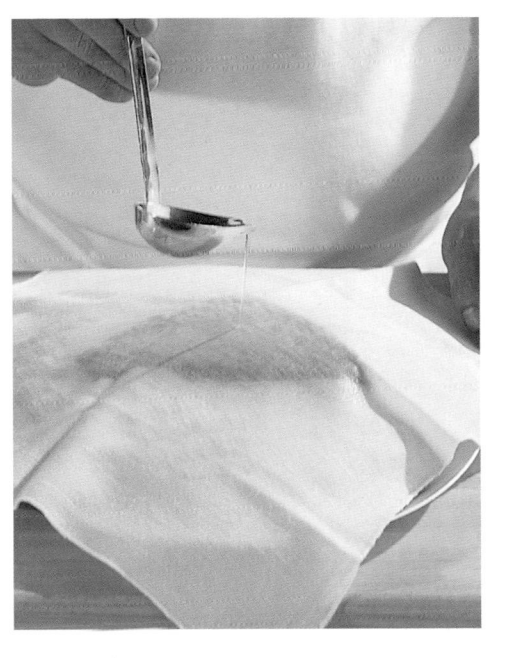

2 Bring 300ml [10fl oz] of water to the boil. Carefully pour the freshly boiled water over the covered fillet.

3 Cool the fillet by plunging it into cold water or by holding it under a cold-running tap. The flesh should have whitened and the skin shrunk.

4 For scattered sushi or sashimi, slice the fillet into strips about 1cm [½ in] thick.

Shellfish and roe
kai rui

It is imperative that you buy the freshest fish for sushi and sashimi, and the same applies to shellfish. Ideally, shellfish such as crab, lobster, shrimps, prawns, scallops, oysters and abalone should be bought while still alive, although this isn't always possible or practical. They can live for up to two days if kept in shallow water at a temperature of 5–6°C [35–40°F]. Check the following to ensure freshness:

• Shrimps and prawns in particular should be active and clear grey in colour. If no longer alive, select ones with clear, distinctive body markings.

• Scallops, oysters and abalone should not float and should feel heavy; their shells should remain tightly closed and not be chipped.

• If buying a whole octopus, check that the eyes are clear and bright, not cloudy.

• Sea urchin is almost always bought ready-prepared, removed from its spiky shell. It should be mustard-coloured, moist and firm, not greyish yellow and slimy.

• Fish roes tend to have longer shelf-lives as they are often sold in jars or tins, which make them good store-cupboard ingredients for sushi.

< Octopus is rarely sold whole outside Japan: only the tentacles are used for sushi

> It takes a firm hand to prise the precious oyster from its shell, but it makes a delicate topping for battleship sushi

Crab
kani

Whatever the local variety may be, in a sushi shop, crab is always served cooked and referred to as *kani*. The 'California roll', an invention originally created for American palates, uses cooked crabmeat, avocado and mayonnaise in an inside out rolled sushi. If the thought of buying a live crab and boiling it whole is too daunting, buy a ready-boiled or, better still, a dressed crab for making sushi at home.

white, coral-flecked crabmeat

Cooked crab
It takes some effort to extract the meat from a cooked crab – only white crabmeat is used for sushi.

Availability
Crabs come into season in Europe between April and December and in Australia, during spring and summer. Available throughout the year in North America, they are most tasty in autumn and winter. Frozen white crabmeat can be used for sushi, but beware of 'crab sticks' – actually cheap, processed fish, not crab.

Crab claws contain sweet, white meat and are bigger on male crabs.

Female crabs have larger 'aprons' under their body and their meat is said to be sweeter than male crabs.

Preparing crab
for sushi

Whole cooked crabs are available from most fish-mongers but it is easy to cook a fresh crab at home. Place the live crab in a large pot of cold salted water. Put the lid on, bring quickly to the boil and cook for five to six minutes per 500g [1lb]. Drain the crab, cool and extract the meat as below. Only white meat is used for sushi, not the more strongly flavoured brown meat.

Specialized equipment

claw cracker or nutcracker

seafood pick or skewer

Preparation time
15–20 minutes
[excluding cooking time]

---

1 Set the cooked crab on its back on a chopping board, and twist and break the claws and legs from the body.

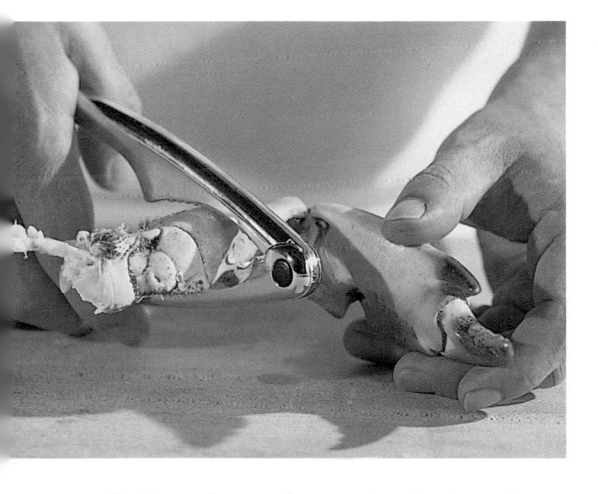

2 Use a claw cracker or nutcracker to crack open the large claws. All the crab's legs will contain some meat, although the very small legs will hardly be worth the effort.

3 Flake the meat from the cracked claws using a seafood pick or skewer.

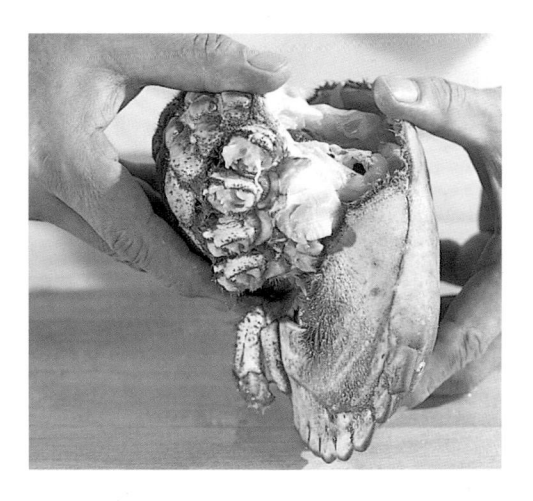

4 Using the heel of a knife, firmly cut through the join where the crab's tail meets the body.

5 Ease the main part of the crab's body out of the shell.

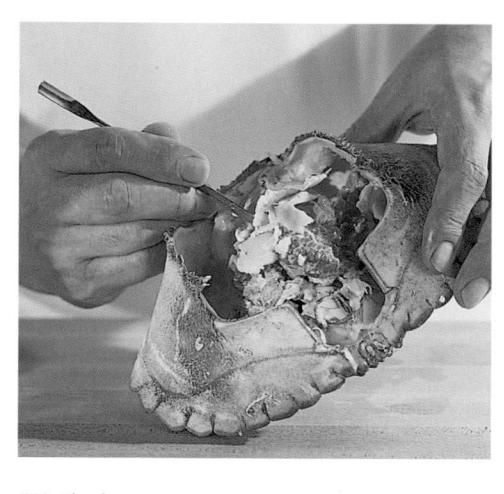

6 Most of the white meat is contained in the body of the crab, while the brown meat is left in the shell.

7 The brown meat and red coral can easily be scraped from the shell if desired. Be sure to discard the pale paper-like head sac and stomach found just behind the crab's mouth.

8 Remove and discard the grey looking gills or 'dead man's fingers' from the sides of the central body section.

9 Pull the tail flap or apron from the main body section.

10 Using a heavy knife, cut the body in half to get to the meat.

11 Clean away any remaining coral or brown meat using a seafood pick or skewer.

12 Carefully pick the white meat out of all the sections of body, discarding any small pieces of membrane or shell.

13 If necessary, cut the body into quarters to enable you to reach all the inaccessible areas and remove the white meat.

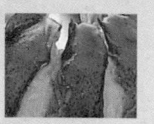

Lobster
ise ebi

Revered as the king of the prawn family, the lobster's
high price reflects its high rank. Although it is not
considered a traditional Japanese sushi ingredient,
its firm flesh and excellent flavour have made it
popular with innovative sushi chefs outside of
Japan. There are two types of lobster – those with
large claws and those without, known as spiny
lobsters. Both can vary in length from 30–80cm
[12–32in] and weigh as much as 3kg [6lb]. Buy
small to medium-sized lobsters as larger ones tend to
have drier, less succulent flesh and blander flavour.

Turn the lobster
over and check
that the tail is
filled with meat.

Cooked lobster
Lobsters come in a wide variety
of colours but they all turn a
deep burgundy red when
properly cooked.

most of the
meat is in
the tail

Choose lobsters with the least barnacles.

Claws should feel heavy and solid.

Spiny lobsters have two large antennae instead of claws.

Availability

Australia and North America are renowned as good sources of lobster. They come into season in Australia from mid-November to June. They are available all year round in North America, but are generally at their tastiest between October and May; Maine, in the US, is a good source during the summer months. They come into season in Europe between April and November.

Preparing lobster
for sushi

Like crabs, lobsters contain white and brown meat, but only the white meat is used in sushi. If buying a live lobster, choose a lively one that feels heavy for its size. To cook it, put it in a large pan of cold salted water and bring it to the boil with the lid on. Cook for five to six minutes per 500g [1lb]. Alternatively, buy a ready-cooked lobster. Follow the steps below to extract the meat.

> **Specialized equipment**
> *heavy knife or nutcracker*
> *seafood pick or skewer*
>
> **Preparation time**
> 10–15 minutes
> [excluding cooking time]

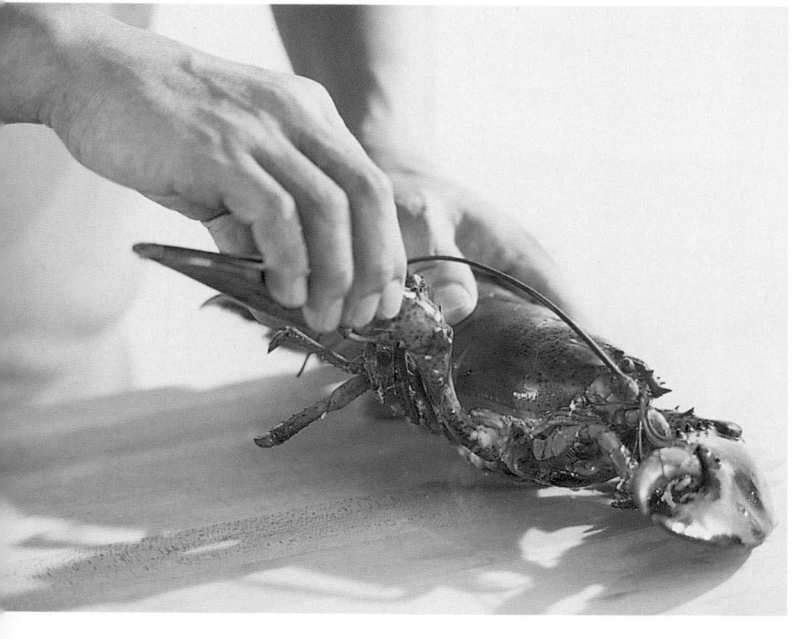

1 Most of the white meat is found in the muscular tail and, for clawed lobsters, in the two large claws.

2 Use the heel of a heavy knife blade to crack open the claws, or alternatively, use a nutcracker. Pick out the meat with a seafood pick or skewer.

3 Grasp the lobster in both hands and detach the head where it joins the body.

4 Using a sharp, heavy knife, cut through the translucent shell covering the bottom of the tail on both sides, at the point where it meets the upper shell.

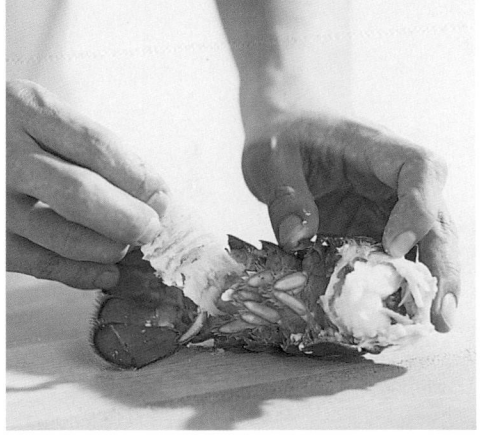

5 Pull away and discard the translucent covering to get to the meat.

6 Pull the white meat out of the tail – it should come out in one large piece.

Prawns and shrimps
ebi

There are many varieties and sizes of prawns, both wild and farmed; smaller prawns are classified as shrimps. For sushi, both prawns and shrimps are referred to as *ebi*. They are usually served cooked and have a delicate flavour and a firm texture. Raw shrimp, *ama ebi,* is considered a great delicacy among sushi connoisseurs. A cleaned, raw shrimp has a jewel-like, glossy, almost transparent appearance and is sweet in flavour with a tender texture. Demand for both prawns and shrimps is more than wild supplies can meet, so even sushi bars in Japan import frozen stocks from other parts of Asia.

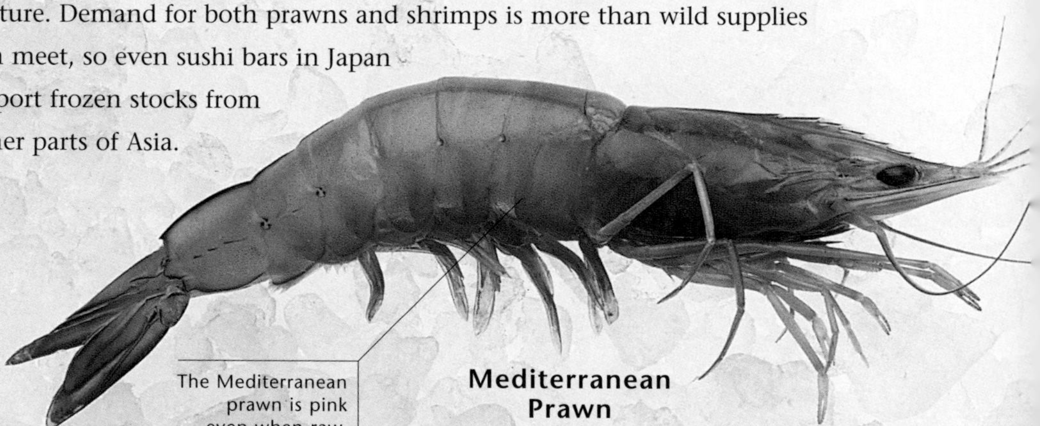

The Mediterranean prawn is pink even when raw.

Mediterranean Prawn

The tiger prawn has characteristic dark grey stripes on its body.

Tiger Prawns

Mediterranean prawns
Cooked prawns, such as these Mediterranean prawns, can be bought peeled or with the heads and shells intact.

intact antennae and eyes indicate the prawns are more likely to be fresh

the whole prawn turns pink and white when cooked

Availability
As a general rule, prawns that live in warmer waters are larger. Fresh prawns are generally available in Europe all year round. In the US, excellent quality shrimps are caught off the Maine coast, especially in winter between November and March. Australia probably has the widest variety of large prawns – they come into season in April and last until the end of November. The raw shrimp, *ama ebi*, are best bought ready-prepared from specialist Japanese shops.

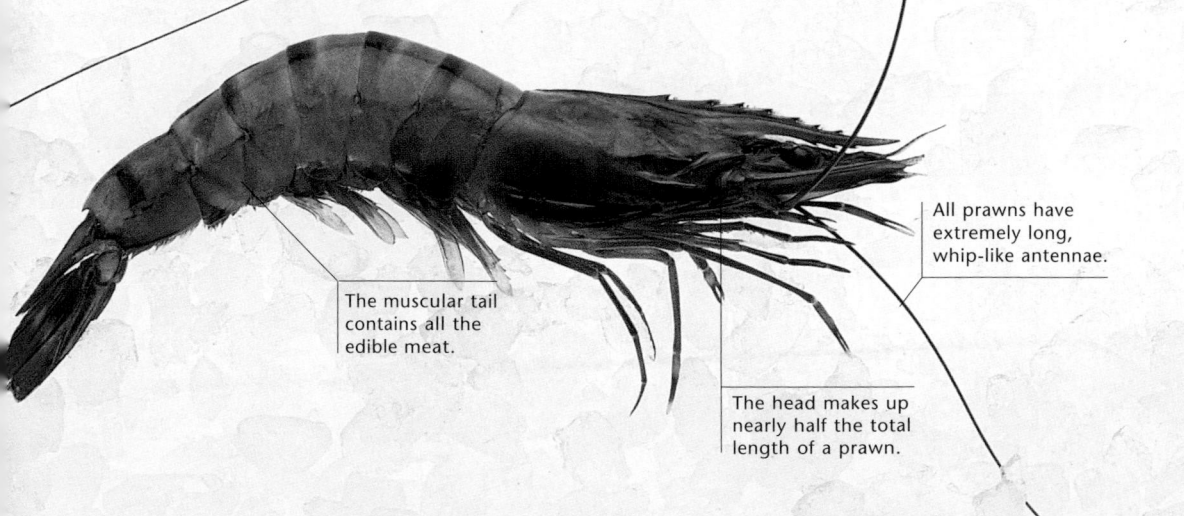

The muscular tail contains all the edible meat.

All prawns have extremely long, whip-like antennae.

The head makes up nearly half the total length of a prawn.

Preparing prawns
for sushi

Their firm sweet flesh makes king and tiger prawns popular ingredients in all types of sushi. Inserting a skewer along the underside of the prawn before cooking prevents it from curling. Take care not to overcook them as this can give them a rubbery texture.

> **Specialized equipment**
> *bamboo skewers*
>
> **Preparation time**
> 10 minutes

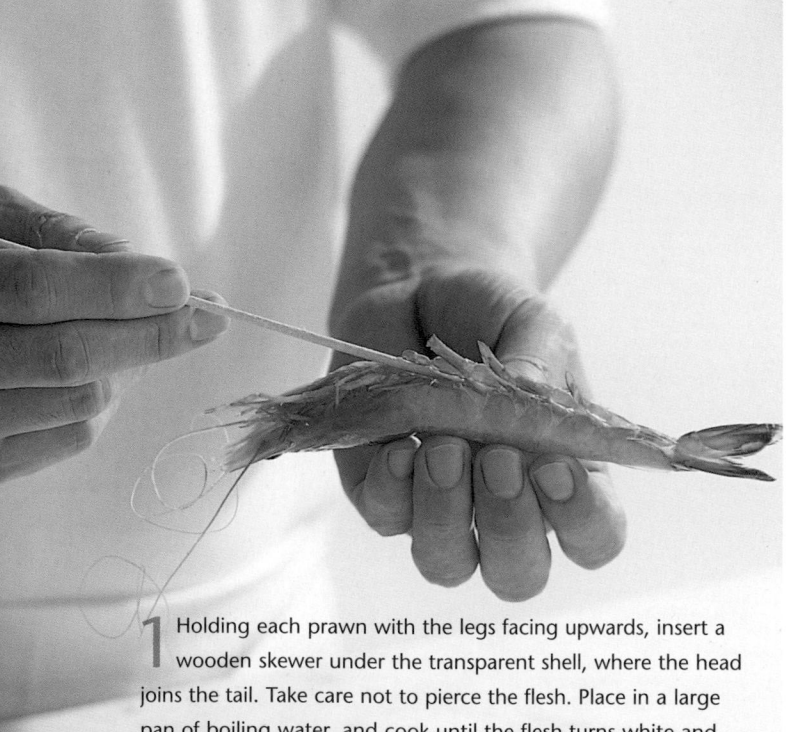

1 Holding each prawn with the legs facing upwards, insert a wooden skewer under the transparent shell, where the head joins the tail. Take care not to pierce the flesh. Place in a large pan of boiling water, and cook until the flesh turns white and pink, about 2–3 minutes. Drain, and set aside to cool.

2 Remove the skewer from the prawn. Gently but firmly, pull the head to separate it from the body. Discard the head.

3 Holding the prawn with the legs facing upwards, use your thumbs to remove the legs and peel away the outer shell. Leave the tail intact.

4 Using a sharp knife, cut along the underside of the prawn until you reach the dark vein that runs the length of its body.

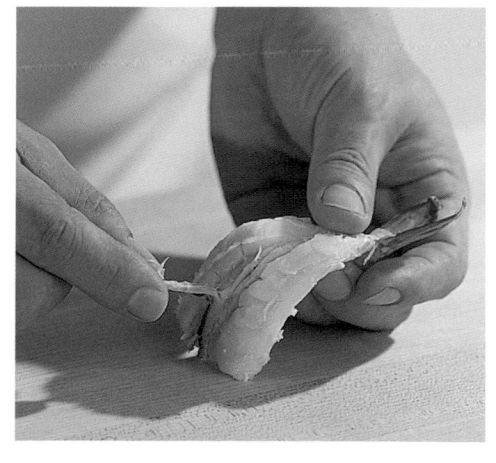

5 Use a knife or the wooden skewer to scrape out the dark vein. You may need to wipe any remaining vein away with a damp cloth.

6 Trim and tidy the ends of the tail. This gives an elegant presentation but for some sushi, such as hand-formed sushi, you might want to carefully pull off the tail shell.

Squid and octopus
ika / tako

The Japanese word *ika* refers to many different varieties of squid, but *ma ika* and *yari ika* are most preferred for sushi. Always buy squid fresh, if possible; it freezes well if you have too much, which makes it a convenient ingredient for home sushi-making. The octopus feeds on other sushi ingredients such as crab, lobster and scallops – this gourmet diet makes it high in protein and gives it excellent flavour. It has a firm texture and makes a very good sushi topping. Larger octopus have thicker tentacles which are easier to slice for hand-formed sushi [p116–7].

Squid

The body and tentacles are used to make many different types of sushi.

Octopus

Fresh squid

Its pearly white, glossy flesh has a sticky, almost resistant, texture. Squid is nearly always served raw.

Cooked octopus

For sushi, octopus is boiled, which tenderizes and firms the flesh. Its grey skin turns burgundy, and its flesh whitens.

Only the octopus's tentacles are used as a sushi topping.

Availability

Squid and octopus are widely available all year round, which makes them good sushi and sashimi ingredients. However, squid is at its best in Europe in autumn and winter, and during spring in North America. Octopus is generally at its best during winter and spring in the northern hemisphere.

Look for squid and octopus that still have their tentacles intact and most of their skin on – these are signs that they have been handled well. Fresh seafood should smell like the ocean, never fishy, and look shiny and firm. Remember, high quality frozen squid or octopus is a lot better than low quality fresh.

Preparing squid
for sushi

A popular sushi ingredient, squid is extremely simple
to clean. Choose only the freshest squid – it should
look glossy and have shiny black eyes. Use the method
below to prepare squid for Scattered Sushi [p132–49]
or Hand-formed Sushi [p208–17]. For Stuffed Squid
Sushi [p154–7], keep the body and tentacles intact.

**Specialized
equipment**

clean cloth or tea towel

Preparation time
10 minutes

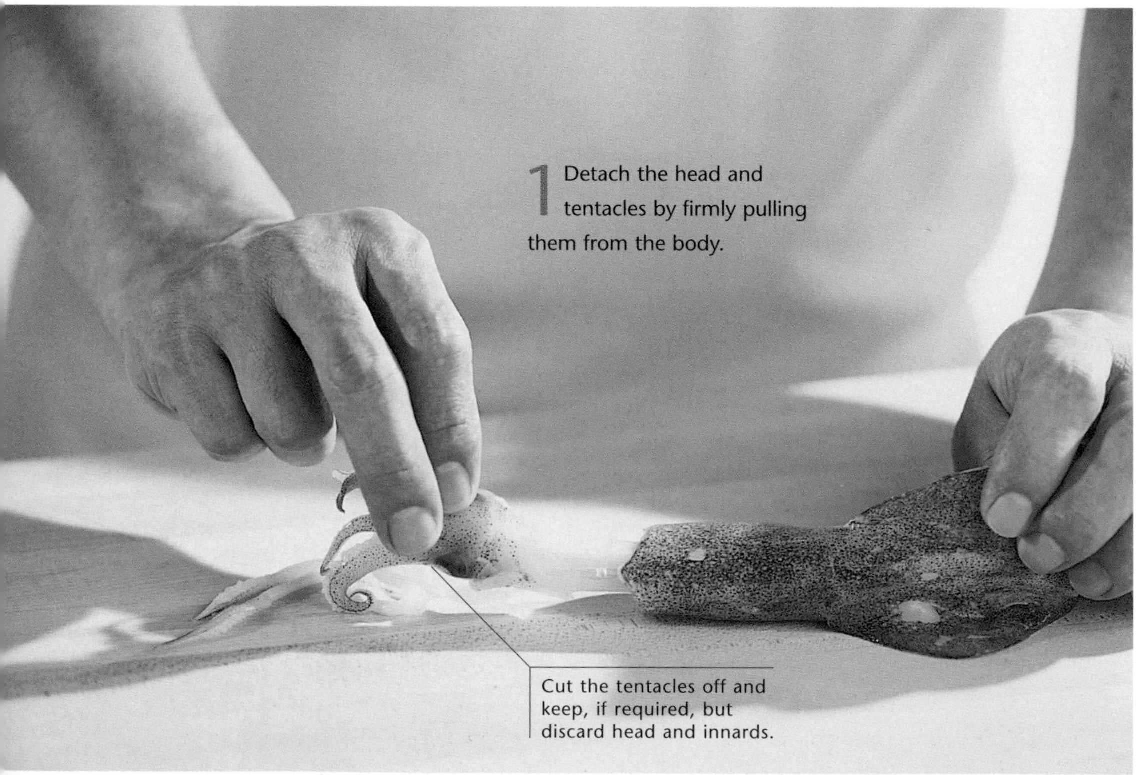

1 Detach the head and
tentacles by firmly pulling
them from the body.

Cut the tentacles off and
keep, if required, but
discard head and innards.

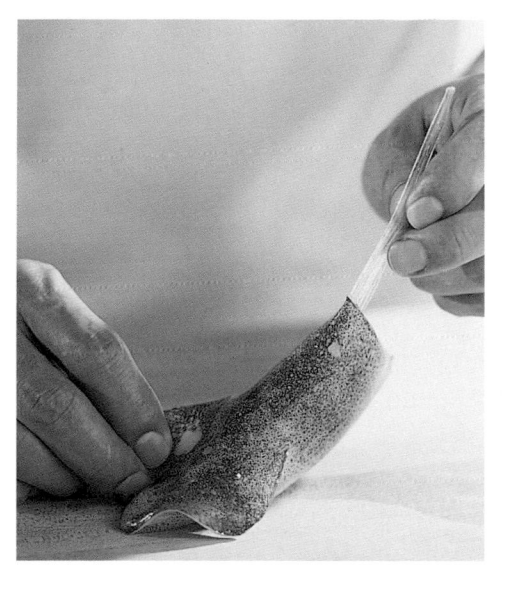

2 Pull the translucent, quill-shaped piece of cartilage out of the body and discard it.

3 If stuffing the squid, keep the body whole and go to the next step. Otherwise, insert a sharp knife into the body and carefully slit it down one side.

4 Either open the body and lay it flat, skin side up, or lay the intact body on a clean surface or chopping board. Grasp the two triangular fins and pull upwards. Discard the fins and the skin.

5 Use a clean, damp cloth to wipe away the mucous lining on one side and any pieces of skin left behind on the other. If using the squid whole, turn it inside out and wipe with a cloth.

Preparing octopus
for sushi

Although the whole of an octopus can be eaten raw, normally only the boiled tentacles are used for sushi. Boiling tenderizes the meat and gives it a sweet flavour, but keep the heat as low as possible as rapid boiling toughens it. Fresh octopus needs to be rubbed clean with salt before cooking. Clean the suckers and ends of tentacles as they may contain mud or sand.

Specialized equipment
200g [7oz] salt, or enough to coat the tentacles
bamboo strainer or colander
Preparation time
45 minutes

The very tops of the tentacles are tough and should be discarded.

1 Using a sharp knife, cut the tentacles off just below the eyes.

2 Put the tentacles in a bowl or on a chopping board and pour over the salt. Rub the salt into the tentacles to tenderize and clean them.

3 Bring a large pan of salted water to the boil, and add the tentacles. Bring back to the boil, then reduce the heat and simmer gently for about 10 minutes.

4 Drain in a bamboo strainer or colander, and set aside to cool. The skin should have turned a deep pink/red with the tentacles tightly curled, showing clean white suckers.

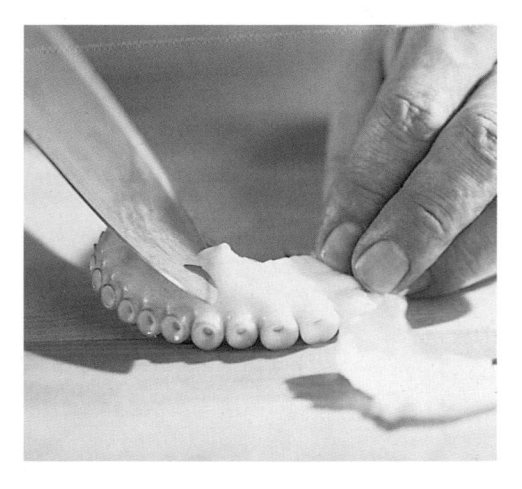

5 Cut the tentacles away from the central section which contains the octopus's mouth parts or 'beak'. This section should be discarded.

6 With the blade of the knife at a 45° angle, to the chopping board, cut the tentacles diagonally into 3–4mm [⅛ in] slices.

Abalone, oysters, scallops
awabi / kaki / hotate gai

One of the earliest ingredients to be used in sushi, abalone is also one of the most highly prized and expensive toppings. It has a unique, subtle flavour and chewy flesh that doesn't appeal to everybody. Oysters, eaten raw even outside Japan, have a light salty flavour. They are usually served as a topping for battleship sushi [p218–21]. The delicately flavoured flesh of the scallop is served as a topping for hand-formed sushi [p208–17]; smaller ones are served on battleship sushi.

Abalone

Abalone can grow up to 30cm [1ft] wide, but the larger they are the more rubbery their flesh.

Look for a yellow tag, which shows that it is farmed.

The shell is lined with mother-of-pearl.

Fresh oysters should always be firmly closed.

Availability

The Japanese love abalone and as demand far exceeds the wild supply, they are commercially cultivated. Only buy abalone with the yellow tags that show they are farmed – wild they are a protected species. In Japan, they are available all year round, but are best between April and June. In North America, they are found off the Pacific coast. Oysters can be eaten all year round but they tend to be less flavoursome from May to August when they spawn. Scallops are widely available all around the world and are also commercially farmed.

Oyster shells are often dotted with barnacles.

Scallops

Fresh shellfish close their shells sharply when tapped.

Oysters

All of the watery grey body of the oyster is edible.

Only the scallop's large white muscle is used for sushi.

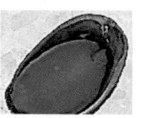

Preparing abalone
for sushi

In Japan, abalone is considered to be a delicacy, but many non-Japanese sushi lovers can't get excited about it as they find it bland and chewy. The best way to enjoy its texture and delicate flavour is to eat it raw and to slice it as thinly as possible.

Specialized equipment

oyster knife or any short strong knife

clean cloth or tea towel

small brush for cleaning shellfish

Preparation time
45 minutes

Cut as close to the shell as possible.

1 Slide an oyster knife or short strong knife under the abalone in the shell, and cut the attached muscle.

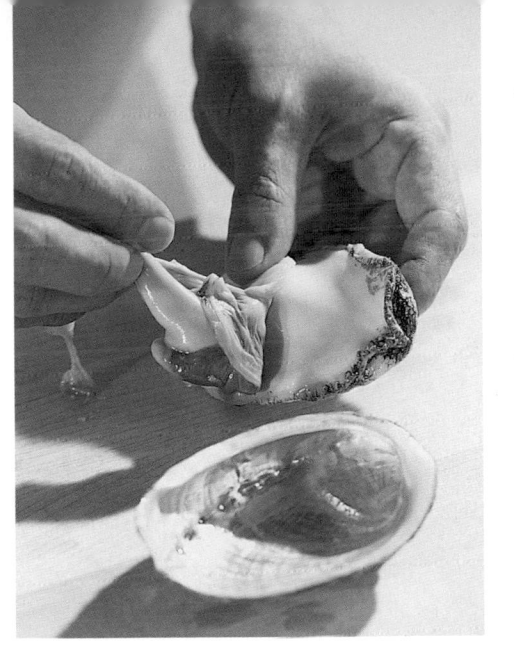

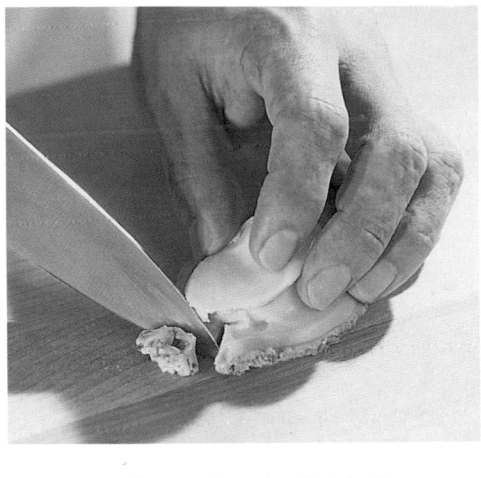

2 Carefully pull off the dark intestines and discard. Wipe clean with a damp cloth.

3 Cut out the mouth at the slightly thinner end of the abalone and discard.

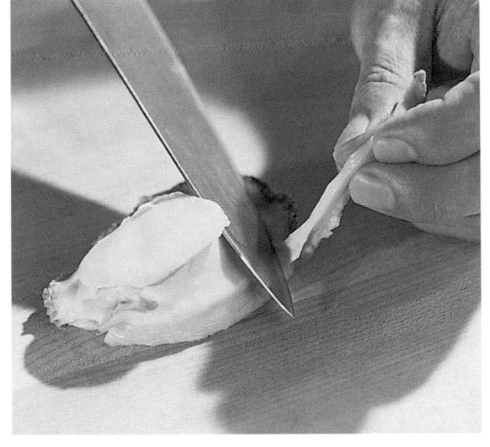

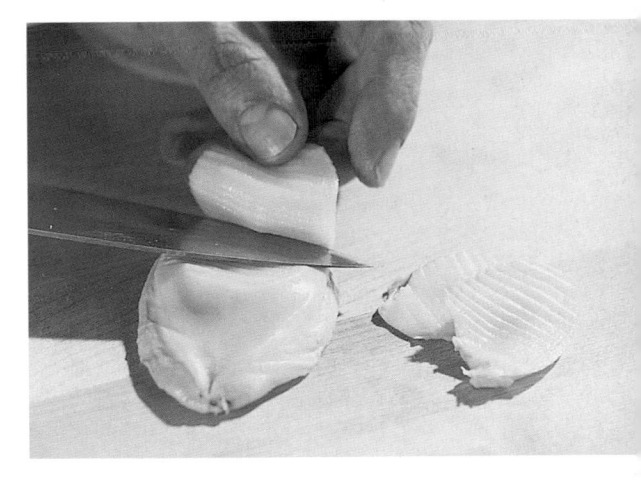

4 Trim off the dark fringe with a knife and discard. Wash the abalone under cold running water, scrubbing off any mucus with a brush.

5 Slice the abalone horizontally into 3–4mm [⅛ in] slices and use for hand-formed sushi, scattered sushi or sashimi.

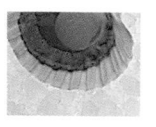

Preparing oysters and scallops for sushi

Because of their runny consistency, oysters are used in battleship rolls [see p218–21]. Thin slices of raw scallop, which have a delicate sweet flavour, are used as a topping for Hand-formed Sushi [see p208–17] and for Scattered Sushi [see p132–49]. Discard oysters and scallops with cracked, chipped or broken shells.

Specialized equipment

oyster knife or any thin, sharp knife

tea towel

Preparation time
about 1 minute per oyster or scallop

Shucking oysters

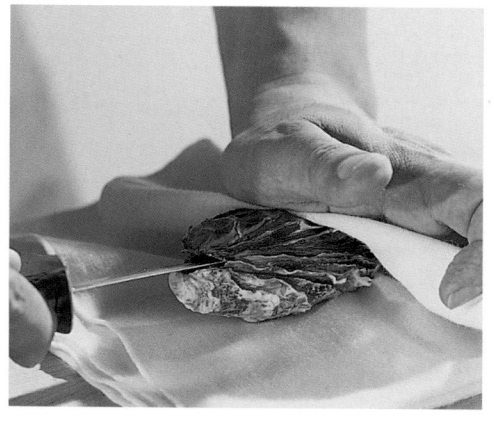

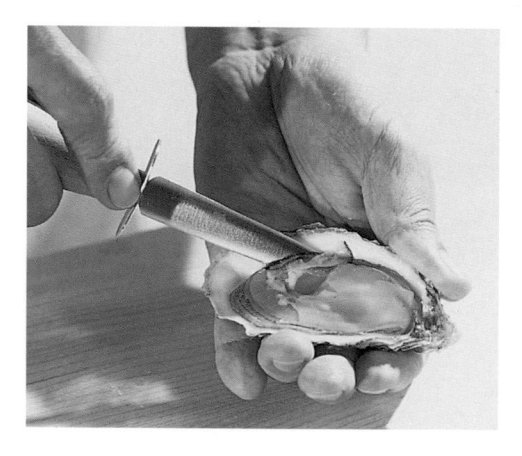

1 Place the oyster on a firm surface. Use a cloth to protect your hand from the sharp shell. Work the knife into the hinge, the narrowest point of the shell. Twist the blade to separate the shells slightly. Slide the blade into the oyster shell, keeping it flat against the upper shell, and scrape it from one side to the other to cut the muscle. The upper shell can now easily be removed.

2 Cut through the muscle that attaches the oyster to the lower shell, and carefully remove the oyster. Use immediately.

Shelling scallops

1 Slide an oyster knife or a thin sharp knife into the shell and cut the muscle that attaches the upper and lower shells. Keep the blade flat against the upper shell and work the blade from side to side.

2 Noting the position of the cut part of the muscle, insert the blade under the scallop at the same spot and cut through the muscle attaching the scallop to the lower shell.

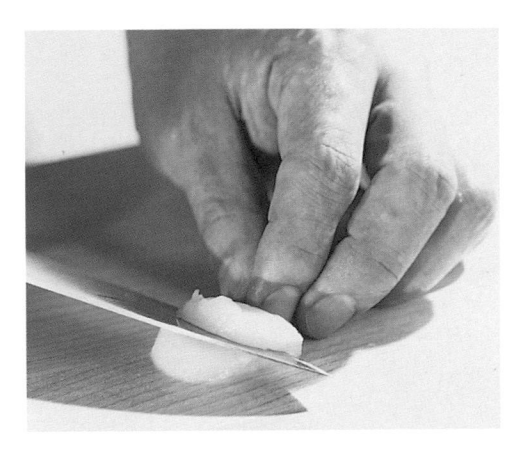

3 Tear off the frilly fringe and bright orange coral – only the round, white muscle is used for sushi.

4 Rinse in cold water and cut into thin slices about 3–4mm [⅛ in] thick by cutting across the top of the scallop. Use immediately.

Fish roe, caviar and sea urchin

Because of their unmanageable nature, fish roe and caviar are usually served in the form of battleship-shaped sushi, where a sheet of nori holds the topping in place. Some of the smaller roes, such as flying fish roe, or *tobiko*, are used as coatings to add colour to inside out rolled sushi. Fish roe and caviar are considered to be delicacies and often command exorbitant prices. Herring roe, or *kazunoko*, for example, was once so abundant on the coasts of Japan that it was used as fertilizer. These days it is so expensive, it has earned the name 'yellow diamond'.

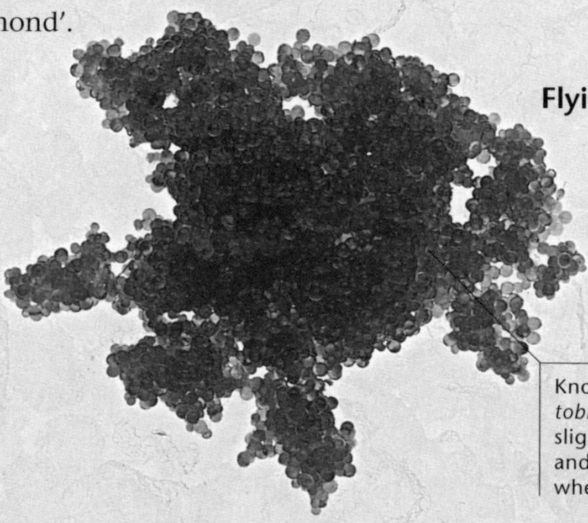

Flying Fish Roe

Sevruga Caviar

Known in Japanese as *tobiko*, these have a slightly crunchy texture and burst in your mouth when you bite into them.

The sushi conoisseur's favourite, sea urchin or *uni* has a subtle nutty flavour when fresh; freezing it can make it less palatable.

The eggs of the Sevruga sturgeon are small, grey and often saltier in flavour than the other varieties.

Sea Urchin

Availability

Caviar and lumpfish caviar are widely available in small jars or tins. Genuine caviar is expensive and, although not a traditional sushi ingredient, its silky texture and luxurious taste have made it popular amongst more innovative sushi chefs. Once opened, caviar should be refrigerated and used within one week. Salmon roe is available in small jars and can be soaked in sake for 1–2 minutes to separate the eggs. It should also be refrigerated once opened and used within one week. Japan and North America are the primary sources of sea urchin.

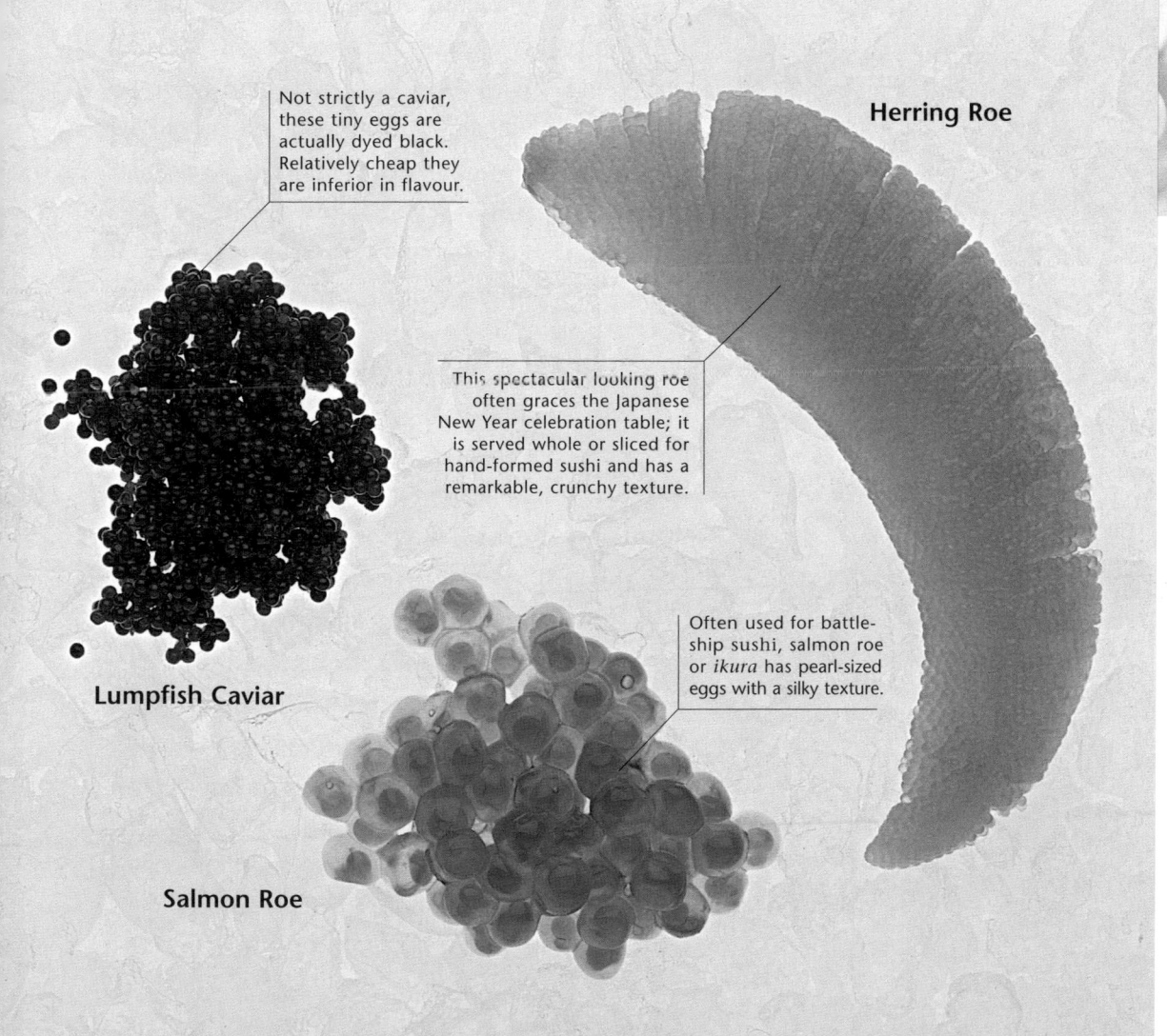

Not strictly a caviar, these tiny eggs are actually dyed black. Relatively cheap they are inferior in flavour.

Herring Roe

This spectacular looking roe often graces the Japanese New Year celebration table; it is served whole or sliced for hand-formed sushi and has a remarkable, crunchy texture.

Lumpfish Caviar

Often used for battle-ship sushi, salmon roe or *ikura* has pearl-sized eggs with a silky texture.

Salmon Roe

∧ Crack open the huge legs of the Alaskan king crab to get to the succulent meat inside

Alaskan king crab [kani]

These large crabs are available ready-cooked from most good fishmongers, but tend to be more expensive than other varieties. The legs, which need to be cracked open, contain more of the sweet, white and red meat than the body. Alaskan crab makes a good topping for hand-formed sushi and is often held in place with a strip of nori. Buy fresh crabmeat if possible, but frozen is also available.

Freshwater eel [unagi]

Grilled eel is traditionally eaten on the Day of the Cow – the Japanese believe that it keeps them healthy for the rest of the year and nearly 1000 tons of it are consumed over the 24-hour period. Freshwater eel is never eaten raw, even in sushi. It is filleted and steamed first, then cut into small pieces, skewered and dipped in a sweet sauce of reduced eel stock, sugar and soy sauce. It is then grilled over a charcoal fire. Most of the *unagi* found in sushi bars is imported ready-prepared from Japan. It has a rich, nutty flavour and is very tender. Ready-prepared *unagi* is available vacuum-packed from Japanese food stores.

Conger eel [anago]

This sea eel grows much bigger than its freshwater cousin – up to 3 metres [10ft] in length – but it is best eaten when it is younger and smaller. Preparing *anago* is a highly skilled job and is considered a good test of the quality of a sushi shop. Preparation is similar to that of the freshwater eel. *Anago* is a popular sushi ingredient, but its flesh is leaner than *unagi* so not as rich in flavour. Conger eel is widely available all year round.

Dover sole [shita birame]

The Japanese name means 'tongue' – an apt description of this odd-looking fish with its disproportionately small head and tapering tail. It grows to no more than 30cm [1ft] in length, but it has wonderfully delicate flavour and texture. It is available all year around except in April.

Yellowtail [hamachi]

These sleek migratory fish cruise around the open sea. Yellowtail is the common name for a specific type of amberjack. The Japanese variety has light golden flesh and very little fat. *Hamachi* is best eaten young when its rich, smooth, buttery texture and slightly smoky flavour can be enjoyed to the full. The meat around the pectoral fins, just behind the gills, is considered the best and, in a sushi shop, is often reserved for special customers. It is used for hand-formed sushi in Japan; some sushi connoisseurs prefer it to tuna.

Swordfish [makajiki]

Its rarity and exquisitely flavoured pink flesh make swordfish one of the most sought after sushi ingredients in Japan. There are several different varieties available: *makajiki* [swordfish], *mekajiki* [broadbill] and *shirokawa* and *kurokawa*, which do not have English names. The most highly regarded of all is *makajiki*, a handsome fish that can grow to 2 metres [6½ ft]. *Makajiki* comes into season in Japan in the autumn. It can be difficult to buy swordfish fresh enough for sushi outside Japan. Beware of grey, watery steaks with gaps appearing in the flesh.

∨ Most swordfish steaks in fishmongers are not of high enough quality for sushi

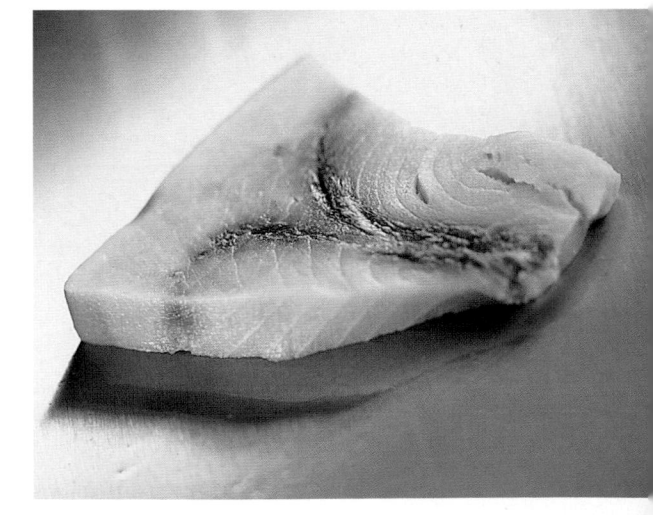

Making

Scattered sushi
chirashi zushi

This is the easiest type of sushi to prepare. It makes a satisfying one-course meal and is served either in individual bowls or brought to the table on a larger plate. *Chirashi* means 'to scatter' and rather than shaping the rice as with other types of sushi, ingredients such as fish and vegetables are arranged on top of it or mixed into it.

There are two basic types of scattered sushi. *Edomae chirashi zushi,* or Tokyo-style sushi, consists of a few slices of sashimi-cut fish decoratively arranged on a bed of sushi rice [see p134–7]. For *gomoko zushi*, or Kansai-style sushi, the ingredients are often cooked and mixed together with the sushi rice [see p138–9]. This is the most versatile form of sushi and something closer to a rice salad, so experiment and use the recipes that follow as guidelines rather than following them strictly.

As with all sushi, start cooking the rice first and then prepare the rest of your ingredients. At the end, the actual assembly takes very little time at all. Please note, the preparation times in the recipes that follow do not include the time that it takes to prepare the rice as it is so easy to make in advance.

< Save time when making sushi by preparing your ingredients in advance

> Tokyo-style sushi [see p134–7] – an artistic arrangement of fish and vegetables on a bed of rice

Tokyo-style sushi
edomae chirashi zushi

Originally, this dish would have been a simple one-course meal – a bowl of rice topped with a few slices of raw fish and whatever vegetables were cheap and good on the day. It was popular in Edo, which is now Tokyo. There is no strict rule as to what seafood to use – try to combine good colours and textures. Unlike many other scattered sushi, *edomae chirashi zushi* is best served in individual bowls. Arrange the ingredients however you like, but try to mix shapes and colours. To speed assembly, prepare everything beforehand.

Ingredients

1 quantity prepared sushi rice [p36–8]

4 tbsp shredded daikon or cucumber

4 perilla leaves or mustard cress to garnish

1 skinless fillet of tuna, about 150g [5oz], cut as for sashimi [p89] into 12 slices

1 thick Japanese omelette [p40–43], cut into 8 strips, 1cm [½ in] thick

1 medium squid body, about 90g [3oz], cleaned [p114–15] and cut into 4 strips

1 skinless fillet of salmon, about 150g [5oz], cut as for sashimi [p89] into 8 slices

4 prepared tiger prawns [p110–11]

1 vinegar-marinated mackerel fillet [p92–3] about 120g [4oz], cut into 8 slices

4 scallops, cut in half

4 white fish roses made using 120g [4oz] skinless fillet of white fish [p242]

4 tsp salmon roe

4 wasabi paste leaves made with 4 tsp paste [p51]

1 baby cucumber, cut into pine branch garnishes [p50]

Serves 4

Preparation time
1 hour

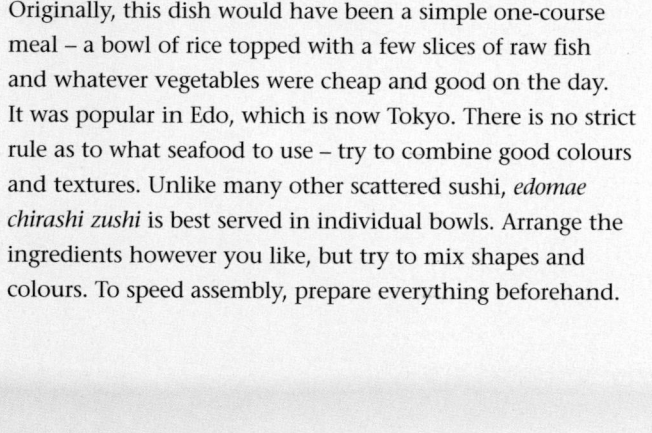

1 Fill each bowl two-thirds full with sushi rice. Place a small, loose ball of shredded daikon or cucumber against one side of each bowl; lean a perilla leaf against it; or use mustard cress.

2 Position 3 slices of tuna and 2 pieces of omelette in front of the perilla leaf or mustard cress.

3 Curl each piece of squid, and place in front of the omelette. Arrange 2 slices of salmon next to the tuna.

4 Cut a prawn so that it folds in half and add it to the arrangement.

5 Arrange 2 slices of mackerel with silver skin showing, 2 scallop halves and a white fish rose in the bowl.

6 Add a spoonful of salmon roe, and finally, garnish with a wasabi leaf and a cucumber pine branch.

Tokyo-style scattered sushi – a feast for the mouth and for the eyes

Vegetarian scattered sushi
gomoko zushi

This is one of the easiest types of sushi to prepare at home. In Japan it is made with the offcuts of whatever vegetables are found in the refrigerator. You could add asparagus to this dish – I've even been known to throw in a handful of frozen peas. It makes an ideal lunch dish, is great for picnics and can even be served as a light dinner party starter. Save time by preparing the shiitake mushrooms, kampyo and tofu pouches in advance.

1   Steam or blanch the mangetout until tender, about 4–5 minutes. Reserve a few whole mangetout to use as a garnish and chop the rest.

2   Spread the rice in the bottom of a large serving dish, or divide between 4 individual bowls. Keep the rice as loose as possible.

3   Scatter the shiitake mushroom slices, the kampyo and the tofu pouch slices over the rice.

4   Set aside a few slices of lotus root and a few carrot flowers to use as a garnish. Add the remaining lotus root slices, the carrot flowers and the chopped mangetout.

5   Cut the omelette into fine shreds and scatter over the rice. Garnish with the slices of lotus root and the reserved carrot flowers and mangetout.

6   Sprinkle with the shredded nori just before serving. Add this at the very last minute, otherwise it will go soggy.

Ingredients

30g [1oz] mangetout

1 quantity prepared sushi rice [p36–8]

4 large seasoned shiitake mushrooms [p31], thinly sliced

30g [1oz] prepared kampyo [p30], chopped into 2cm [1in] lengths

2 seasoned deep-fried tofu pouches [p46], unseparated, thinly sliced

60g [2oz] lotus root, thinly sliced

1 carrot, cut into flowers [p48]

3–4 thin Japanese omelettes [p44–5]

2 sheets nori seaweed, thinly shredded

Serves 4

Preparation time
40 minutes

Vegetarian scattered sushi is a mix of different tastes, textures and colours

Asparagus and scrambled egg sushi

I like to serve this sushi in the spring when asparagus comes into season, but you can make it at any time of year and use whatever green vegetable is in season.

1 Steam the asparagus for 2–3 minutes. Reserve the tips to use as a garnish, and chop the stalks into small pea-sized pieces.
2 Mix the sushi rice and chopped asparagus stalks together in a large mixing bowl, and spread the mixture in a large serving dish or divide between 4 individual bowls.
3 Scatter the scrambled egg over the rice and garnish with the asparagus tips.

Ingredients

500g [1lb] asparagus, trimmed

1 quantity prepared sushi rice [p36–8]

1 quantity scrambled eggs [p43]

Serves 4

Preparation time
40 minutes

Mangetout and vine tomato sushi

This is an excellent light lunch in the summer. The combination of slightly crunchy bright green mangetout and sweet, succulent vine tomatoes is quite refreshing.

1 Blanch the mangetout and cool immediately in cold water. Reserve a few whole mangetout to use as a garnish, and cut the remaining ones into thin strips.
2 Mix the sushi rice with the mangetout and chopped tomatoes in a large mixing bowl. Spread the mixture in a large serving dish, or divide between 4 individual bowls.
3 Sprinkle over the toasted sesame seeds and garnish with the reserved mangetout.

Ingredients

150g [5oz] mangetout

1 quantity prepared sushi rice [p36–8]

150g [5oz] vine tomatoes, seeded and finely chopped

1 tbsp toasted sesame seeds

Serves 4

Preparation time
40 minutes

Fresh seasonal vegetables add a delicious bite to scattered sushi

Broccoli and shredded omelette sushi

Take care to steam the broccoli only briefly as this retains its vibrant colour and its crunchiness.

1 Cut the broccoli into small, bite-size pieces. Steam for 2 minutes, then set aside to cool.
2 Stack the omelettes on top of each other and roll up tightly. Finely shred by cutting very thin slices at an angle. Mix the sushi rice, broccoli and shredded omelette in a large bowl.
3 Transfer the rice mixture to a large serving dish, or divide between 4 individual plates and scatter broccoli on top.
4 Place a small mound of ginger on top of the rice. Sprinkle over the seasame seeds before serving.

Ingredients

500g [1lb] purple sprouting broccoli, tough stems removed

4 thin omelettes [p44–5]

1 quantity prepared sushi rice [p36–8]

4 tbsp shredded red or pink pickled ginger

2 tbsp toasted sesame seeds

Serves 4

Preparation time
40 minutes

Mushroom and egg sushi

Mushroom and egg complement each other perfectly in this dish. Use fresh enoki, shiitake or oyster mushrooms.

1 Heat the oil in a large frying pan or wok, and stir-fry the mushrooms for 2 minutes. Remove from the heat, add the soy sauce and stir gently for a further 30 seconds. Drain and set aside.
2 Combine the sushi rice with the cooked mushrooms and sesame seeds in a large bowl.
3 Transfer the rice mixture to a large serving dish, or divide between 4 individual plates. Cut the omelette into fine shreds, then sprinkle over the rice. Garnish with the shredded nori just before serving.

Ingredients

2 tbsp vegetable oil

500g [1lb] mushrooms, sliced into 1cm [½in] strips

1 tbsp soy sauce

1 quantity prepared sushi rice [p36–8]

2 tbsp toasted sesame seeds

4 thin omelettes [p44–5]

shredded nori to garnish

Serves 4

Preparation time
40 minutes

Pink pickled ginger tops broccoli and shredded omelette sushi

Sun-dried tomato and mozzarella sushi

My parents would be horrified by this fusion sushi – or what they would call 'confusion sushi', but it really works.

1   Mix the sushi rice, sun-dried tomatoes and mozzarella cheese together in a large mixing bowl.
2   Transfer the rice mixture to a large serving dish, or divide between 4 individual bowls.
3   Garnish with basil leaves and serve.

Ingredients

1 quantity prepared sushi rice [p36–8]

100g [3½ oz] sun-dried tomatoes, drained and sliced

175g [6oz] fresh mozzarella cheese, drained and cubed

large bunch of fresh basil leaves to garnish

Serves 4

Preparation time
30 minutes

Crabmeat, chilli and lime sushi

This is fusion sushi that combines fresh crab and chillies, two favourites of mine. Vary the amount of chilli to suit your taste and add a little lime juice to help bring the contrasting flavours together. You might find it more economical to buy frozen white crabmeat.

1   Combine the prepared sushi rice, crabmeat and chopped chillies in a large mixing bowl.
2   Cut each piece of nori to plate size, and lay a sheet on each plate.
3   Divide the rice mixture between the individual plates, piling it on top of the nori squares. Squeeze a little lime juice over the rice; garnish with the coriander leaves and slices of lime, and serve.

Ingredients

1 quantity prepared sushi rice [p36–8]

175g [6oz] crabmeat

2–4 large red chillies, seeded and finely chopped

4 sheets nori seaweed

juice of 1 lime

fresh coriander leaves and slices of lime to garnish

Serves 4

Preparation time
40 minutes

Garnish sun-dried tomato and mozzarella sushi with basil leaves

Seared beef fillet and red onion sushi

This recipe uses the traditional Japanese method for cooking bonito fish, *tataki*, to cook beef, but it works just as well with tuna steak. The beef is briefly seared to seal in the flavour while the centre remains almost rare. Submerging the seared beef in ice-cold water instantly halts the cooking process and also washes away excess fat. You can save time by preparing up to step 5 in advance. This is a robust dish that should be enjoyed with a full-bodied red wine.

Ingredients

1 medium red onion, peeled and halved

500 g [1lb] beef fillet

1 tbsp vegetable oil

100 ml [3½ floz] sake

100 ml [3½ floz] soy sauce

1 quantity prepared sushi rice [p36–8]

2 spring onions, finely chopped, to garnish

chilli daikon relish [p33]

salt and freshly ground black pepper

Serves 4

Preparation time
1 hour 30 minutes

1 Cut the onion into thin slices and place in a bowl of cold water. Set aside to soak for 10 minutes. Pat dry the beef fillet with kitchen paper. Rub salt and pepper into it, and set aside to season for 30 minutes.

2 Heat the oil in a large heavy-bottomed frying pan and sear the beef until brown, about 2 minutes on each side.

3 The surface of the beef should be well-browned, but the inside should be raw. However, you can cook the meat for longer if you prefer it less rare.

4 Transfer the beef to a bowl of iced water and leave to stand for 10 minutes. Combine the sake and soy in a shallow dish.

5 Wipe the beef dry with kitchen paper and transfer to the dish of sake and soy mixture. Set aside to marinate for at least 30 minutes, or leave to marinate overnight in the refrigerator.

7 Fill each bowl two-thirds full with sushi rice, and top with the slices of beef.

6 Remove the beef from the marinade and pat dry with kitchen paper. Slice into 5 mm [¼ in] thick pieces or as thinly as possible.

8 Drain the onion slices and use to garnish. Sprinkle over the spring onions, and serve with chilli daikon relish.

Seared beef fillet, an unconventional but delicious sushi ingredient

Stuffed sushi
inari zushi

This form of sushi uses cooked ingredients such as thin omelettes, cabbage leaves or deep-fried tofu as a wrapping material for sushi rice and other cooked ingredients. Vegetarian stuffed sushi, especially the traditional *inari zushi* which is made with delicious pouches of seasoned deep-fried tofu, is great to take on a picnic – it is easy to transport and tends not to spoil quickly.

The Japanese prepare stuffed sushi at home and eat the tasty little parcels under cherry trees in spring which are famous for their beautiful, fragrant blossom. The fillings can vary from simple plain sushi rice mixed with a few chopped fresh herbs to whatever seasonal ingredients are available. There are no strict rules as to what you can or cannot use – I have included a recipe for one of my personal favourites, stuffed squid sushi. Because most types of stuffed sushi can be prepared up to six hours in advance, it also makes a convenient party food.

< Cooked ingredients are mixed with rice and then used as a stuffing or wrapped to create a parcel

> Deep-fried tofu makes a wonderful container for thinly sliced shiitake mushrooms and rice

Stuffed tofu pouches
inari zushi

This conveniently portable form of sushi is a popular choice for sushi lunch boxes. The tofu pouches have a distinctive sweet and savoury flavour and are also highly nutritious because of their soy content. The pouches taste delicious even with plain sushi rice but you can try adding other ingredients such as chopped perilla leaves or lemon zest.

1   Mix the sushi rice with the sesame seeds and mushrooms in a large mixing bowl. Carefully spoon the filling into each tofu pouch until about one half full.
2   Make a parcel by carefully folding one side of the tofu pouch under and then the other.

Ingredients

1 quantity prepared sushi rice [p36–8]

2 tbsp toasted sesame seeds

6 seasoned shiitake mushrooms [p31], very finely sliced

6 seasoned tofu pouches, [p46]

Makes 12 pieces

Preparation time
45 minutes

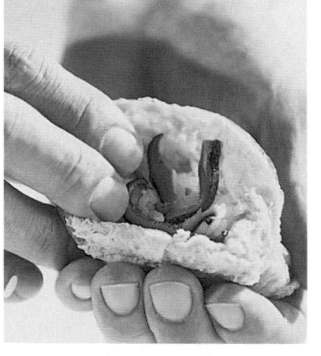

Use your fingers to loosely pack the filling; make sure you don't overfill the pouch.

Carefully fold the edges over to make a parcel.

Stuffed tofu pouches with simple fillings make perfect picnic food

Stuffed squid sushi
ika zushi

Here, squid is first cooked in a sweet vinegar mix, amazu, and then stuffed with a mixture of seasoned rice and vegetables. Experiment with different stuffings, but as *ika zushi* is always served sliced, use vegetables such as green beans, carrots, cucumbers and chillies that add colour.

Ingredients

for amazu:
3 tbsp Japanese rice vinegar

1 tbsp sugar

1 tsp salt

for squid:
2 medium squid with tentacles, about 300g [10oz] each, cleaned and body intact [p114–15]

1 tbsp soy sauce

60g [2oz] green beans, trimmed

1 quantity prepared sushi rice [p36–8]

5cm [2in] piece fresh ginger, grated

5 perilla leaves, chopped, or 2 tbsp chopped fresh coriander leaves

Serves 4

Preparation time
1 hour

1 Mix the ingredients for the amazu together in a small bowl. Add to the squid with the soy sauce in a non-aluminium pan. Cook gently for 2–3 minutes.

2 Drain the squid and set to one side. Once cool enough to handle, chop the tentacles. Steam or blanch the green beans until tender, about 2–3 minutes, then chop into small pea-sized pieces.

3 Mix the sushi rice with the chopped green beans, grated ginger, chopped tentacles and chopped perilla leaves or coriander in a bowl.

4 Spoon the rice mixture into each of the marinated squid bodies.

5 Gently pack the filling into the squid with a pair of cooking chopsticks or a spoon. Set aside to stand at room temperature for between 30 minutes and 1 hour to allow the flavours to develop.

6 Use a sharp knife dipped in water to slice the stuffed squid into 2 cm [¾ in] thick rounds. Arrange on a plate and serve.

Green beans and perilla leaves add colour to stuffed squid

Omelette purses
chakin zushi

Omelette makes a colourful wrapping material, and here each
stuffed purse is tied together with a bright green coriander
stalk. This sushi is popular with my vegetarian friends.

1 Mix the sushi rice with the
shiitake mushrooms and
sesame seeds in a bowl. Place
an omelette on a clean surface
or chopping board and spoon
about 2 tablespoons of rice
stuffing into the middle of it.

Ingredients

*1 quantity prepared
sushi rice [p36–8]*

*4 seasoned shiitake
mushrooms [p31],
thinly sliced*

2 tbsp toasted sesame seeds

*8 thin Japanese omelettes
[p44–5]*

*8 coriander or flat leaf
parsely stalks, leaves
removed, 15 cm [6 in] long*

Serves 4

Preparation time
1 hour 30 minutes

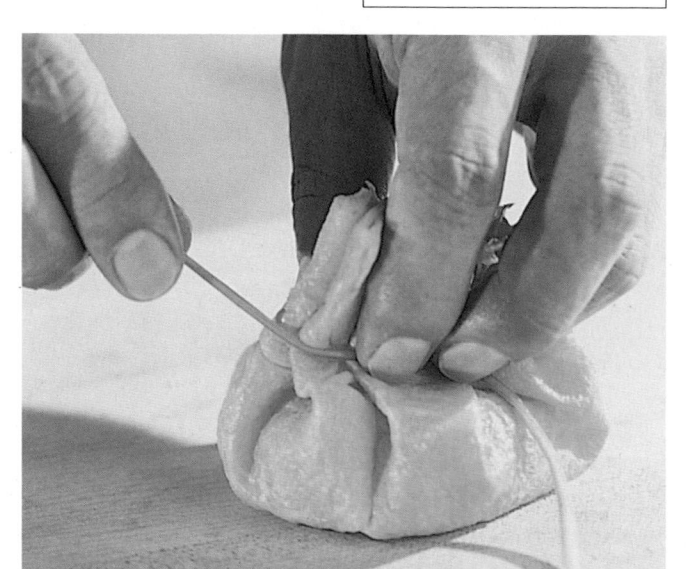

2 Run the back of a knife
along the coriander or flat
leaf parsley stalk to tenderize
it. Gather up the edges of the
omelette and tie together
with the stalk.

Purses and parcels can be tied
with coriander stalks or kampyo

 # Savoy cabbage leaves with herb and egg rice

The bright green colour and crinkled texture of savoy cabbage make it an interesting wrapping material. The leaves are blanched very briefly then immersed in cold water, which helps them to retain their colour. Be sure to pat any excess water off the leaves otherwise the stuffing can become soggy. Use the same technique to fold these parcels as for omelette parcels [see p158–59].

1   Cut out and discard the thick stems at the base of each of the cabbage leaves. Bring a large pan of water to the boil, and blanch the cabbage leaves for about 2 minutes. Remove and immerse immediately in a bowl of cold water. Pat any excess water off the leaves.

2   Mix the sushi rice with the herbs, scrambled eggs and sesame seeds in a bowl.

3   Place a cabbage leaf on a clean surface or chopping board; put a tablespoonful of the rice mixture in the middle of it.

4   Fold over the near and far edges of the leaf so that they overlap in the middle. Then fold the other opposite edges over to make a parcel.

5   Secure the parcel by piercing it with a small wooden skewer or toothpick. Repeat the process to make 8 parcels. Be sure to remind people to remove the skewers or toothpicks before eating.

Ingredients

8 large savoy cabbage leaves

½ quantity prepared sushi rice [p36–8]

30g [1oz] mixed herbs such as flat leaf parsley, coriander, spring onions or mint, finely chopped

1 quantity scrambled eggs [p43]

2 tbsp toasted sesame seeds

8 wooden skewers or toothpicks

Makes 8 parcels

Preparation time
45 minutes

Choose tender young cabbage for this fresh-tasting stuffed sushi

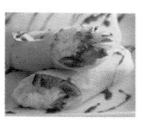

Seared duck breast in rice paper parcels

Pan-fried duck breast is wrapped in Thai rice paper and drizzled with traditional Japanese teriyaki sauce in this innovative recipe. Teriyaki sauce can be bought ready-made but it's worth taking a little extra time to make this delicious version yourself. Serve it as a dipping sauce or keep it for up to a week in a sealed container in the refrigerator.

Ingredients

for savoury teriyaki sauce:
60ml [2fl oz] mirin

60ml [2fl oz] soy sauce

30g [1oz] sugar

5cm [2in] piece fresh ginger, peeled

5cm [2in] piece carrot, peeled

1 medium onion, peeled and halved

for parcels:
1 duck breast

4 round sheets rice paper

½ quantity prepared sushi rice [p36–8]

½ a cucumber, cut into thin strips

Makes 4 parcels

Preparation time
45 minutes

1 Put the ingredients for the teriyaki sauce in a small saucepan and heat gently. Stir until the sugar dissolves, then leave to simmer until the sauce has thickened to a syrupy consistency, about 20 minutes. Meanwhile prepare the duck.

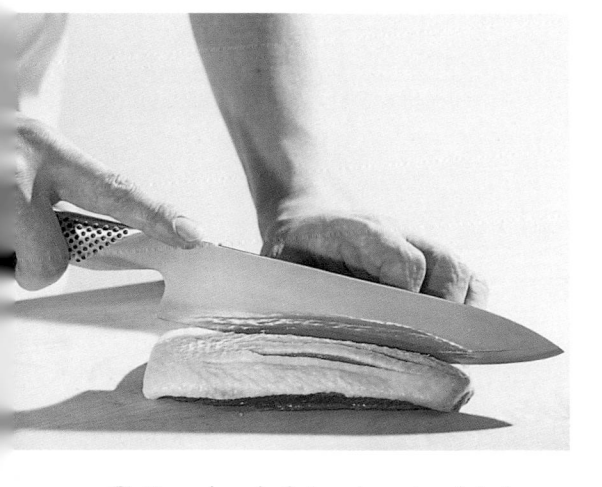

2 Use a sharp knife to cut a series of shallow slits in the skin of the duck breast to help the fat drain away.

3 Heat a heavy-bottomed frying pan over a medium heat. Cook the duck breast skin-side down until brown and crispy, about 5–10 minutes. Turn over and cook for a further 3–5 minutes.

4 Remove the duck from the heat and plunge into a bowl of boiling hot water, or pour over boiling water to wash off excess fat. Remove from the water; set aside to cool to room temperature.

5 Fill a baking tray with warm water, lay in the sheets of rice paper and soak until soft, about 2–3 minutes. Remove, and drain on kitchen towel. Cut the duck into 5mm [¼ in] thick slices.

7 Add 2–3 slices of duck and a few thin strips of cucumber.

6 Spread the rice paper on a clean surface or chopping board. Put a large tablespoon of rice in the centre and flatten slightly with the back of a spoon.

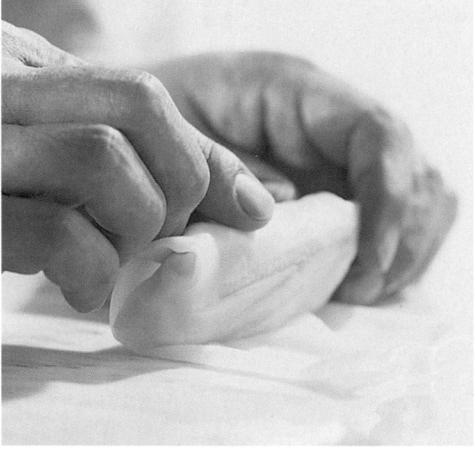

8 To wrap, bring the bottom edge of the rice paper over the filling, then fold in the sides. Continue to wrap to make a small parcel.

9 To serve, cut the parcel diagonally and arrange on a serving plate. Strain the teriyaki sauce and drizzle over the parcels.

Stuffed sushi inspired by Peking roast duck pancakes

Pressed sushi
oshi zushi

This is the oldest form of sushi and probably developed from the ancient method of preserving fish by packing it tightly in boxes of fermented rice. Rice and other ingredients are pressed together in a wooden sushi mould to form a block, which is then cut into bite-sized pieces. Until the mid-nineteenth century when hand-formed sushi, or *nigiri zushi*, was invented, all sushi was made in this way. Today, pressed sushi made with vinegar-marinated mackerel is the most popular take-away food bought at airports by Japanese travellers going abroad.

The recipes for pressed sushi that follow use a wooden pressed sushi mould [see p23], but a cake tin lined with clingfilm makes a very good substitute. Of the many different types of sushi, pressed sushi is most suited to advance preparation. In fact, I prefer to make it up to six hours in advance as this allows time for the flavours of the sushi rice and topping to develop. Wrap each pressed block in clingfilm and store at a cool room temperature, then cut into small pieces to serve. Prepare a selection with different toppings, and serve them as elegant and delicious canapés.

< Use a knife dipped in vinegared water or wiped with a wet cloth to ensure clean cuts when slicing pressed sushi

> Create designer sushi by arranging strips of ingredients in the bottom of the sushi mould to give a striped effect when turned out

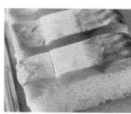

Pressed sushi
oshi zushi

All the pressed sushi recipes that follow use a rectangular mould that measures 15cm [6in] x 7.5cm [3in] x 5cm [2in]. Soak the mould in a bowl of water for about 15 minutes beforehand with a weight, such as a plate, on it to stop it from floating – this prevents the rice from sticking to it. You can prepare as far as step 7 up to six hours in advance.

Ingredients

1 marinated mackerel fillet [p92–3], about 150g [5oz]

wasabi

½ quantity prepared sushi rice [p36–8]

Makes 6 pieces

Preparation time
30 minutes

1 Trim the mackerel fillet so it is as thin and flat as possible. The offcuts can be used to fill gaps in the mould, so don't discard them.

2 Cut the fillet to fit the base of the mould, and lay it skin side down inside the box. Fill any gaps with smaller pieces of mackerel.

3 Cover the bottom of the mould with a patchwork of fillet cuts. Spread a few dabs of wasabi over the mackerel.

4 Add the sushi rice to the mould – it should be about two-thirds full – and use your fingers to pack it down evenly over the mackerel fillets.

5 Put the lid on the mould and press it down firmly to compact the rice.

6 With both thumbs on the lid of the mould, holding it in place, lift off the sides. Then take the lid off and carefully turn the mould over onto a chopping board, so the mackerel is on top.

7 Remove the base of the mould. If preparing in advance, wrap the block in clingfilm and store in a cool place for up to 6 hours, but don't refrigerate.

8 Dip a sharp knife in water, wiping off the excess, and cut the block of sushi in half.

9 Cut each half into 3 equally sized pieces to make 6 pieces and serve with pickled ginger.

Pressed mackerel sushi – excellent served with pickled ginger

Soy-basted conger eel sushi

Conger eel or *anago* is available cooked and basted in soy, and either frozen or in vacuum packs from Japanese food shops. Try microwaving it for 20–30 seconds to revive its flavour before you use it in this sushi.

Follow the recipe for Pressed Sushi [see p170–73], but substitute the conger eel for the mackerel and omit the wasabi.

Ingredients

250g [8oz] soy-basted conger eel

½ quantity prepared sushi rice [p36–8]

Makes 6 pieces

Preparation time
20 minutes

Prawn and nori sushi

Prawns make a good sushi ingredient for those who are wary of uncooked fish. Remember to lay the prawns pink side down in the mould.

1 Open the prawns flat and lay them pink side down on the bottom of the wet sushi mould, covering the entire bottom of the box. Dab a little wasabi on the prawns, if using.
2 Fill the mould with half of the prepared sushi rice.
3 Cut a sheet of nori to fit the mould and gently press it down on to the rice.
4 Add the rest of the rice so the mould is nearly full. Put the lid on the mould, and press down gently.
5 Unmould the rice and prawn block, and use a knife dipped in water to cut it into 6 equally-sized pieces.

Ingredients

Approximately 12 medium prawns, cleaned and butterflied [p110–11], tail shells removed

wasabi [optional]

½ quantity prepared sushi rice [p36–8]

2 sheets nori seaweed

Makes 6 pieces

Preparation time
20 minutes

Lunch box favourites prawn and nori, and conger eel pressed sushi

Omelette and mustard cress sushi

This simple recipe adds an exotic twist to the classic combination of egg and cress. Make sure you buy proper cress – not the bland supermarket substitute, rape seedlings.

1   Line the base of a wet sushi mould with a layer of omelette. Fill the mould two-thirds full with sushi rice, put the lid on it and press gently to compact the rice.
2   Unmould the rice and egg block, and use a knife dipped in water to cut it into 6 equally sized pieces.
3   Trim the root ends off the cress, and top each piece of sushi with a small peppery bunch of cress.

Ingredients

2 thin Japanese omelettes [p44–5]

½ quantity prepared sushi rice [p36–8]

2 cartons mustard cress

Makes 6 pieces

Preparation time
45 minutes

Asparagus and red pepper sushi

Here, the sushi mould is used to shape the rice, and the toppings are added later.

1   Grill the red pepper whole until the skin blackens. Put it in a bowl, cover with clingfilm and set aside to cool.
2   Meanwhile, steam or blanch the asparagus until tender, about 4 minutes, then plunge into a bowl of ice cold water.
3   Peel the skin off the red pepper and discard the seeds and the pith. Slice into thin strips.
4   Fill a wet sushi mould two-thirds full with sushi rice and put the lid on it. Press gently to compact the rice.
5   Unmould the block of rice, and use a knife dipped in water to cut it into 6 equally sized pieces.
6   Cut the asparagus stalks in half lengthways and trim to the length of the rice blocks. Arrange them in a row on the rice and make a criss-cross pattern on top with the red pepper.

Ingredients

1 large red pepper

12 small asparagus spears

½ quantity prepared sushi rice [p36–8]

Makes 6 pieces

Preparation time
40 minutes

Vegetarian sushi makes a colourful and appetizing meal for everyone

 # Avocado and shiitake mushroom sushi

This recipe combines eastern and western ingredients in a simple and light sushi. The vinegar in the rice balances the high oil content of the avocado.

1   Line the base of a wet sushi mould with the avocado slices, then add the sushi rice. Put the lid on the mould, and press gently to compact the rice.
2   Unmould the rice and avocado block, and use a knife dipped in water to cut it into 6 equally sized pieces.
3   Top each piece of sushi with the shiitake mushroom slices.

Ingredients

1 ripe avocado, sliced

½ quantity prepared sushi rice [p36–8]

6 seasoned shiitake mushrooms [p31], sliced

Makes 6 pieces

Preparation time
30 minutes

Smoked salmon and cucumber sushi

The skill is in arranging the strips of salmon and cucumber. This sushi looks impressive but takes practice to perfect.

1   Trim the salmon and cucumber strips so that they fit the mould exactly when placed diagonally in it. Line the base of the wet sushi mould with alternating diagonal strips of smoked salmon and cucumber.
2   Add the sushi rice, then put the lid on the mould and press gently to compact it.
3   Unmould the rice, salmon and cucumber block, and use a knife dipped in water to cut it into 6 equally sized pieces.

Ingredients

100g [3½ oz] smoked salmon, cut into strips

15 cm [6 in] piece of cucumber, cut lengthways into thin strips

½ quantity prepared sushi rice [p36–8]

Makes 6 pieces

Preparation time
30 minutes

Multicolour toppings can make spectacular pressed sushi

Shiitake mushroom and zasai sushi

This Chinese-inspired sushi uses zasai, a pickled vegetable with dark green knobbly skin and a crunchy texture. Look for it in jars or tins in any South East Asian food shop.

1 Soak the zasai in water for about an hour, then drain and cut into thin slices.
2 Line the bottom of a wet sushi mould with the slices of zasai. Fill the mould half full with sushi rice.
3 Add a layer of shiitake mushroom slices. Put the lid on the mould, and press gently to compact the rice.
4 Unmould the zasai, mushroom and rice block, and use a knife dipped in water to cut it into 6 equally sized pieces.

Ingredients

100g [3½ oz] pickled zasai root

½ quantity prepared sushi rice [p36–8]

8 seasoned shiitake mushrooms [p31], sliced

Makes 6 pieces

Preparation time
30 minutes

Sea bass and perilla leaf sushi

The chilli garnish gives a fiery boost to this delicate sushi. Try to cut the sea bass thinly enough for the green of the perilla leaf to show through the translucent fish.

1 Line the bottom of a wet sushi mould with a thin layer of sea bass. Add a thin layer of perilla leaves.
2 Add the sushi rice, put the lid on the mould and press gently to compact the rice.
3 Unmould the sea bass, perilla leaf and rice block, and use a knife dipped in water to cut it into 6 equally sized pieces.
4 Garnish each piece of sushi with a couple of slices of chilli.

Ingredients

90–120g [3–4oz] sea bass fillet, thinly sliced [p88–9]

½ quantity prepared sushi rice [p36–8]

about 10 perilla leaves

1 hot red chilli, cut into thin rounds, to garnish

Makes 6 pieces

Preparation time
30 minutes

Sea bass and perilla sushi in front of shiitake mushroom and zasai sushi

Children's sushi
kodomo zushi

There is no reason why children should be excluded from the pleasures of eating sushi. The most enthusiastic and obliging guinea pigs for testing my recipes have been my three children. Start with more familiar toppings such as ham, cheese and smoked salmon, and use biscuit cutters to create fun shapes; use the offcuts as garnishes.

1   Moisten the biscuit cutters with water to prevent the rice from sticking to them. Use one third of the rice to make shapes in the first biscuit cutter [see below]. Cut corresponding shapes out of the omelette and use as a topping. Repeat with the second third of rice in another biscuit cutter and use smoked salmon as a topping. Make shapes with the remaining rice and sprinkle soboro on top of the rice.

2   Garnish each shape with cucumber, offcuts from the toppings or with other smaller cut out shapes.

Ingredients

1 quantity prepared sushi rice [p36–8]

1 thin Japanese omelette [p44–5]

30g [1oz] thinly sliced smoked salmon

½ quantity soboro [p47]

cucumber to garnish

other suggested toppings that use ⅓ of the rice to make 8 pieces each:

½ quantity scrambled eggs [p43]

8 cheese slices

60g [2oz] thinly sliced honey roasted ham

Makes about 24 pieces

Preparation time
45 minutes

Use the back of a teaspoon to compact the rice.

Hold the rice in place as you lift off the biscuit cutter.

Children's sushi can be as much fun to make as to eat

Rolled sushi
maki zushi

The perfect party food or dinner party starter, rolled sushi is probably the most recognizable sushi. It consists of rice and fish, vegetables or omelette rolled into a cylinder with nori seaweed around it and may also be called *nori maki*. There are many different types of rolled sushi: thin rolls, *hoso maki*, contain a single ingredient such as tuna or cucumber; thick rolls, *futo maki*, have several different fillings and combine a variety of flavours, colours and textures; inside-out rolls, *uramaki*, have rice on the outside and nori on the inside; hand-rolled sushi, *temaki zushi*, are cornet-shaped.

Once prepared, rolled sushi should be eaten straight away as the nori quickly absorbs the moisture from the rice and becomes soggy. If left too long, the sushi rice expands and can split the nori. However, it is less important that the nori in the inside-out roll remains crisp so they can be prepared up to three hours in advance. Rolled sushi is not as difficult as hand-formed sushi and the Japanese often prepare it at home. With a little practice and a bamboo rolling mat, it's not difficult to achieve impressive results. As always, prepare your rice and other ingredients in advance.

< Once you've mastered the technique, experiment with combinations of fillings with different textures and colours for impressive effects

> Hand-rolled sushi is party sushi and very easy to do; simply prepare platters of different fillings and let your guests roll their own

Thin roll sushi
hoso maki zushi

This is believed to be the original form of rolled sushi and uses a single filling such as tuna, cucumber or seasoned kampyo. Use whatever filling you prefer, but keep it simple. Once you have mastered thin roll sushi, the other varieties are easy. This elegant bite-size sushi makes wonderful finger food and is a guaranteed success as a dinner party starter.

1 Mix the ingredients for the vinegared water in a small bowl and set aside. Lay a sushi rolling mat on your work surface. Fold a sheet of nori in half across the grain, and pinch along the folded edge to break it in two. Place a halved sheet along the edge of the rolling mat with the shiny, smooth side facing downwards.

Ingredients

for vinegared water:
1–2 tbsp rice vinegar
250 ml [8 fl oz] water

for sushi rolls:
4–5 sheets nori seaweed

1 quantity prepared
sushi rice [p36–8]

wasabi paste

1 skinless fillet of tuna,
about 125 g [4 oz], cut into
pencil-thick strips [p89–91]

½ cucumber, cut into
1 cm [½ in] square strips

½ quantity thick Japanese
omelette [p40–42], cut into
1 cm [½ in] square strips

other suggested fillings that
make about 3 rolls each:
1 skinless fillet of salmon,
about 125 g [4 oz], cut into
pencil-thick strips [p89–91]

125 g [4 oz] crabmeat

1 medium carrot, cut into
1 cm [½ in] square strips
and lightly steamed

Makes 8–10 rolls

Preparation time
45 minutes

2 Dip your hands in the vinegared water to prevent the rice from sticking to them. Take a handful of rice and form it into a log shape.

3 Place the rice in the centre of the sheet of nori and use the tips of your fingers to spread it evenly over it. Leave about a 1cm [½ in] margin of nori along the edge furthest from you.

4 If using a fish filling, dab a thin line of wasabi paste across the centre of the rice. Don't overdo the wasabi – it should complement the flavour of the sushi, not overpower it.

5 Arrange a strip of tuna (or cucumber or omelette) on top of the wasabi. You may need to use two or three short pieces, but line them up close to each other with no gaps between them.

6 Lift up the edge of the mat closest to you, and slowly roll away from you in a smooth movement.

7 Roll the mat over so that the top edge of the nori meets the edge of the rice. You need to keep a gentle pressure on the roll to keep it neatly compacted.

8 You should be able to see the strip of nori not covered by rice. Gently shape the length of the roll using both hands and applying even pressure.

9 Lift the edge of the mat slightly and push the roll forward a little so that the uncovered strip of nori seals the roll. The moisture from the rice acts as an adhesive.

10 Push in any stray grains of rice to tidy the ends. Set aside in a cool place – but not the refrigerator – while you make more.

11 Dip a cloth or tea towel in the vinegared water, moisten a sharp knife and cut each roll in half.

12 Moisten the knife with the cloth between each cutting. Place the two halves next to each other and cut them twice to make 6 equal bite-sized pieces. Arrange on a serving plate and serve immediately.

Simple and elegant thin roll sushi with tuna, cucumber and omelette

Thick roll sushi
futo maki zushi

Because of their colourful assortment of fillings, *futo maki* are also known as *date maki* or 'dandy rolls'. The rolling technique is similar to thin rolls, but these larger rolls use a whole sheet of nori instead of half of one. Experiment with different combinations of fillings to create colourful patterns, but be sure to prepare all the fillings before you start assembling the rolls. Eat theses rolls immediately once prepared.

Ingredients

for vinegared water:
1–2 tbsp rice vinegar
250 ml [8 fl oz] water

for sushi rolls:
3 sheets nori seaweed

1 quantity prepared sushi rice [p36–8]

1 carrot, cut into pencil-thick strips and steamed

30g [1oz] green beans, trimmed and lightly steamed

30g [1oz] seasoned shiitake mushrooms [p31]

1 thick Japanese omelette [p40–42], cut into 1cm [½ in] strips

30g [1oz] prepared kampyo [p30]

other fillings that could be substituted for any of the above:

60g [2oz] skinless fish such as salmon, tuna or red snapper, cut into pencil-thick strips [p89–91]

60g [2oz] crabmeat or lobster meat

30g [2oz] spinach or avocado

3 seasoned tofu pouches [p46], cut into 1cm [½ in] strips

Makes 3 rolls

Preparation time
45 minutes

1 Mix the ingredients for the vinegared water in a small bowl and set aside. Lay a bamboo rolling mat on your work surface and place a sheet of nori shiny side down on it. Dip your hands in the vinegard water, form two handfuls of rice into log shapes and place at the centre of the nori.

2 Spread the rice evenly across the whole width of the nori, leaving a 4cm [1¾ in] margin on the edge of the nori furthest from you.

3 Lay one third of the carrot strips in the centre of the rice with a third of the green beans and a third of the shiitake mushrooms on either side.

4 Arrange a third of the omelette strips and a third of the kampyo on either side of the green beans and shiitake mushrooms.

5 Place your thumbs under the rolling mat and lift the near edge of the mat with your thumbs and index fingers. Hold the fillings in place with the rest of your fingers.

6 Holding a small flap at the top of the mat, bring the near side of the roll over so that it covers the fillings.

7 Bring the rolling mat down to meet the strip of nori, and gently squeeze along the length of the roll to tuck in the near edge of the nori.

8 Lift the front edge of the mat slightly with one hand and use the other to gently push the roll forward so that the strip of nori not covered by rice seals the roll.

9 Pull back the mat and tidy the ends. Set aside in a cool place, but not the refrigerator, while you prepare the remaining 2 rolls. Use a knife moistened with vinegared water to cut the roll in half. Cut each half into six slices. When you get more confident you can place the 2 halves alongside each other and cut them together.

Slices of thick roll sushi, or *futo maki*, always look impressive

Inside-out roll sushi
uramaki

Despite appearances, this type of rolled sushi is easier to prepare than the traditional nori-outside version. The stickiness of the rice ensures that the sushi holds together and is surprisingly rigid. Another advantage of this type of sushi is that inside-out rolls can be prepared in advance as it is less important for the nori to stay crisp. The 'California roll' demonstrated here traditionally contains crab and avocado. It was first created by an American born Japanese chef in the early 70s to overcome early squeamishness about eating raw fish – it has since become a classic.

Ingredients

for vinegared water:
2–3 tbsp rice vinegar
250ml [8floz] water

for sushi rolls:
3 sheets nori seaweed

1 quantity prepared
sushi rice [p36]

120g [4oz] crabmeat [p98]

1 baby cucumber
[¼ of a large one], cut into
pencil-thickness strips

125g [4oz] mayonnaise

wasabi paste, if desired

1 medium avocado,
halved and stoned, sliced
lengthways into thin strips

6 tbsp flying fish roe

Makes 6 rolls

Preparation time
35 minutes

1 Mix the ingredients for the vinegared water in a small bowl and set aside. Lay a bamboo rolling mat on your work surface, and cover it with clingfilm.

2 Break the nori sheet in half [see p186] and place it on the mat. Dip your hands in the vinegared water, take a good handful of rice and place it in the middle of the nori. Use your fingers to spread an even layer of rice to the edges of the nori. Pick up the rice-covered nori and quickly turn it over on the mat.

3 Lay the crab and cucumber along the centre of the nori. Add a line of mayonnaise on one side and a thin smear of wasabi on the other, if using. Arrange the avocado on top.

4 Lift up the near edge of the mat, holding the fillings in place with your fingers, if necessary. Start rolling to join the 2 edges of the rice and nori sheet together.

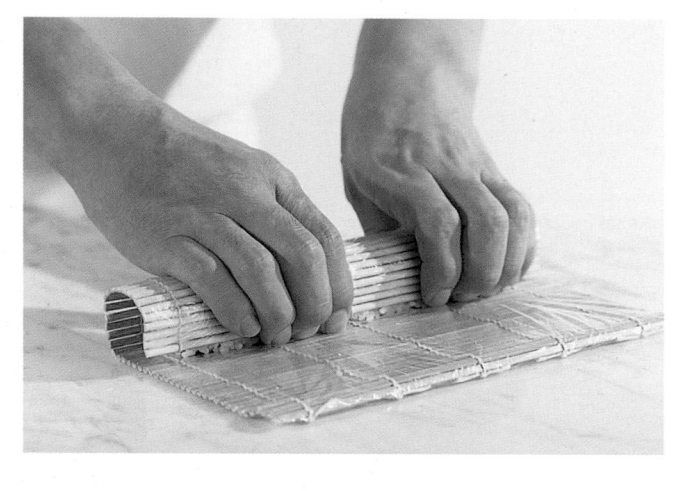

5 Gently squeeze along the length of the roll to mould it together, then lift up the front edge of the mat and push the roll forward to join the 2 edges of nori. Use gentle but firm pressure to shape the log into a round or square shape.

6 Open the mat. Spoon the fish roe onto the sushi roll, and use the back of a spoon to spread the roe over it. Turn the roll over to coat the underneath. The roe does not have to cover the sushi perfectly.

7 Dip a cloth or tea towel in the vinegared water, moisten a sharp knife and cut each roll in half. Place the 2 halves next to each other, moisten the knife and cut twice to give 6 equally sized pieces.

Flying fish roe adds a touch of vibrant orange to inside-out rolls

Log roll sushi
bō zushi

This simple but delicious rolled sushi uses vinegar-marinated mackerel as a wrapping material instead of nori. It is an excellent way to enjoy the taste of marinated mackerel if you don't have a pressed sushi mould. Be sure to leave adequate time to prepare the fish, and let the roll stand for 30 minutes at room temperature before cutting as this allows time for the flavours to develop.

Ingredients

for vinegared water:
2–3 tbsp rice vinegar
250ml [8 floz] water

for sushi roll:
1 quantity prepared sushi rice [p36–8]

2 vinegar-marinated mackerel fillets [p92], about 150g [5oz] each

wasabi paste [optional]

Makes 2 rolls

Preparation time
45 minutes

1 Mix the ingredients for the vinegared water in a small bowl and set aside. Lay a rolling mat on your work surface and cover both sides of it in clingfilm.

2 Wet your hands with vinegared water. Place two small handfuls of rice in the centre of the rolling mat and shape into a mackerel-length log.

3 Dab the underside of the mackerel with a little wasabi, if using. Place the fillet on top of the mound of rice, skin side up.

4 Lift the mat over the rice and mackerel so that it is completely covered.

5 Work your hands along the length of the sushi log, squeezing it firmly but gently. If the mackerel is longer than the rice, neaten it by pressing the ends of the fish over so that they stick to the rice.

6 Set aside to stand for 20 minutes at room temperature. Dip a cloth or tea towel in the vinegared water and moisten a sharp knife. Slice the log into bite-size pieces.

Easy to make, beautiful to look at and quick to eat – log roll sushi

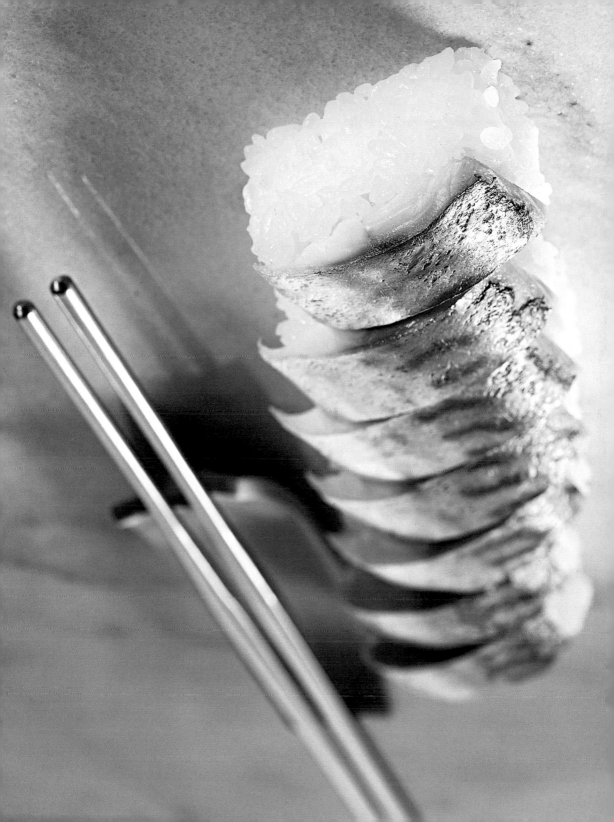

Hand-rolled sushi
temaki zushi

This sushi makes a perfect dinner party starter and involves very little effort on the host's part. Simply prepare the sushi rice and cut up a colourful selection of fillings, then let your guests roll their own sushi. Use 100g [3½ oz] of skinless fish fillet per person as a rough guide (try to use at least two kinds of fish), but err on the generous side rather than risk running out.

1 Hold a piece of nori in your left hand, and put a generous tablespoon of rice in the top left hand corner.

Ingredients

10 sheets nori seaweed, halved [p186]

1 quantity prepared sushi rice [p36–8]

wasabi paste

your choice of fillings such as:

400g [14oz] fish in total, cut for hand-rolled sushi [p88–91] any of:
sea bass or red snapper;
tuna or salmon;
turbot, brill or lemon sole;
vinegar-marinated mackerel or smoked salmon

100g [3½ oz] salmon roe or flying fish roe

½ quantity thick Japanese omelette [p40–42]

400g [14oz] vegetables in total, cut into pencil-thick strips 6cm [2¾ in] long, any of:
avocado, stoned;
cucumber;
fresh carrot;
pickled daikon;
green beans, trimmed and blanched;
1 carton mustard cress;
10 perilla leaves

Makes 20 cornets

Preparation time
45 minutes

2 Spread the rice to the centre of the bottom edge of the nori. Use your finger to flatten the rice slightly, then dab a little wasabi paste on it.

3 Arrange your choice of fillings on top of the rice so they point diagonally to the top left corner of the nori.

4 Fold the bottom left-hand corner of the nori towards the top right hand corner, wrapping it around the rice and fillings.

5 Continue rolling until the nori forms a cornet shape that holds the rice and fillings.

Create your own combinations with hand-rolled sushi

Hand-formed sushi
nigiri zushi

A relatively new addition to the sushi repertoire, *nigiri zushi* is less than 200 years old. It was first invented as a street food in the old capital Edo, now Tokyo, and totally revolutionized sushi because it took so little time to make. *Nigiri* means 'to squeeze' – when a sushi chef makes *nigiri zushi*, he gently squeezes a small quantity of rice into an oval, adds a perfectly judged amount of wasabi paste, then presses on a topping, usually of fish. But there is more to it than simply making balls of rice and putting slices of fish on top. The perfect piece of *nigiri zushi* should be the right size to eat in one mouthful and the rice should gently fall apart on your tongue, not in your fingers or chopsticks. The gentle tartness of the sushi rice should complement the topping, not compete with it, and a hint of wasabi should enhance the flavour.

Start with Easy Hand-formed Sushi [see p214–17], and progress to the expert's method when you have perfected the technique. While the rice is cooking, prepare the toppings. Have a bowl of vinegared water nearby to dip your fingers in from time to time as this prevents the rice from sticking to them, then begin the assembly.

< *Nigiri zushi* is the most popular type of sushi and is what many people think of when the word sushi is mentioned

> Toppings have changed with the times: abalone, sea bream and flounder were traditional; tuna and mackerel only became popular after World War II

Expert hand-formed sushi
nigiri zushi

This is the ultimate sushi. It looks deceptively simple when prepared by a sushi chef, but is in fact one of the most difficult. A sushi master spends years perfecting his technique and produces each piece of sushi in what appears to be one smooth movement taking only a matter of seconds. In his expert hands the pieces tend to be marginally smaller than Easy Hand-Formed Sushi [see p214–7], and use less rice but slightly more fish.

Ingredients

1 quantity prepared sushi rice [p36–8]

500g [1lb] skinless fillet of any fish such as red snapper, salmon, tuna, sole, brill or sea bass, cut for hand-formed sushi [p88–91]

wasabi paste

Makes 40–50 pieces

1 Mix 250ml [8fl oz] water and 2–3 tbsp vinegar in a small bowl and wet hands in it to prevent the rice from sticking to them.

2 Take a small handful of rice in your right hand and gently mould it into a rounded oblong.

3 Holding the ball of rice loosely in your right fist, pick up the topping with your left hand. Lay the topping across your fingers, and dab a little wasabi paste on it.

4 Hold the rice between your right thumb and index finger, and gently press it on to the topping with your left thumb.

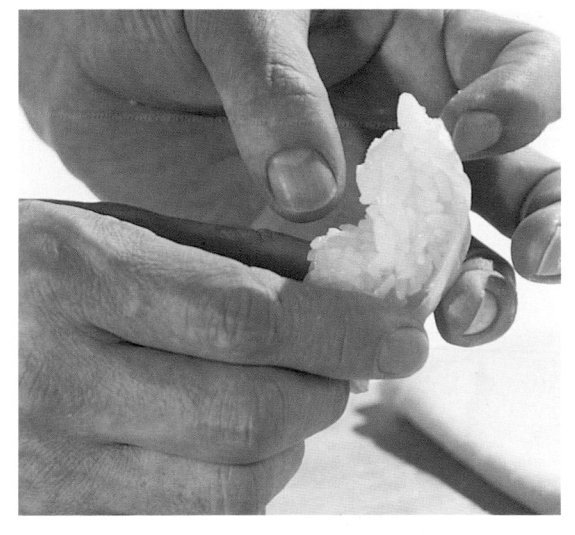

5 Hold the sushi halfway along its sides, between your thumb and index finger. Spin the sushi 180° so the topping is on top.

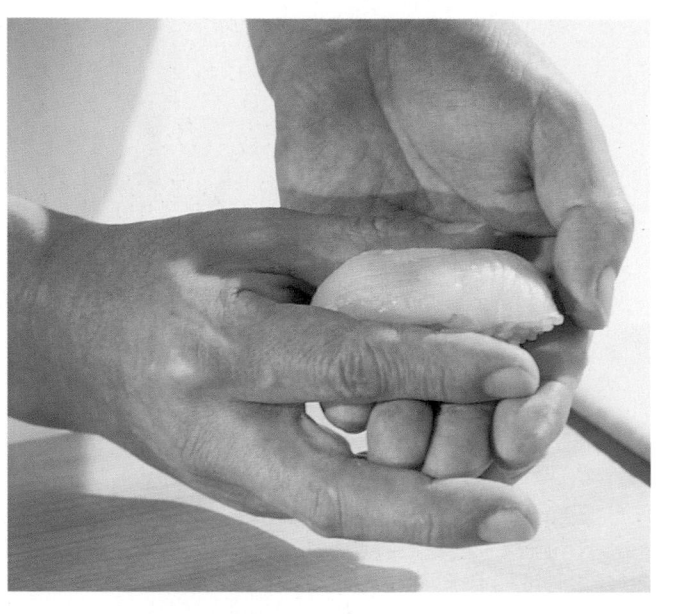

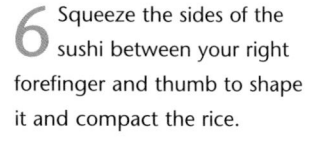

6 Squeeze the sides of the sushi between your right forefinger and thumb to shape it and compact the rice.

7 Cup the sushi in your left hand and use two fingers to press gently on the top to compact it further.

8 Open your left hand and spin the sushi round, keeping the topping on top. Repeat steps 6 and 7 to shape the sushi.

Red snapper makes a delicate topping for *nigiri zushi*

Easy hand-formed sushi
nigiri zushi

Nigiri zushi is the most difficult sushi to master – even the Japanese rarely make it at home. This is an easier – and quicker – basic method of preparation. The results are really the same, although a sushi master might disagree. Use 100g [3½ oz] fish per person, which makes five pieces, as a rough guide. As with the expert's version, prepare your toppings beforehand.

Ingredients

for vinegared water:
2–3 tbsp rice vinegar
250ml [8floz] water

for hand-formed sushi:
1 quantity prepared
sushi rice [p36–8]

400g [14 oz] fish preferably
several different types
[p52–129], cut for
hand-formed sushi [p88]

wasabi paste

½ quantity thick Japanese
omelette [40–42], cut into
slices 0.5cm [¼ in] thick

5 strips nori seaweed
1cm [½ in] x 7.5cm [3in] for
tying the omelette topping

Makes 24–32 pieces

Preparation time
45 minutes

1 Mix the ingredients for the vinegared water in a small bowl. Dip your hands in the mixture and pick up a ball of rice about the size of an egg. Gently roll it in the palm of your hands, shaping it into an oblong. Place it on a clean work surface or chopping board. Prepare several at a time.

2 Tidy up the shape of the rice balls, if necessary, but don't over-handle the rice.

3 Lay the toppings out next to each oblong of rice. Dab a little wasabi paste on each oblong of rice. Omit wasabi if using omelette as a topping.

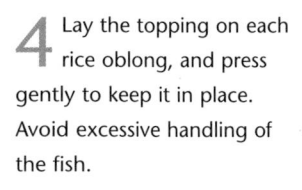

4 Lay the topping on each rice oblong, and press gently to keep it in place. Avoid excessive handling of the fish.

5 If using fish as a topping, use your thumb and forefinger to press the ends of the fish to the rice.

6 Gently shape the sides of the rice. If using omelette as a topping, tie the sushi with a strip of nori.

Sushi with tuna, sea bass, salmon, marinated mackerel and omelette

Battleship sushi
gunkan maki

Sushi toppings such as fish roe and oysters simply will not stay on the sushi rice without some form of containment. This type of sushi is called *gunkan maki* because the strip of nori seaweed that keeps the topping in place gives it a battleship shape. The nori absorbs the moisture from the rice and the topping and becomes soggy if left too long, so make this type of sushi last if you are making a selection.

Ingredients

for vinegared water:
2–3 tbsp rice vinegar
250 ml [8 fl oz] water

for sushi:
3 sheets nori seaweed,
each cut into 6 equal strips

½ quantity prepared
sushi rice [p36–8]

wasabi paste

120g [4oz] of flying fish roe,
[can be dyed red, green or
natural coloured]

6 oysters

60g [2oz] salmon roe

Makes 18 pieces

Preparation time
30 minutes

1 Mix the ingredients for the vinegared water in a small bowl and set aside. Put 2 sheets of nori on top of each other, and cut into 6 equal-sized strips about 2½ cm [1in] wide and 15 cm [6in] long.

2 Wet your hands in the vinegared water. Shape about a tablespoon of sushi rice into an oblong-shaped ball. Wipe your right hand dry and pick up a strip of nori. Wrap it around the rice ball with the smooth side of the nori facing outwards.

3 Crush a grain of cooked rice at the end of the strip of nori so that it sticks the nori down where it overlaps to form a ring around the rice.

4 Dab a little wasabi paste on the rice and flatten the rice slightly.

5 Spoon the topping onto the rice, keeping it inside the ring of nori.

Dyed flying fish roes, salmon roe, oyster and natural flying fish roe

Clingfilm sushi
temari zushi

This is one of the easiest types of sushi to make and you don't need any specialized equipment – just some clingfilm. Prepare these pretty canapés up to a day in advance; keep them wrapped in cling film until needed.

1   Divide the rice in half. Lay a piece of clingfilm, about 10cm [4in] square, on a clean work surface and place a piece of smoked salmon at the centre of it. Mould a teaspoonful of sushi rice into a loose ball and place on top of it.

2   Pick up all four corners of the clingfilm and gather them in the middle. Twist the clingfilm to compact the rice and form a small ball. Repeat the process to make 10 smoked salmon balls. Make 10 prawn balls in the same way, but put half a teaspoonful of caviar in the crescent of each prawn.

3   Keep each piece of sushi wrapped in the clingfilm until just before serving. Put a dab of wasabi on each of the smoked salmon balls just before serving.

Ingredients

½ quantity prepared sushi rice [p36–8]

30g [1oz] smoked salmon, cut into 10 postage stamp size pieces

wasabi

10 cooked prawns

30g [1oz] flying fish roe

other toppings that use the same quantity of rice to make 10 pieces each:

½ cucumber, sliced wafer thin and cut into postage stamp size

30g [1oz] any variety of caviar

30g [1oz] rare roast beef, thinly sliced and cut into postage stamp size

wasabi paste

Makes 20–30 pieces

Preparation time
25 minutes

Form the rice into a loose ball, but don't overhandle it.

Adjust the shape of the ball with your fingers, if necessary.

Smoked salmon with wasabi and prawn and fish roe sushi balls

Eating

At a sushi bar
a unique experience

Whether you have discovered sushi already or are just trying it for the
first time, there is something very special about a visit to a sushi bar –
you receive highly personalized service and almost all the food you eat
is prepared in front of you. Marvel at the sushi chef's expertise, and rely
on him for guidance – he will look after you.

Inside the sushi bar

Sushi bars tend to be small, intimate
places and although interiors may vary,
you will usually find a long, spotlessly
clean counter with a refrigerated glass
case behind it where the day's carefully
prepared fish, shellfish and roe are
beautifully displayed. The master sushi
chef stands behind the counter.

Most sushi bars do not accept
reservations at the counter, which tends
to operate on a first-come-first-served
basis. Some customers simply pop in for
a quick snack while others linger for the
whole evening. However, you can usually
book a table in a large restaurant.

Never feel intimidated or awkward –
the aim of a good sushi bar is to provide
excellent food and service in a relaxed
atmosphere. The sushi master chef prides
himself on maintaining the highest level
of service possible.

< The sushi chef can cast his trained eye over the
entire shop from his position behind the counter

> Order individual pieces of sushi or try a combination set, a good introduction to sushi

No menu

Sushi bars are unique in that often there is no real menu – you order the toppings of your choice by simply pointing at the fish in the display case in front of you. In Japan, sushi bars often don't display prices as fresh fish is bought daily and prices inevitably fluctuate. As a result, there may be some uncertainty over your final bill, but if you feel uncomfortable about this, opt for a combination set. This usually consists of a selection of hand-formed and rolled sushi, or *nigiri zushi* and *maki zushi*, for a fixed, normally more reasonable price. You can always order individual pieces on top of the set.

The bill

A professional trained sushi chef may be given written orders by waiters if the sushi bar is part of a restaurant, but he very rarely writes anything down. Instead, he keeps track of each customer's order, for as many as six people at a time, and discreetly adds up the total in his head when he is asked for the bill.

Tipping

The sushi chef takes pride in performing his craft and would not dream of asking for a tip. A gracious way of thanking him is to offer him a sake or a beer. If he accepts, order it from the waiter. The sushi chef will raise a toast to thank you, and you should drink to the good sushi you had with him. Outside Japan, unless a service charge has been included in your bill, a standard tip is customary.

Etiquette
dos and don'ts

There is something about the formal and orderly atmosphere of the sushi
bar that can make even the most beautifully mannered non-Japanese
diner feel awkward. Sushi bars are intimate but relaxed places without
strict rules of conduct. Feeling at ease with the etiquette will not only
help you relax, it will enhance your enjoyment of the meal.

Structuring the meal

The absence of a menu means that there
is no obvious guidance as to how to
structure your meal. There is no correct
order in which to eat sushi, though a
sushi connoisseur might disagree.

Choose whatever takes your fancy and
consider these conventional guidelines,
but don't regard them as gospel.

• A few slices of sashimi can be a gentle
start to a sushi meal – ask the sushi chef
what he recommends.

• If you want to taste the sushi bar's
vinegar mixture – a fair indication of
the chef's skills – start with omelette as
its subtle flavour allows you to taste the
rice. However, I have known sushi gurus
to end a meal with omelette, treating it
more like a sweet dessert.

• Start with blander tasting white fish
and work your way towards richer
fish with red meat and more strongly
flavoured toppings. A logical enough
approach, but if your favourite topping
is fatty belly of tuna, start with that.

• Some say that you should finish a meal
with rolled sushi. This may be because

Chopstick etiquette

In a sushi bar, you are given a pair of disposable wooden chopsticks in a paper sleeve when you take your seat. Take the chopsticks out of the sleeve, break them apart and rest them on the small chopstick rest in front of you.

• Don't pass food from your chopsticks to another person's chopsticks as this is considered to be extremely bad luck. In the traditional Japanese funeral ceremony, relatives pass the cremated bones of the deceased with chopsticks before collecting them in a burial pot.

• If you are helping yourself to food from a communal plate or serving someone else, it is polite to turn your chopsticks around and use the top ends.

they contain more rice and are therefore more filling than hand-formed sushi, but I don't think you should have to wait.

Fingers or chopsticks?

If you don't feel comfortable using chopsticks, it is perfectly acceptable to use your fingers [see p230]. Remember that hand-formed sushi was originally invented as a snack to be eaten at a street stall. You should be given a wet towel at the start of a meal at a sushi bar, so wipe your fingers on this before you begin.

The correct use of soy sauce

One of the most wonderful seasonings, soy sauce appears in almost every aspect of Japanese cooking. I love it and use it all the time, but for sushi, it should be used sparingly – for dipping and not for drowning the food.

There is an art to dipping a piece of hand-formed sushi into soy sauce without it disintegrating and leaving grains of rice floating in the dish. Whether you are using chopsticks or your fingers [see below], try to eat hand-formed sushi in one mouthful; it is considered impolite to bite a piece of sushi in half and then put the remaining half back on your plate.

When dipping a piece of rolled sushi, dip only a small corner of it in the soy sauce. Don't submerge the sushi as not only will it fall apart, but the rice will quickly absorb all the soy sauce and the delicate flavours of the roll will be totally overwhelmed.

The same technique applies for dipping battleship sushi in soy sauce.

how to dip your sushi

1 Pour a little soy sauce into a small dipping bowl. Tip the piece of sushi to one side on the plate and pick it up, holding it between your thumb and middle finger.

2 Turn your hand slightly to dip only the topping in the soy sauce. Pop the piece of sushi into your mouth upside down, so you taste the topping and soy first.

∧ Pickled ginger

Sushi is served with a little heap of thinly sliced pink pickled ginger. It is intended as a palate cleanser and should be eaten a slice at a time in between different flavours of sushi. Although pickled ginger's refreshing taste is rather addictive for some people, it is meant as an accompaniment to sushi or sashimi, not a side salad, even though the sushi chef will happily keep replenishing it.

> Wasabi

I have watched people dissolve an entire mound of wasabi paste in their soy sauce dipping dish and then proceed to drown a piece of sushi or sashimi in it. Up until now I have recommended that you eat according to your personal tastes and are not intimidated by convention, but this is where I draw the line. Wasabi is an essential accompaniment to sushi and sashimi, but it is intended to enhance the flavour of the food and should never be regarded as a proof of bravery.

At a sushi bar, if you like the taste and sensation of wasabi, ask the chef to apply a little more to your sushi and he will be more than happy to oblige. If you are eating sashimi, dab a little wasabi paste on an individual slice and then dip it briefly in the soy sauce. This way, you can savour the unique flavour of the fish and yet still enjoy the essence of the wasabi and soy sauce.

What to drink
tea, beer, sake and wine

Good sushi restaurants and bars offer a wide range of beverages, and the Japanese drink whatever they wish with their meal. The most traditional drinks in a sushi bar are probably hot green tea or sake, Japanese rice wine, but Japanese beer is also available. Sushi has become such an international food that both red and white wine are also popular choices.

Green tea

A cup of hot green tea, called *agari* in sushi bars, is not only refreshing but cleanses the palate during a sushi meal. It is a gentle digestive aid and contains vitamins A, B and C.

Beer

There are three main breweries in Japan, but good sushi bars usually stock many different Japanese and non-Japanese beers – *birru*. Japanese beers tend to be closer in flavour to American and European lagers and are always served cold. Beer has a crisp, refreshing quality that goes well with sushi and sashimi.

Sake

The smooth and subtle flavour of sake enhances almost all Japanese food. It is quite potent, with an alcohol content of

about 17 percent. Sake should be drunk at room temperature or even slightly chilled. You may, however, be served hot sake in a small bottle with a tiny cup. The practice of serving sake hot dates back to the post-war period when food scarcity meant that sake had to be made artificially and it was heated to disguise the inferior smell and flavour.

It is pleasant to drink warm sake in the winter – some say that the heat makes it more potent – and there are plenty of die-hards who insist on heating it up regardless of the time of year.

The Japanese rediscovered sake during the economic prosperity of the 80s and many small local brands have since become available even outside Japan. Sake comes in three grades: *tokkyu*, premium class, is the best and the most expensive; *ikkyu*, first class, is still excellent and *nikyu*, second class, is perfectly drinkable table wine grade. However, the grading system gives no indication of the flavour, which can range from dry to sweet, it is only for the purposes of the tax system.

Wine

Any good Japanese restaurant or sushi bar should have a respectable wine list, and I often serve wine with sushi at home. I would always recommend that you should drink whatever wine you like drinking, but for those that want to choose a wine depending on the topping or filling, here are my guidelines:

For vegetables, egg or white fish, choose a full-bodied white wine such as a Burgundy, a crisp Sauvignon Blanc or a ripe Chardonnay. For more robustly flavoured vegetables such as mushrooms, try a light- or medium-bodied red such as a Pinot Noir or Chianti Classico, but otherwise a dry white such as a Reisling. **For shellfish** such as tiger prawns or crab, try champagne or sparkling white wine. **For strongly flavoured fish** such as tuna, salmon or marinated mackerel, choose a medium- to full-bodied white such as a Burgundy or Chardonnay, or even a full-bodied red such as a Gamay.

Sushi at home
entertaining

Sushi is such an artistic and yet delicious food that it never fails to impress. Start simple, with scattered sushi for example, and progress to more challenging types as your sushi-making skills improve. Remember that hand-formed sushi requires a little more expertise, so if you want to impress your guests at a dinner party, try to have a practice run first.

Entertaining at home

Provide chopsticks, a chopstick holder and a small dipping bowl at each place setting. Offer wasabi and pickled ginger in communal bowls or arrange small mounds of each on a serving plate for people to help themselves. Put soy sauce on the table in a small jug.

Easy lunch menu Make a large dish of any scattered sushi [see p132–45] except Tokyo-style Sushi – this should be offered in individual bowls.

Easy dinner menu Start with Spring Miso Soup [see p238], then as a main course, provide a platter with a selection of fillings for hand-rolled sushi [see p204–7]. What could be simpler than letting your guests roll their own sushi?

Easy vegetarian menu Start with Inside Out Roll Sushi [see p196–9] substituting strips of cucumber and toasted sesame

which is similar to a sophisticated consommé, is served at the start. *Miso shiru*, or miso soup, served with a bowl of rice and a small dish of pickles usually signifies the end of the meal [see pages 236–39 for soups].

Sashimi makes a perfect starter for a sushi meal, typically accompanied by soy sauce, wasabi, pickled ginger and shredded daikon [see p240–43].

Finish the meal with a selection of refreshing fresh fruit sliced attractively.

seeds for the crab and flying fish roe. Follow with Asparagus and Scrambled Egg Sushi, Mangetout and Vine Tomato Sushi [see p140–41] or any other vegetarian scattered sushi.

A light spring or summer menu
Prepare individual plates of sashimi [see p240–43]. Follow with rolled sushi made with three to five different fillings or toppings [see p184–203].

A warming autumn or winter menu
Begin with a hot soup such as Clear Soup with White Fish [see p236–7], then follow with a plate of two to four different types of pressed sushi [see p168–83] or with indvidual bowls of Tokyo-style Sushi [see p134–7].

What to serve with sushi
The Japanese often serve soup at both ends of the meal. Traditionally, *sui mono*,

Clear soup with egg and shiitake mushrooms

The egg in this soup separates into strands and provides a soft, delicate contrast to the earthy flavour of the shiitake mushrooms. Try to be artistic as you ladle it into bowls.

1   Heat the dashi stock in a small saucepan until it reaches boiling point, then remove from the heat.
2   Add the beaten egg, pouring it through a wire sieve to create strands. Use a whisk to make gentle waves in the pan to separate the strands. Don't whisk the soup.
3   Add the mushroom caps, and season with soy sauce, sake and salt to taste. Bring back to the boil over a low heat, then immediately remove from the heat.
4   Ladle the soup into serving bowls, garnish with whole coriander leaves and serve.

Ingredients

1 quantity dashi stock [p39]

2 eggs, beaten

4 fresh shiitake mushrooms, stems removed

1 tbsp light soy sauce

1 tbsp sake

fresh coriander to garnish

salt

Serves 4

Preparation time
25 minutes

Clear soup with white fish

Use any white fish such as red snapper, sole or sea bass for this soup. Leaving the skin on the fish helps to keep its shape and also adds a decorative touch.

1   Bring the dashi stock to the boil in a small saucepan. Add the soy sauce, mirin and salt to taste. Reduce the heat and simmer gently.
2   Add the fish to the pan and bring back to the boil, then immediately remove from the heat.
3   Put two pieces of fish skin side up in each individual bowl.
4   Gently ladle the soup over the fish, garnish with the spring onion slices and serve.

Ingredients

1 quantity dashi stock [p39]

1 tbsp light soy sauce

1 tbsp mirin

125g [4oz] white fish fillets such as red snapper, sole or sea bass, cut into 8 pieces

4 spring onions, finely sliced

salt

Serves 4

Preparation time
20 minutes

Soup can be served either at the beginning or the end of the meal

Clam miso soup
asari miso shiru

This classic miso soup is easy to prepare as the cooking water is used for the broth. The colour of miso paste ranges from light cream to dark brown, but generally the darker it is, the saltier it tastes.

1   Dissolve the miso paste in a little hot water and add to a saucepan with the dashi stock and clams. Bring gently to the boil, skimming any residue from the surface, then remove from the heat.

2   Leave the lid on the saucepan for 1–2 minutes until the clams have opened; discard any clams that have not opened. Season the soup with salt to taste.

3   Ladle the soup into individual bowls, garnish with the spring onion slices and serve.

Ingredients

4 tbsp miso paste

1 quantity dashi stock [p39]

20 clams, washed thoroughly [p126]

2 spring onions, finely sliced

salt

Serves 4

Preparation time
20 minutes

Spring miso soup

I use purple sprouting broccoli in this soup, but you could substitute mangetout or asparagus. Use light miso paste as it won't overwhelm the delicate flavour of the vegetables.

1   Dissolve the miso paste in a little hot water and add to a saucepan with the dashi stock and broccoli. Bring to the boil over a gentle heat, then reduce the heat and simmer for 3 minutes. Season with salt to taste.

2   Add the cubed tofu and bring back to the boil, then remove from the heat.

4   Ladle the soup into individual bowls, garnish with the toasted sesame seeds, if using, and serve.

Ingredients

4 tbsp light miso paste

1 quantity dashi stock [p39]

250g [8oz] purple sprouting broccoli

60g [2oz] firm tofu, cut into 1cm [½ in] cubes

1 tbsp toasted sesame seeds to garnish [optional]

salt

Serves 4

Preparation time
20 minutes

Spring miso soup with tofu in front of clam miso soup

Sashimi
an introduction

To some, sashimi looks like sushi without the rice, but there is more
to it than sliced raw fish. Sashimi is one of the oldest Japanese cuisines
and has a history all of its own. It may be incomprehensible to some,
but the Japanese believe that in most cases the less a food is cooked
the better, and the best way to cook a fish is not to cook it at all.

The origins of sashimi

In 123 AD the reigning Emperor was
served raw bonito and clams with
vinegar by his head chef – this was
sashimi in its earliest form. By the
middle of the 15th century, it was
recognised as a dish in its own right.

Known as *namasu*, it was eaten with
seasoned vinegar, not with soy sauce
as it is today. By the mid-17th century,
sea bass, red snapper, bonito, shark, eel,
perch, carp, shellfish, pheasant and duck
were all used for sashimi. Many of these
were eaten raw but some were blanched
or lightly cooked. At around the same
time, soy sauce became widely available
and sashimi, in the form that we know
today, became popular.

Today, sashimi is regarded as the
perfect start to a Japanese meal. It is
served with soy sauce, wasabi, shredded
daikon and sometimes fresh seaweed and
perilla leaves – accompaniments chosen
not just for their colours and flavours
but for their ability to aid digestion.

< Begin a sushi meal with a few slices
of sashimi – fish in its purest form

 # Arranging a sashimi plate
and making garnishes

Generally, any fish that is suitable for sushi can also be used for sashimi. The most crucial factor is freshness, even more so than for sushi, as with sashimi there are no other ingredients to disguise the fish's flavour. Fish with red meat such as tuna, bonito and mackerel are cut into thick slices, and white fish such as snapper, sole and sea bass are sliced thinly as they tend to be firmer in texture [see p88–91]. Choose fish with both red and white meat for an arrangement, and decorate the plate with a few carefully chosen garnishes. Estimate about 125g [4oz] fish per person.

Garnishes
thin slices of lemon or lime
wasabi leaves [p51]
perilla leaves
shredded daikon [p49]
prawn funtails [see below]
white fish roses [p242]
flying fish roe

prawn fantails

A specialist Japanese fishmonger will sell raw prawns glazed in a sugar and vinegar syrup. Make a prawn fantail by laying a prawn on its side on a chopping board. Hold it by its tail and and twist so that the body coils around the tail. Separate the individual shell pieces in the tail to make a decorative fan.

making a white fish rose

1 Use a 7.5cm [3in] wide fillet of white fish (about 120g or 4oz) such as red snapper, sole or sea bass. Slice at a 45° angle and cut 3–4 thin strips as for hand-formed sushi [see p88–91]. Lay them in a line with each strip overlapping by about 2.5cm [1in]. This amount of fish will make four roses.

2 Roll up the line of fish strips. Use chopsticks, if necessary, to pick up the ends of each strip and to roll.

3 Set the rose on its base, and use chopsticks or your fingers to gently shape the 'petals'.

A skillfully arranged sashimi plate is an edible work of art

Troubleshooting
problems and solutions

It takes years of practice and hard work to become a fully-fledged sushi chef so don't be disappointed if you can't produce to sushi bar standards to begin with. If your first attempts aren't perfect, in most cases they will still be salvagable. Here are solutions to some of the more common problems that you might encounter in the earlier days of sushi making.

Scattered sushi

Problem The rice has solidified and it is difficult to mix in other ingredients.

Solution The rice may have become too cold. Sprinkle a tablespoonful of Japanese rice vinegar over it, then fold in gently to separate the grains. Always allow the rice to cool once prepared, but never refrigerate it as this will cause it to harden. Mix in other ingredients when the rice is room temperature.

Stuffed sushi

Problem The rice has solidified and become unmanageable.

Solution See Scattered sushi [left].

Problem The wrapping material has torn.

Solution You may have overstuffed the sushi. Continue to wrap or stuff as best you can, and serve with the torn part underneath so it is concealed. 'What the eyes do not see, the heart will not grieve.' If it is too bad you may have to take out some filling and start again.

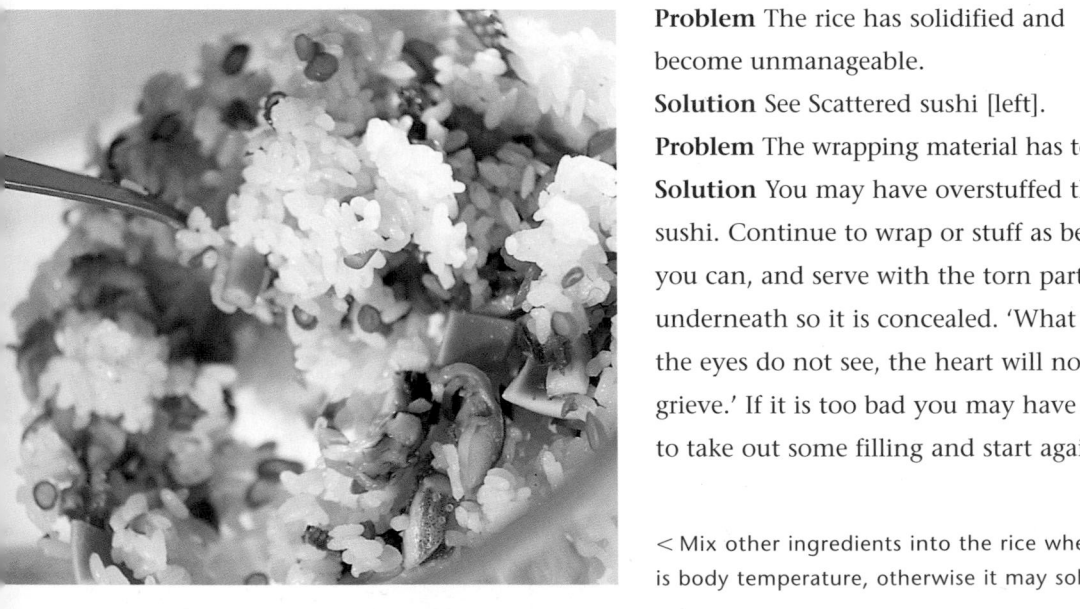

< Mix other ingredients into the rice when it is body temperature, otherwise it may solidify

∧ Soak the sushi mould in cold water beforehand to prevent rice from sticking

Pressed sushi

Problem The block of sushi is stuck in the pressed sushi mould.

Solution You may not have soaked the sushi mould in cold water for long enough beforehand [see p23]. Wet a pallet knife with water and cut around the edges of the block to unstick the rice. When the block is free, tidy the edges with the wet knife.

Rolled sushi

Problem The filling is off-centre.

Solution You may have positioned the filling wrongly before rolling. Cut the roll into bite-size pieces and use your fingers to try to recentre the fillings individually. If this does not work,

gently shape each piece into a tear drop shape with the filling at the narrow end. To serve, arrange the pieces of sushi in a circle with the fillings towards the centre to make a sushi flower.

Problem The nori has split.

Solution You may have overfilled the roll with rice or with fillings. Place another sheet of nori seaweed on the rolling mat, put the roll split side down on it and re-roll it. Although the roll has double layers of nori, the moisture from the rice will meld them together. Alternatively, turn it into an inside out roll [see p196–99].

∨ Don't fill rolled sushi with too many ingredients, otherwise the nori may split

鮨 Glossary
useful japanese terms

Abura age	Puffy, brown deep-fried tofu [p46, 152]
Agari	Green tea served in sushi bars
Aji	Spanish or horse mackerel [p54]
Akami	Lean tuna, cut from the back of the fish [p60]
Aka gai	Ark shell clam [p126]
Ama ebi	Sweet shrimp, usually served raw [p108]
Anago	Conger eel [p128, 174], served basted in a sweet soy sauce
Asari	Common clam [p126]
Awabi	Abalone [p118]
Baka gai	Round clam [p126]
Battera	Pressed mackerel sushi [p62, 170]
Birru	Beer
Bō zushi	Log roll sushi [p200]
Chakin zushi	'Stuffed purse' sushi [p160]
Chirashi zushi	Scattered sushi [p132]
Chu toro	Medium fatty tuna, from the upper belly [p61]
Daikon	Long white radish [p33] also known as a mouli
Dashi	Basic fish stock [p39]
Dashi maki tamago	Thick, sweet omelette [p40]
Deba bōchō	Type of knife – cleaver [p20]
Edomae chirashi zushi	Tokyo-style scattered sushi [p133]
Fukin	Cloth used in the kitchen [p18]
Fukusa zushi	Sushi wrapped in a pancake omelette [p158]
Futo maki	Large roll sushi also known as *date maki* [p192]
Gari	Pickled ginger [p28, 231]
Gomoko zushi	Scattered sushi – 'five item sushi' [p138]
Gunkan maki	Nigiri sushi wrapped with nori to hold loose toppings [p218]
Hamachi	Yellowtail tuna [p129]
Hamaguri	Venus clam [p126]
Hangiri	Wooden rice tub [p18]
Hashi	Chopsticks
Hōchō	General term for knives [p20]
Hikari mono	Term for shiny, oily fish [p54, 56]
Hirame	Term for flat fish with eyes on the left side of the head [p76, 78]
Hoso maki	Thin rolled sushi [p186]
Hotate gai	Scallops [p118, 122]
Ika	Squid [p112]
Ikura	Salmon roe [p125]
Inari zushi	*Abura age* stuffed with sushi rice [p150, 152]
Iri goma	Toasted sesame seeds [p32], can be white or black
Ise ebi	Lobster [p104]
Itamae	The sushi chef [p11]
Iwashi	Sardine [p56]
Kaki	Oysters [p118, 122]
Kampyō	Strips of dried gourd [p24, 30]
Kani	Crab [p98, 128]
Karei	Term for flat fish with eyes on the side of the head [p80, 82]
Katsuo	Bonito [p58]
Katsuo bushi	Dried bonito flakes [p32, 39]
Kazunoko	Herring roes [p56, 125]
Kodomo zushi	Children's sushi [p182]
Kome	Japanese-style rice [p26]
Konbu	Kelp, usually dried [p32]
Maguro	Tuna [p60]
Makajiki	Swordfish [p129]

Maki zushi	Rolled sushi, called *nori maki* if made with nori seaweed [p184]
Makisu	Mat made of bamboo strips for making roll sushi [p23, 184]
Matsukawa zukuri	'Pine bark method' of fish skin [p94]
Matō dai	John Dory [p66]
Mirin	Sweet rice wine for cooking [p29]
Miru gai	Horse clam [p127]
Miso shiru	Soup made with soy bean paste [p235, 238]
Nigiri zushi	Sushi rice with fish, vegetables or omelette
Nishin	Herring [p56]
Nori	Dark seaweed pressed into thin sheets [p26]
Oho toro	Fattiest cut of tuna [p61]
Ohyō garei	Halibut [p82]
Omakase	Chef's choice
Oshi zushi	Pressed sushi [p168]
Oshibako	Pressed sushi mould [p23, 168]
Oshibori	Moistened heated towel
Oshi zushi	Pressed sushi [p168]
Renkon	Lotus roots [p33]
Saba	Mackerel [p62]
Sai bashi	Cooking chopsticks [p19]
Sake	Rice wine [p29, 233] – the same word is used for salmon [p64]
Sanmai oroshi	Three piece filleting technique for round fish [p72]
Sashimi	Sliced or prepared raw fish [p240]
Sayori	Garfish [p127]
Shamoji	Flat rice-serving spoon [p18]
Shako	Mantis shrimp [p127]
Shari	Term for sushi rice
Shime saba	Vinegar-marinated mackerel [p92]
Shiitake	Type of Japanese mushroom [p31]
Shiso	Japanese mint, perilla [p31]
Shita birame	Dover sole [p129]

Shōyu	Japanese soy sauce [p28, 230]
Soboro	Ground fish, usually pink [p47]
Su	Rice vinegar [p29]
Sui mono	Clear soup [p235, 236]
Sushi meshi	Prepared rice for sushi [p34]
Suzuki	Sea bass [p68]
Tai [also Ma dai]	Japanese red snapper [p70, 94]
Tako	Octopus [p112]
Tamago soboro	Scrambled eggs [p43]
Tamari	Wheat-free soy sauce [p28]
Tataki	Cooking method – rapid searing then cooling of the meat [p146]
Temaki zushi	Hand rolled sushi [p204]
Temari zushi	Sushi balls [p222]
Teriyaki sauce	Thicker, sweetened soy sauce [p164]
Tobiko	Flying fish roe [p124]
Tofu	Soybean curd [p238]
Toro	Cut of tuna – see *chu toro, oho toro*
Tsuma / kazari	Garnishes / decorations [p48]
Unagi	Freshwater eel [p128]
Uni	Sea urchin [p124]
Uramaki	Inside-out rolled sushi [p196]
Usuba bōchō	Vegetable knife [p20]
Usuyaki tamago	Thin, pancake omelette [p44]
Wakita	'Side chopping board' or assistant sushi chef [p11]
Wasabi	Green, hot Japanese type of horseradish [p27]
Yanagi bōchō	Vegetable knife [p20]
Zaru	Bamboo strainer [p19]
Zāsai	Chinese pickled vegetable [p180]

Restaurant directory
sushi bars

Australia

MELBOURNE

Mizu
133 Commercial Road,
South Yarra
Tel: 9827 1141

Misuzu's
7 Victoria Avenue,
Albert Park
Tel: 9699 9022

**Japonica Japanese
Restaurant**
Shop 6/180 Toorak Road,
South Yarra
Tel: 9827 2968

Sozai
1221 High Street,
Malvern
Tel: 9824 8200

Yuu
137 Flinders Lane,
Melbourne
Tel: 9639 7073

**Kanpai Japanese
Restaurant**
569 Chapel Street,
South Yarra
Tel: 9827 4379

**Kazen
Japanese Cafe**
201 Brunswick Street,
Fitzroy
Tel: 9417 3270

Akari 177
177 Brunswick Street,
Fitzroy
Tel: 9419 3786

**Aya Japanese
Restaurant**
1193 High Street,
Armadale
Tel: 9822 9571

**Hibari Japanese
Restaurant**
479 Malvern Road,
South Yarra
Tel: 9827 0155

SYDNEY

**Ju Ju's Japanese
Restaurant**
Shop 320, Kingsgate
Shopping Centre,
Kings Cross
Tel: 9357 7100

**Asakusa Japanese
Restaurant**
119 King Street,
Newtown
Tel: 9519 8530

Sushi Suma
421 Cleveland Street,
Surry Hills
Tel: 9698 8873

BRISBANE

Domo
Shop 1,
421 Brunswick Street,
Fortitude Valley
Tel: 3252 2588

Kabuki
The Stamford Plaza,
Edward Street
(cnr Margaret Street),
Brisbane
Tel: 3221 1999

Oshin
256 Adelaide Street,
Brisbane,
Tel: 3229 0410

Canada

VANCOUVER

Tojo's Restaurant
202–777 Broadway Street,
Vancouver,
BC V5Z 4J7
Tel: 604-872-8050
www.tojos.com

**Shijo Japanese
Restaurant**
1926 4th Avenue,
Vancouver,
BC V6J 1M5
Tel: 604-732-4876

Zen Japanese Restaurant
2232 Marine Drive,
West Vancouver,
BC V7V 1K4
Tel: 604-925-0667

TORONTO

Hiro Sushi
171 King Street East,
Toronto,
ON M5A 1J4
Tel: 416-304-0550

Tempo
596 College Street,
Toronto, ON M6G 1B4
Tel: 416-531-2822

Nami
55 Adelaide Street East,
Toronto, ON M5C 1K6
Tel: 416-362-7373

OTTAWA

Kinki
41 York Street,
Ottawa, ON K1N 5S7
Tel: 613-789-9559

Suisha Gardens
208 Slater Street,
Ottawa,
ON K1P 5H8
Tel: 613-236-9602

MONTREAL

Mikado
368 Laurier West,
Montreal,
QC H2V 2K7
Tel: 514-279-4809

Soto
3527 St. Laurent,
Montreal,
QC H2X 2T6
Tel: 514-842-1150
www.restaurantsoto.com

United Kingdom

LONDON

Café Japan
626 Finchley Road,
London, NW11 7RR
Tel: (020) 8455 6854

Defune
34 George Street,
London, W1U 7DP
Tel: (020) 7935 8311

Matsuri
15 Bury Street,
London, SW1Y 6AL
Tel: (020) 7930 7010

Shogun
Britannia Hotel, Adams Row, London, W1K 2HP
Tel: (020) 7493 1255

Sushi Hiro
1 Station Parade,
Ealing Common,
London, W5 3LD
Tel: (020) 88963175

Yoshino
3 Piccadilly Place,
London, W1V 9PD
Tel: (020) 7287 6622

OUTSIDE LONDON

Azuma
4 Byron Place,
Triangle South,
Bristol, BS8 1JT
Tel: (0117) 927 6864

Chikako's
10–11 Mill Lane,
Cardiff, CF1 1FL
Tel: (029) 2066 5279

Daruma-ya
Unit 5, Commercial Quay,
82 Commercial Street,
Edinburgh, EH6 6LX
Tel: (0131) 554 7660

Fumi
248 Durham Road,
Gateshead, NE8 4JR
Tel: (0191) 477 1152

Fusion
41 Byres Road,
Glasgow, G11 5RG
Tel: (0141) 339 3666

Notsushi
Imperial Court,
Exchange Street East,
Liverpool, L2 3PH
(0151) 236 0643

Sapporo Teppanyaki
38–40 Preston Street,
Brighton, BN1 2HP
Tel: (01273) 777 880

United States

ATLANTA, GA

Nakato
1776 Cheshire Bridge Rd,
NE Atlanta, GA,
30324-4922
Tel: (404) 873-6582

BOSTON, MA

Ginza
19 Hudson Street,
Boston, MA, 02111-1902
Tel: (617) 383-2261

Fugakyu
1280 Beacon Street,
Brookline, MA,
02446-3718
Tel: (617) 734-1268

CHICAGO, IL

Kamehachi
1400 N Wells,
Chicago, IL, 60610
Tel: (312) 664-3663

Sushido
1443 W Fullerton Ave.,
Chicago, IL, 60614
Tel: (773) 472-9066

DENVER, CO

Japon
1028 South Gaylord Street,
Denver, CO, 80209
Tel: (303) 744-0330

FLORIDA

Sushi Rock Café
1351 Collins Avenue,
Miami Beach, FL,
33139-4259
Tel: (305) 532-2133

HONOLULU, HI

Kyo-Ya
2057 Kalakaua Avenue,
Honolulu, HI, 96815-2044
Tel: (808) 947-3911

LOS ANGELES, CA

Sushi Nozawa
11288 Ventura Boulevard,
Suite C, Studio City,
CA, 91604-3149
Tel: (818) 508-7017

Nobu
3835 Cross Creek Road,
Malibu, CA, 90265
Tel: (310) 317-9140

NEW ORLEANS, LA

Ninja Restaurant
8433 Oak Street,
New Orleans, LA, 70118
Tel: (504) 866-1119

NEW YORK, NY

Honmura An
170 Mercer Street,
New York, NY,
10012-3244
Tel: (212) 334-5253

Nobu
105 Hudson Street,
New York, NY,
10013-0500
Tel: (212) 219-0500

Tomoe Sushi
172 Thompson Street,
New York, NY,
10012-2576
Tel: (212) 777-9346

NEW JERSEY

Nikko
881 Route 10 E,
Whippany, NJ,
07981-1104
Tel: (973) 428-0787

PHILADELPHIA, PA

Hikaru Restaurant
4348 Main Street,
Philadelphia, PA,
19127-1438
Tel: (215) 487-3500

PHOENIX, AZ

Ra Sushi Bar and Restaurant
3815 N Scottsdale Road,
Scottsdale, AZ, 85251
Tel: (480) 990-9256
www.rasushi.com

SAN FRANCISCO, CA

Kabuto Sushi
5116 Geary Boulevard,
San Francisco, CA, 94118
Tel: (415) 752-5652

Tokyo Go Go
3174 16th Street,
San Francisco, CA, 94110
Tel: (415) 864-2288

SEATTLE, WA

I Love Sushi
1001 Fairview Avenue N,
Seattle, WA, 98109
Tel: (206) 625-9604

Shiro's
2401 2nd Avenue,
Seattle, WA, 98121
Tel: (206) 443-9844

TEXAS

Nara Restaurant & Sushi Bar
11124 Westheimer,
Houston, TX,
77042-3291
Tel: (713) 266-2255

WASHINGTON, DC

Makoto
4822 MacArthur Boulevard NW,
Washington, DC,
20007-1557
Tel: (202) 298-6866

Kaz Sushi Bistro
1915 I Street NW,
Washington, DC,
20006-2107
Tel: (202) 530-5500

Japanese retailers and fish suppliers

Most of the ingredients mentioned in this book are readily available in good supermarkets. If your supermarket doesn't stock a certain item and there is no specialty Japanese store nearby, you can usually order the specific product over the internet. It can sometimes be difficult to find a good fishmonger, but when you do keep hold of them. Be sure to tell them that you are going to use the fish for sushi.

Australia

Anegawa Supermarket
Specialist Asian supplier
7/17 Waters Road,
Neutral Bay, Sydney
Tel: 9904 4177

Asian Foods Ltd
Specialist Asian supplier
101–105 Grafton Street,
Cairns QLD 4870
Tel: 4052 1510

Burlington Supermarket
Asian supplier
TC Beirne Centre Shop 27,
Chinatown Mall,
Brisbane 4000
Tel: 3216 0828

Claringbold's Seafood
Seafood supplier
Prahran Market,
Commercial Road,
Prahran, Melbourne
Tel: 9826 8381

Fisch Shop
Seafood and sushi supplies
251A Chadstone
Shopping Centre,
Chadstone 3148
Tel: 9568 1138

Mackay Reef Fish Supplies
Fresh fish supplier
2 River Street,
Mackay 4740
Tel: 4957 6497

Randwick Oriental Supermarket
Specialist Asian supplier
61 Belmore Road,
Randwick, Sydney
Tel: 9398 2192

Sushi Sushi
Sushi supplies
Chadstone Shopping
Centre, Chadstone
Tel: 9568 3882

Sydney Fish Market
*Many suppliers of
excellent fresh fish*
cnr of Pyrmont Bridge Road
and Bank St, Pyrmont,
NSW 2009
Tel: 9660 0866

Tokyo Mart
Specialist Asian supplier
Shop 27, Northbridge
Plaza, Cnr of Eastern Valley
Way and Sailors Bay Road,
Northbridge, Sydney
Tel: 9958 6860

www.seafoodshop.com.au
*Online seafood
supplier*
Seafood shop,
PO Box 1167,
Stafford City,
QLD 4053
Tel: 3355 4333

Canada

Fujiya
*Fish and Japanese
foods retailer*
912 Clark Drive,
Vancouver,
BC V5L 3J8
Tel: 604-251-3711

Fujiya
*Fish and Japanese
foods retailer*
Suite 112,
1050 W. Pender Street,
Vancouver BC
Tel: 604-608-1050

Lapointe Fish
Online fish supplies
445 Catherine Street,
Ottawa,
Ontario K1R 5T7
Tel: 613-233-6221

**Pacific Coast
Wasabi Ltd.**
Fresh wasabi growers
450–1050 Alberni Street,
Vancouver BC, V6E 1A3
www.wasabia.ca

Sanko
Japanese groceries
730 Queen Street West,
Toronto, ON M6J 1E8
Tel: 416-703-4550
www.toronto-sanko.com

United Kingdom

Akaneya
Japanese food store
81 Northumberland Ave.,
Reading, RG2 7PT
Tel: (0118) 931 0448

Arigato
Japanese supermarket
48–50 Brewer Street,
London, W1F 9TG
Tel: (020) 7287 1722

Atari-ya
Fish and Japanese foods
Monkville Parade,
Finchley Road, London,
NW11 0AL
Tel: (020) 8458 7626

Atari-ya
Fish and Japanese foods
West Acton Branch,
7 Station Parade,
Noel Road,
London, W3 0DS
Tel: (020) 8896 1552

Chalmers & Gray
Fresh and smoked fish
67 Notting Hill Gate,
London, W11 3JS
Tel: (020) 7221 6177

Miura Foods
Japanese food suppliers
44 Coombe Road,
Norbiton,
Nr Kingston,
Surrey, KT2 7AE

Miura Foods
Japanese food suppliers
5 Limpsfield Road,
Sanderstead,
Surrey, CR2 9LA
Tel: (020) 8651 4498

Intel Supermarket
Japanese food suppliers
126 Malden Road,
New Malden,
Surrey, KT3 6DD
Tel: (020) 8942 9552

Jasmin
c/o Stanton House Hotel
Japanese food suppliers
The Avenue,
Station Fitzwarren,
Swindon, Wiltshire,
SN6 7SE
(Wed, Fri, Sun 3–6pm)
Tel: (01793) 861777

Midori c/o
Anglo-Japan Services Ltd
Japanese food suppliers
19 Marlborough Place,
Brighton,
East Sussex, BN1 1UB
Tel: (01273) 601460

Mount Fuji International
Japanese food online
Shrewsbury,
SY4 1AS
Tel: (01743) 741169
www.mountfuji.co.uk

Oriental City
Japanese food suppliers
399 Edgeware Road,
Colindale,
London, NW9 0JJ
Tel: (020) 8200 0009

Setsu Japanese Food
Japanese food suppliers
196a Heaton Road,
Newcastle Upon Tyne,
NE6 5HP
Tel: (0191) 265 9970

Steve Hatt Fishmongers
Fresh and smoked fish
88–90 Essex Road,
London,
N1 8LU
Tel: (020) 7226 3963

T K Trading
Japanese food supplies
Unit 6/76,
The Chase Centre,
8 Chase Road,
North Acton,
London,
NW10 6QD
Tel: (020) 8453 1001

United States

99 Ranch/Tawa Market
Japanese food market
7330 Clairemont
Mesa Blvd.,
San Diego,
CA 92111
Tel: (858) 974-8899

99 Ranch/Tawa Market
for other outlets see:
www.99ranch.com

The CMC Company
Online exotic food outlet
P.O. Drawer 322 Avalon,
NJ 08202
Tel: 1-800-262-2780
www.thecmccompany.com

Katagiri
Large Japanese market
224 East 59th Street,
New York,
NY 10022
Tel: (212) 755-3566
www.katagiri.com

Maine Coast Sea
Vegetables
Specialist seaweed supplier
3 Georges Pond Road,
Franklin, ME 04634
Tel: (207) 565-2907
www.seaveg.com

Mistuwa Market
Japanese food market
333 S. Alameda Street,
Los Angeles,
CA 90013
Tel: (213) 687-6699

Mistuwa Market
Japanese food market
675 Saratoga Avenue,
San Jose, CA 95129
Tel: (408) 255-6699

Mistuwa Market
Japanese food market
100 E. Algonquin Road,
Arlington Heights,
IL 60005
Tel: (847) 956-6699

Mistuwa Market
Japanese food market
595 River Road,
Edgewater, NJ 07020
Tel: (201) 941-9113

Mistuwa Market
for other outlets see:
www.mitsuwa.com

Ohana Seafood Market
Fresh fish supplier
168 Lake Street South,
Kirkland,
Washington 98033
Tel: 1-800-347-4754
www.fish2go.com

Pacific Farms USA LP
Fresh wasabi supplier
88420 Highway 101 N,
Florence, OR 97430
Tel: (800) 927-2248
www.freshwasabi.com

Pure Food Fish Market
Fresh fish supplier
Pike Place Market,
Seattle, WA
Tel: 206-622-5765
www.freshseafood.com

www.asiafoods.com
Online Asian food supplier
Mailing address:
AsiaFoods.com
18-20 Oxford Street,
Boston,
MA 02111
Tel: 1-877-902-0841

www.quickspice.com
Asian food supplier
Tel: (800) 553-5008

Sushi Foods Company
*Online supplier of sushi
supplies and utensils*
San Diego, California
Tel: 1-888-81-78744
Tel: 1-619-222-3732
www.sushifoods.com

Uwajimaya
*Japanese food and
equipment*
600 5th Avenue South,
#100, Seattle, WA 98104
Tel: (206) 624-6248

Index

Acknowledgments

Author's Appreciation
I would like to thank Rosie and Eric of Books for Cooks who supported me throughout and without whose help this book would not have started. A big thank you to Ian O'Leary and his French assistant, Ludo, for taking beautiful photographs and providing good music during the long photo shoot. I also would like to thank all the members of the team of Dorling Kindersley but especially Mary-Clare Jerram, Tracy Killick, Sara Robin and Hugh Thompson for their very professional but human support. A huge gratitude goes to Nasim Mawji for her transatlantic editing. My special thank you to Jasper

Morris of Morris & Verdin [Wine Merchants] for sharing his wine expertise. Thank you to Kalpana Brijnath, Eve Pleming and Simon May for lending me 'hands' for the party photo shoot. But my final and biggest thank you goes to my long-suffering English husband, Stephen, for his unlimited support and Maxi, Frederick and Dominic, my three sons for being tireless guinea pigs.

Dorling Kindersley would like to thank Jenny Jones for her editorial work at the beginning and Rosie Hopper for her inspirational work as a stylist.

The authors

Kimiko Barber

Kimiko left her native Japan to go to an English boarding school in 1972, and quickly realized that she would have to recall her grandmothers' cooking skills if she was to survive. After over ten years working in finance in Tokyo and London, a chance visit to Books for Cooks, a mecca for foodies, inspired her to change her career and focus on cooking and entertaining.

Kim now inspires others with her demonstrations of Japanese and Asian cooking at Books for Cooks, Notting Hill, London.

Hiroki Takemura

Hiroki completed a sushi chef apprenticeship in Osaka, Japan. To broaden his experience, he then moved to Europe and arrived in a cold and rainy London in February 1982 with just a small suitcase and his sushi knives. For the next ten years he worked in the city's noted Japanese restaurants. In 1996, Nobu Matsuhisa asked Takemura to head up Nobu London's opening team. Takemura accepted, and then worked briefly in Nobu's New York restaurant, to attune himself with the cooking (Takemura still refers to Nobu Matsuhisa as 'oyaji' – 'honourable father'). Takemura is now Executive Chef of Zuma in London's Knightsbridge, a new restaurant boasting sushi, tempura and yakitori bars.

Credits

Picture credits:
Peter Wilson 6bl, 8tl.

Ceramica Blue www.ceramicablue.co.uk

New Wave Tableware supplied by Villeroy and Boch Tel: (020) 8871 0011

The Conran Shop Ltd, Michelin House, 81 Fulham Rd, London SW3 6RD www.conran.com Tel: (020) 7589 7401

NOM, 7–9 Exhibition Road, South Kensington, London, SW7 6RD Tel: (020) 7590 0890

Handmade boat dishes by Sarah Vernon www.studiopottery.co.uk

Thanks to Jasper Morris for his expertise and donating all the wines for the photo shoot. Mr. Jasper Morris of Morris & Verdin Unit 2, Bankside Industrial Estate, Sumner Street, London SE1 9JZ Tel: (020) 7921 5300

Finally many thanks to Valerie Chandler for the index.

ThEme
Restaurants

THEME
Restaurants

Michael Kaplan

interview with
David Rockwell

PBC INTERNATIONAL, INC.

Distributor to the book trade in the United States and Canada
Rizzoli International Publications
through St. Martin's Press
175 Fifth Avenue
New York, NY 10010

Distributor to the art trade in the United States and Canada
PBC International, Inc.
One School Street
Glen Cove, NY 11542

Distributor throughout the rest of the world
Hearst Books International
1350 Avenue of the Americas
New York, NY 10019

Library of Congress Cataloging-in-Publication Data
Kaplan, Michael (Michael A.)
    Theme Restaurants / by Michael Kaplan.
              p.   cm.
    Includes index.
    ISBN 0-86636-542-7 (alk. paper). — ISBN 0-86636-579-6 (pb :
alk. paper)
    1. Restaurants—Decoration—United States 2. Restaurants—Lighting—
United States.   I. Title.
NK2195.R4K36 1997
747'.8571'0973—dc21   97-5302
                                                 CIP

CAVEAT—Information in this text is believed accurate, and will pose no
problem for the student or casual reader. However, the author was often
constrained by information contained in signed release forms, information
that could have been in error or not included at all. Any misinformation
(or lack of information) is the result of failure in these attestations. The
author has done whatever is possible to insure accuracy.

Color separation by Fine Arts Repro House Co., Ltd., Hong Kong
Printing and binding by South China Printing Co. (1988) Ltd., H.K.

10 9 8 7 6 5 4 3 2 1

Printed in Hong Kong

Contents

An Interview with David Rockwell

Among the most innovative architects working today, David Rockwell has created a wide range of restaurants at all sorts of price points. Projects include everything from Manhattan's super-chic Monkey Bar to the world's superstar-studded chain of Planet Hollywoods. Taking time out from his hectic schedule—currently he is working with Robert DeNiro on renovating the Harlem bebop palace, Mintons—Rockwell sat down with us to discuss state-of-the-art restaurant design and the way it can be translated into investor revenues.

Michael Kaplan: Why have theme restaurants become so pervasive right now?

David Rockwell: I think they've always been pervasive. Even if you go back to the way restaurants are perceived in movies or represented in theater. Look at Harmonia Gardens from *Hello Dolly*. That is one of the first themed restaurants I can think of. Restaurants are about having entertaining experiences. Theming is just another word for evocative design that is narrative and transports you to another time and place. Luchow's, in its day, was themed. When you have a limited amount of time and only so much disposable income, you want to go places that are meaningful, places that touch a nerve and create an emotional response.

MK: Have restaurants become the equal of theme parks?

DR: I see it more as theater. They're immersive, they're involving, they're active instead of passive.

MK: Tell me about your role in designing a restaurant.

DR: It's about listening very hard to the client and understanding what the client is trying to get at. Then we come up with a design response that meets the food, service, and price point goals of the client. If you take a look at Nobu and Planet Hollywood, you'll see very different design responses to different problems. The turnover is different, expectations about the food and environment are different. Designers need to understand and work with all the facets of the restaurant operation.

MK: What specific challenges come with creating a theme restaurant?

DR: I think the same challenges apply to every restaurant. In fact, I can't think of a non-themed restaurant. Republic (a stylish, moderately priced, Japanese noodle house in Manhattan) is as austere as you can get. But it clearly has a very strong point of view that it expresses design-wise. So its decision to be minimal is as conscious as Planet Hollywood's decision to be over-the-top. One challenge in restaurant design is that as people see more and more stuff they become desensitized. It becomes harder and harder to engage people.

MK: What does that mean for you?

DR: It means that we have to really think about where to put the emphasis and impact. Theatrical productions often get very quiet before they get loud in order to emphasize transitions. We do that with our spaces. At Official All Star Cafe in Las Vegas, which recently opened, you enter the main space through a tunnel as you would enter a real sport stadium. That way the scale of the space is brought down, and when the big space opens up, by contrast, it is a stunning transition. We thought that would create additional impact.

MK: You've done a number of restaurants that are

chained around the world. What are the most important elements that can be related to in the creation of restaurants internationally?

DR: You want them to have similar elements so they're a part of a family. They need to have certain features that people might expect and look forward to. With Planet Hollywood, it's the memorabilia, it's the diorama, the lighting concept, the deep-blue sky effect on the ceiling. Within, you have special features that are a little less expected.

MK: *Such as?*

DR: In Washington, D.C., we have a war room. In London, we have a James Bond room. In Paris, there is a film noir room.

MK: *How much research goes into your various restaurant projects?*

DR: For any project we start out with a lot of research about the client. We have a very large library and use it to do quite a bit of historical research. We try to understand the needs of the project. Look at Monkey Bar, a swanky bar/restaurant in Midtown Manhattan. For that project we did a lot of research into nightclubs of the 1930s and '40s. We did a lot of research into movies of the '30s and '40s. The Monkey Bar always had this urban wit to it, so we looked at Hugh Ferris renderings, we looked at the King Cole Room that Maxfield Parish designed in the St. Regis Hotel. We try to inundate ourselves with lots of research to draw from.

MK: *Are there ways to cut corners and reduce costs in the creation of big, elaborate theme restaurant chains?*

DR: You can cut costs by repeating certain elements from one restaurant to the next. Mill work and cast-fiberglass pieces can repeat. You can develop proprietary material usage from place to place; that saves money. If you are building a group of projects you can get a group of subcontractors who understand your needs and buy out the jobs in bulk. If you have certain flagship units—like Planet Hollywood Orlando—then every unit does not need to be as spectacular as that one. So you can pick and choose where to put the money in order to create the most impact.

MK: *Which of your restaurants are you proudest of?*

DR: There are things about all the various projects that I am most proud of. I love the way Planet Hollywood looks at night. I love the translucent quality of the sushi bar at Nobu. I love being at Official All Star Cafe during playoff games. I love to bring people from out of town to the Monkey Bar because it is so romantic about its outlook on New York.

MK: *Are celebrity-sponsored theme restaurants the trend that's particularly hot right now?*

DR: It's a moving target. I don't think there will be any specific themes of the future. The restaurant trend will be to really understand the market: smart operators working with good designers to create places that fill real needs—real food needs, real entertainment needs. There will be places that touch nerves and relate to current culture. Those are the restaurants that will be successful.

MK: *Is there a general direction in public tastes?*

DR: It's really hard to say. I just hope that it won't be staying at home.

Monkey Bar and Nobu are featured in Design Spirits: Bars, Brewpubs & Techno Clubs *by Gail Bellamy, published in 1995 by PBC International, Inc.*

Motown Cafe

Café Centro

Annette's Diner

Harley Davidson Cafe

Pete and Martys

Hang Town Grill

Country Star

Hi-Life Restaurant and Lounge

Motown Cafe

Even before diners enter the musically themed Motown Cafe, they are visually cued by a 20-foot-tall beacon, resembling a song-beaming radio tower, that is planted on the restaurant's roof. Housed in what had once been a Horn & Hardardt cafeteria, this soulful eatery retains posh features from the original 1930s Art-Deco structure: paneled ceiling, stepped pilaster columns, and a glazed-terracotta stairway (detailed with gold records) that connects the main floor with a mezzanine level. Life-size statues of the Supremes, costumes that had been worn by various Motown performers, vintage photos, and an operational, ceiling-high DJ

RIGHT *The world's largest 45-RPM record spins over the main dining room.*

**MOTORTOWN REVUE
LIVE TONIGHT**

location **New York, New York**

architect and interior designer **Haverson Architecture and Design P.C.**

photography **©Paul Warchol**

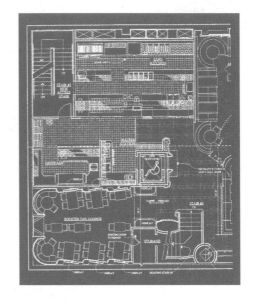

booth combine to immerse visitors in the Motown experience. The 18,100-square-foot space is illuminated with MR-16 recessed fixtures (pinspotting each table), neon-lit coves (they create "horizons" and exaggerate the ceiling height), and warm, white neon strips along the lower-level bar. The overall look of the Motown Cafe echoes classic American architecture from the late '50s to the late '60s, a period during which the record label released more than 100 top-ten hits. Kinetically designed, the Cafe's atmosphere is warm, colorful, dynamic, and resolutely upbeat—just like the music to which it pays homage.

OPPPOSITE *Classic Motown performers' costumes flank the stairwell.*

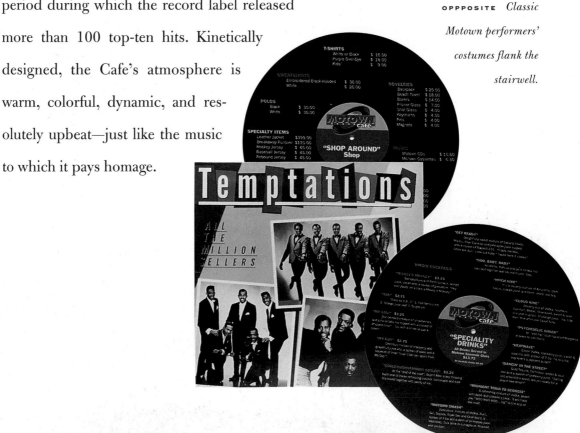

year designed **1995**
square feet **18,100**
budget **$4.9 million $270/sq. ft.**
seats **300**
check average **US $25**
daily covers **1,200**

OPPOSITE *An operational, ceiling-high DJ booth overlooks the multileveled dining area.*
RIGHT *Life-size statues of the Supremes greet diners.*

LEFT *The 600-square-foot gift shop takes up only 3 percent of Motown Cafe's floor space, yet it generates 27 percent of the restaurant's revenues.*

Café Centro

Café Centro recreates the decor, ambience, and cuisine of a bustling 1930s bistro, incorporating Art Deco-style elements that have been inspired by the era's most urbane restaurants in both New York and Paris. Upon entering the 10,932-square-foot eatery, visitors step upon a terrazzo floor and walk among large interior columns that are accented with gold leaf. The ceiling, made from anegré wood and plaster in varying heights, supports Lalique-style chandeliers and custom light fixtures that are adjusted throughout the day to create suitable atmospheres for lunch and dinner. Fitting for a restaurant that is adorned with sculpted zinc friezes depicting various kinds of fish and fowl, Café Centro boasts an open, stainless steel

RIGHT *The restaurant's colors of tan, rose, and verdigris are reflected in this mural, painted by architect Frederick Brush, in homage to Lempika's art from the 1930s.*

CAFÉ CENTRO

kitchen with brass accents that emphasize the light-infused nature of the restaurant. There is a large rotisserie around which guests can sit on semicircular banquettes, and watch meat as it roasts and grills. Bordering the dining area is Café Centro's Beer Bar, a discreet area where microbrews get consumed alongside burl wood walls and in cubicles adorned with museum-quality art objects that recall 1930s travel. The bar's floor is made of black-and-white marble, which is partially covered by a custom-designed rug with a motif of trains, planes, and ships. Black-lacquer panels with chrome accents highlight the bar area, while curved exterior walls of glass-block and stainless steel complete the prewar feel.

ABOVE *Art Deco-style furniture was custom designed by the architect.* LEFT *The concept of "restaurant as theater" inspired this exhibition kitchen, which resembles a glassed-in stage.* OPPOSITE *Gold and reflective surfaces, and the apricot walls, give the restaurant a warm glow.*

location **New York, New York**
architect and interior designer **Frederick Brush**
Design Associates
photography **Roy Wright NYC**

year designed **1993**
square feet **10,932**
budget **$5 million**
seats **306**
check average **US $35.75**
daily covers **590**

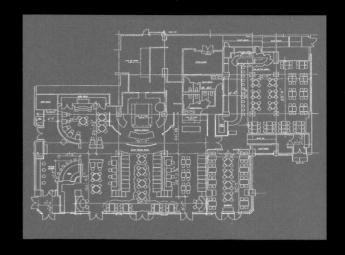

Annette's Diner

Employing moderne-style furnishings, classic colors of pink and blue, and soft curves that define cool '40s/'50s stylings (of everything from coffee tables to Cadillacs), Annette's is the quintessential American diner from that era. Upon entering the sprawling space, guests are greeted by the five-foot-tall statue of the restaurant's namesake—wearing roller skates and appearing ready to take orders. She gives a dramatic introduction to a spectacular dining space that's highlighted by vaulted ceilings and walls of glass. The interior includes a main counter with fixed stools, a large, food pick-up area, and a streamlined dessert/ice-cream counter. Colorful booths and banquettes in salmon and aqua vinyls, hard surfaces of marble floor tiles and laminate counters, and the stainless-steel cooking areas are all softened by boomerang-shaped clouds floating overhead. These acoustical shapes dominate the air space and imbue the design with a unique kind of excitement. All of these classic elements are complemented by the diner's Blue Plate Special menu and coin-operated jukeboxes built into each booth.

LEFT *The five-foot-tall statue of a roller skating waitress sets the tone for Annette's.* BELOW *Boomerang-shaped clouds accent the vaulted ceilings and repeat the wall motif.*

location **Euro Disney, France**

architect **Frank Gehry & Associates, Inc. and Saubot et Jullien Architecture**

interior designer **Morris Nathanson Design Inc.**

photography **Jud Haggard Photography**

year designed **1992**
square feet **6,500**
budget **$1.3 million $200/sq. ft.**
seats **250**

23

Harley Davidson Cafe

Embodying the free and reckless spirit symbolized by Harley Davidson motorcycles, the 5,000-square-foot cafe bearing the same name is passionately designed. Its steel facade appears rebelliously detached from the office building that houses the restaurant, and Twin V Harley Davidson signature engines introduce light sconces that anchor the perimeter. Inside the restaurant, the design is virtually kinetic. Natural timber contrasts against metal, which is highlighted by rotating lights, smoke machines, and strobes. All of this contributes to the overall illusion of actually time traveling through

LEFT *Situated over the main dining room, the American flag is made of hand-lacquered aluminum panels on a metal frame.*

25

year designed **1993**

budget **$2 million $18/sq. ft.**

square feet **5,000**

seats **250**

check average **US $20**

RIGHT *Artifacts of the motorcycle, as it appeared in popular culture, are displayed throughout the restaurant.* **OPPOSITE** *Steel and leather barstools are converted motorcycle seats.*

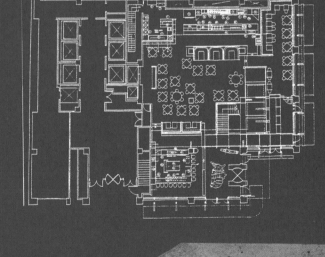

Harley's century-old history. Throughout the Cafe, a motorcycle motif dominates, with new as well as vintage bikes on display and the implementation of lighting fixtures that have been fashioned from Harley parts. Curtains, low partitions, and changes in the floor levels define smaller areas that can be sectioned off for private parties. Wall- and ceiling-surfaces are lit in a manner that is both even and soft. Physical boundaries of the space are used to emphasize a more intimate atmosphere.

location **New York, New York**

interior designers **Tony Chi, Noel Bernardo; Tony Chi & Associates**

photography **©Norman McGrath**

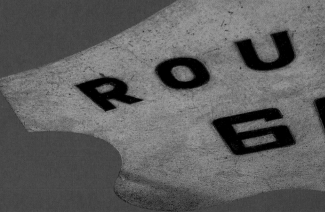

Pete & Martys

Pete & Martys is decked out in classic colors from the 1950s: Coca-Cola red and electric blue. Designed to resemble an idealized malt shop, its interior highlights include a jukebox, music stars' electric guitars, and antique radios. Schoolyard references such as a chain-link fence and classic, rec room accouterments (wall-mounted hubcaps and license plates) complete the '50s theme. The 229-seat, multilevel restaurant was created to accommodate dining as well as dancing and features music from rock 'n' roll's golden age juxtaposed with high-tech video components.

Because Pete & Martys' owners wanted day and night business, the vinyl-upholstered furnishings were carefully chosen to be as appropriate for the bistro as they are for the bar. Theatrical lighting adds a modern sense of drama to this eatery that could have doubled as a set on "Happy Days."

location **Montreal, Canada**

architect and interior designer **DiLeonardo International, Inc.**

photography **Warren Jagger Photography**

The cocktail area resides in an industrial setting with a chain-link fence, ceramic floor tiles, neon signage, and a brick bar.

year designed **1986**
square feet **9,000**
seats **229**

RIGHT *Wall-mounted speakers are reminiscent of rock 'n' roll's golden age.* **FAR RIGHT** *A collection of memorabilia from famous guitarists dominates one wall.*

Hang Town Grill

Hang Town Grill transports diners simultaneously to the future and to the past. This neat trick is accomplished by offering a "Jetsons"-inspired theme of the space age, as it's filtered through a 1950s and 1960s sensibility. Kinetic forms, from the floor to the ceiling, impart the 3,800-square-foot space—redesigned from an existing restaurant—with a sense of cartoonish energy that is further enhanced through vibrant colors and accent lighting. Upwardly angled illumination and cove lighting reinforce the idea of floating planes, which tie into the theme by seeming to defy gravity. Aimed primarily at families, the restaurant features video monitors and a retail display area where logoed caps and

tinguish Hang Town Grill from the relatively staid strip mall into which it has set down.

location **Austin, Texas**

architect and interior designer **Dick Clark Architecture**

photography **© 1996 Paul Bardagjy**

year designed **1996**
square feet **3,800**
seats **164**
daily covers **375**

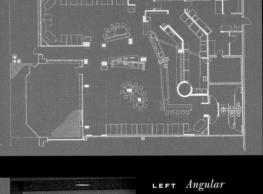

LEFT *Angular columns are lit in a manner that emphasizes the antigravity theme.*
OPPOSITE *Surfboard-shaped menus, tapered columns, and TV monitors impart the space with a sculptural quality.*

Country Star

Western tradition and international style cross paths in this restaurant that celebrates country music and doubles as a venue for the genre's top performers. An enormous, illuminated jukebox facade surrounds the entrance and a bright, white marquee heralds shows by Nashville's biggest names. Inside Country Star, rustic rock formations play off of a dome rotunda illuminated to resemble the nocturnal, desert sky while a walk-of-fame establishes the twanging theme. Immersing visitors in the Music City experience, this 15,000-square-foot

LEFT *Sound is enhanced through acoustical tiles in the main dining area, which is accented by polished silver and light burl woods.* **ABOVE** *The entrance is a multicolored, neon facade resembling an enormous jukebox.*

HOT PICK

Black and Tan
Try this delicious combination of Bass Ale and Guinness Stout stacked ice cold and refreshing.
3.95

It Ain't Country 'til it Cooks!™

LEFT *Video displays and tabletops constructed of 33-RPM records highlight the bar with country-music memorabilia.*

restaurant/entertainment facility has been outfitted with more than 70 video monitors, numerous listening kiosks, and loads of memorabilia. Country Star's dining areas playfully blend various design styles—mostly rooted in classic Americana—in order to create numerous settings within one large space. Those settings are all illuminated by a combination of low voltage and neon lighting that make for atmospherically striking ambience. Additionally, due to the existing building's size and shape, a massive network of HVAC needed to be utilized. Terrazzo floors in saturated, sunset hues flow freely throughout the space—interrupted only by a wooden dance floor—and column enclosures have been fashioned to resemble cowboy boots made from polished and brushed stainless

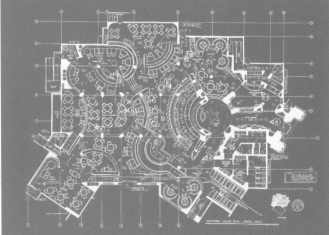

LEFT *Cavernous, rustic rock formations emphasize products for sale in the gift shop.*

steel. Country Star provides customers with a down-home environment, employs cutting-edge technology, and studiously avoids clichés.

year designed **1994**
square feet **15,100**
budget **$3 million $200/sq. ft.**
seats **560**

location **Universal City, California**
architect **James Whaley Architect**
interior designer **Hatch Design Group**
photography **Cameron Carothers Photography**

FIREWATER

COUNTRYSTAR
AMERICAN MUSIC GRILL
LAS VEGAS
ON THE STRIP AT HARMON
BETWEEN TROPICANA AND FLAMINGO
702-740-8400

Country Star's graphics program features die-cut flames and a flaming star logo.

Hi-Life Restaurant & Lounge

A Hi-Life Restaurant & Lounge is a swanky cocktail of curvy, stainless-steel rails, Art Deco-style mirrors, and a classic mahogany bar. The 2,000-square-foot establishment announces its nostalgic theme with a brash, black, baked-enamel facade that's fronted with the words "Hi-Life," in giant neon letters, bookending a martini glass. The exterior entryway is dramatically accented by swimming fish in an octago-

time trip back to the 1940s, Hi-Life Restaurant & Lounge is nal tank embedded in the wall, while the atmosphere inside radiates bygone elegance. Upon entering the restaurant, diners step into a clubby interior that's bordered by dark-green leather walls which are tuffed with brass nail heads in the shapes of clubs, hearts, spades, and diamonds. Vintage light fixtures—taken from an old cruise ship—atmospherically illuminate the way past semicircular, money-colored, Hollywood-style booths. A mounted marlin simultaneously anchors the bar space

and points the way toward a rear dining room, which is intimate and cozy, amusingly decorated with a muraled screen depicting four card-playing dogs. In the rear quarter, customers dine on everything from sashimi to sirloin steak, offerings from an eclectic menu that is anything but dated.

location **New York, New York**

architect and interior designer **Haverson/Rockwell Architects P.C.**

photography **©Paul Warchol Photography**

OPPOSITE *With its neon name playing off of bright black enamel and chrome, the restaurant is simultaneously brash and inviting.* **ABOVE** *Curving booths impart Hi-Life with a sense of alluring motion.* **LEFT** *Heavy drapes with a playing-card motif serve a dual purpose: they divide the bar/restaurant into two distinct spaces and capture a favorite nightclub pastime.*

year designed **1992**

budget **$600,000 $12/sq. ft.**

seats **150**

check average **US $20**

square feet **5,000**

'n'urf

Dive!

Joe's American Bar & Grill

Monte's

Mediterraneo

Surf 'n' Turf

Sullivan's Steakhouse

Oceana

C

rossing an amusement park thrill ride with an Italian deli, Dive! serves sub sandwiches and excites diners with hourly simulations of underwater immersion. Steven Spielberg and Jeffrey Katzenberg conceptualized this Los Angeles restaurant, and created a second Dive! in Las Vegas. They designed Dive! to be as convincing as any Hollywood extravaganza. The 15,400-square-foot, tube-shaped facility has been outfitted with traditional nautical detailing; its special effects—video displays, bubble portholes, and a water wall—are all integrated into the architecture. Lighting is used to reinforce the underwater experience through extensive use of blue and turquoise neon

ABOVE *At Dive! Los Angeles, neon lighting simulates waves and light patterns on the ship's hull exterior.* **OPPOSITE** *A two-story matrix video wall displays images that were shot in the Pacific Islands.*

washes, supplemented with a secondary red tube that is activated during dive sequences. Utilitarian fixtures with blue and amber lamps enhance the sub experience, while exterior lighting is refracted up from a linear pool that simulates light patterns on a ship's hull. Interior furnishings cleverly merge comfortable restaurant design (mahogany stools with linoleum-topped tables) with undersea concessions (banquettes have boat-cushion-style backs in lifejacket-orange canvas). It all combines to create an illusionary experience that takes the notion of a sub sandwich to a whole new depth.

OPPOSITE *Bar stools incorporate bull's-eye seats with torpedo bases.* **ABOVE** *Red chairs with a perforated wood back reinforce the marine theme.* **BELOW** *A periscope allows patrons to monitor activity along Santa Monica Boulevard. A video porthole is built into the rear wall.*

locations **Los Angeles, California ; Las Vegas, Nevada**
architects **Lawrence Berkley & Associates (Los Angeles and Las Vegas),**
Marnell Corrao Associates (Las Vegas),
Meisel Associates Ltd. (Los Angeles and Las Vegas)
interior designer **Meisel Associates Ltd. (Los Angeles and Las Vegas)**
photography **©Karl Herrmann (Los Angeles)**
        Doug Snower (Las Vegas)

location **Los Angeles**
year designed **1993**
square feet **13,500**
seats **300**

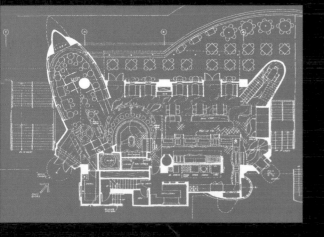

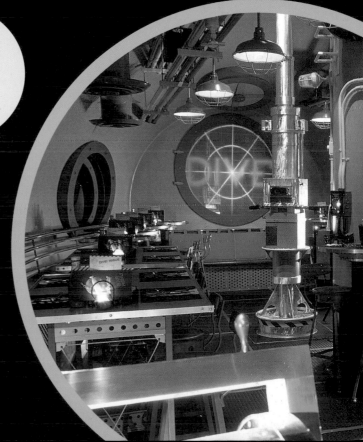

LEFT *The exterior of Dive! Las Vegas provides a backdrop between the gang-plank and the entry hatch, into which customers are transported.* **BELOW LEFT** *Nautical colors of blue and aquamarine are enhanced by bright accents, evoking images of tropical fish.*

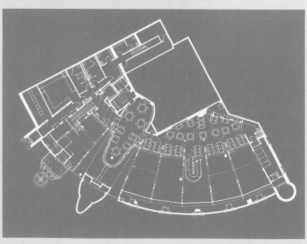

location **Las Vegas**
year designed **1994**
square feet **15,400**
seats **397**

LEFT *A bathysphere, torpedoes, and gauges near the ceiling are wired for activation of lighting, animation, and steam releases.* **BELOW** *The Dive! gift shop is the destination of this tube-shaped space.*

The folks behind Joe's American Bar & Grill have pulled off the neat trick of making something new look like it dates back to the 1920s or

1940s. More precisely, their six-year-old, 6,000-square-foot enterprise resembles a venerable steaks-and-chops eatery that had been built into an old pier warehouse many decades ago. This was achieved by overhauling the space, which had originally housed several retail establishments. Walls were knocked down, brick was put up, ceilings were extended so they soar to warehouse stature. Exposed steel rivets and

year designed **1991**
square feet **6,000**
budget **$750,000 $125/sq. ft.**
seats **150**
check average **US $24**
daily covers **800**

industrial-style details emphasize a faux past, as dark mahogany woods and traditional fabrics imbue the space with a stolid American atmosphere. Large scale portraits, photographs, and busts are adorned with the names of universities and athletes; all lend a clubby feel to the very public restaurant. Illumination comes primarily from bold, public-space lights along with Victorian and Edwardian fixtures that one would find in a grand hotel. An open kitchen, complete with period-looking equipment and exciting culinary performances for diners, completes the trip back into time.

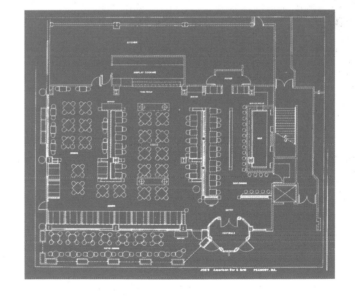

location **Peabody, Massachusetts**
architect **Back Bay Restaurant Group**
interior designer **Morris Nathanson Design, Inc.**
photography **Ron Manville, YUM, Inc.**

Monte's

A private club in one of London's most prestigious neighborhoods, Monte's is designed to epitomize the look of the classic men's retreat. It is distinctively laid out in a manner that positions the restaurant, bar, dance floor, and smoking room on separate floors, thus allowing each to have their own ambience and style. Creating such an elaborate facility—out of a space that had previously housed commercial enterprises—required substantial planning and intricate remodeling. Fine furniture, art, and artifacts in the exquisitely finished interiors serve to conceal more than 100,000 pounds of plumbing, wiring, and mechanical systems that had been inserted into the building's framework. The complexity of this project is underscored by the architectural firm's director, Ron

RIGHT *Entry doors are custom-made in bronze and glass, and the floor is patterned in inlaid Verde antique, Boticcino and Rosso Alicante marbles.*

ABOVE *Behind the bar is a glass-enclosed, wood and bronze wine room. The domed ceiling is made from etched glass and gold leaf.*

year designed **1995**
square feet **10,000**
budget **$10 million**

Van Pelt. He describes the finished club as "an extremely expensive Swiss watch where every single item has its own unique and specific place; if it doesn't fit, it won't work."

location **London, England**
architects **Wimberly Allison Tong & Goo and Andrew Young & Co., Inc.**
interior designer **Adam D. Tihany International**
photography **Peter Paige**

LEFT *Walls of bird's eye maple inlaid with mahogany surround the blue-leather and French-silk seating.* BELOW *Within Monte's, the Havana Club is a cigar shop featuring the city's largest walk-in humidor and a selection of 30,000 cigars.*

Sun-drenched colors of the Côte d'Azure merge with the international panache of sailing inside this restaurant that evokes the nautical world—in its theme as well as its cuisine. Mediterraneo's frontage is wrapped with a continuous band of French doors and

MEDITERRANEO

Mediterraneo

white canopies; its interior is adorned with many of the materials found on board a classic yacht including rigging, decking, and assorted hardware. Mediterraneo successfully reinvents this former luncheonette space. The main dining room is primarily lit with a low-voltage cable system that is strung from each side of the ceiling cove, which backsplashes light onto a nautical chart mural. A combination of MR-16 and MR-11 fixtures focuses light on table surfaces and accents the decorative sailing artifacts. The ceiling minimizes reflective sounds, and, considering that the restaurant features an open kitchen, diners can enjoy their Mediterranean-inspired food in a surprisingly placid setting.

location **Greenwich, Connecticut**

architect and interior designer **Haverson Architecture & Design P.C.**

photography **©Paul Warchol**

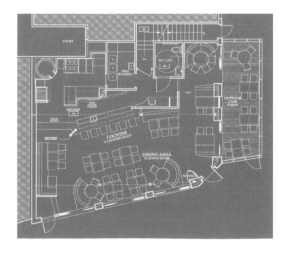

OPPOSITE ABOVE *Maple veneer tabletops are designed by Woodsmiths Company.* **OPPOSITE BELOW** *The bar surface is lit with pinspots from a continuous soffit with MR-16 recessed fixtures.* **ABOVE** *The dining room reflects the rigging, decking, hardware and materials found on board a yacht.*

year designed **1996**

square feet **2,100**

budget **$500,000 $260/sq. ft.**

seats **73**

check average **US $40**

daily covers **200**

Surf 'n' Turf

Dining at Surf 'n' Turf is about as close as you can get to eating a meal inside a cartoon. Practically a virtual reality experience, the 5,900-square-foot restaurant is a wacky mélange of soft curves and swooping forms designed by Jordan Mozer. All of the furnishings and decor are personified with the kinds of details that make the best animation so much fun to watch. The excitement begins at the

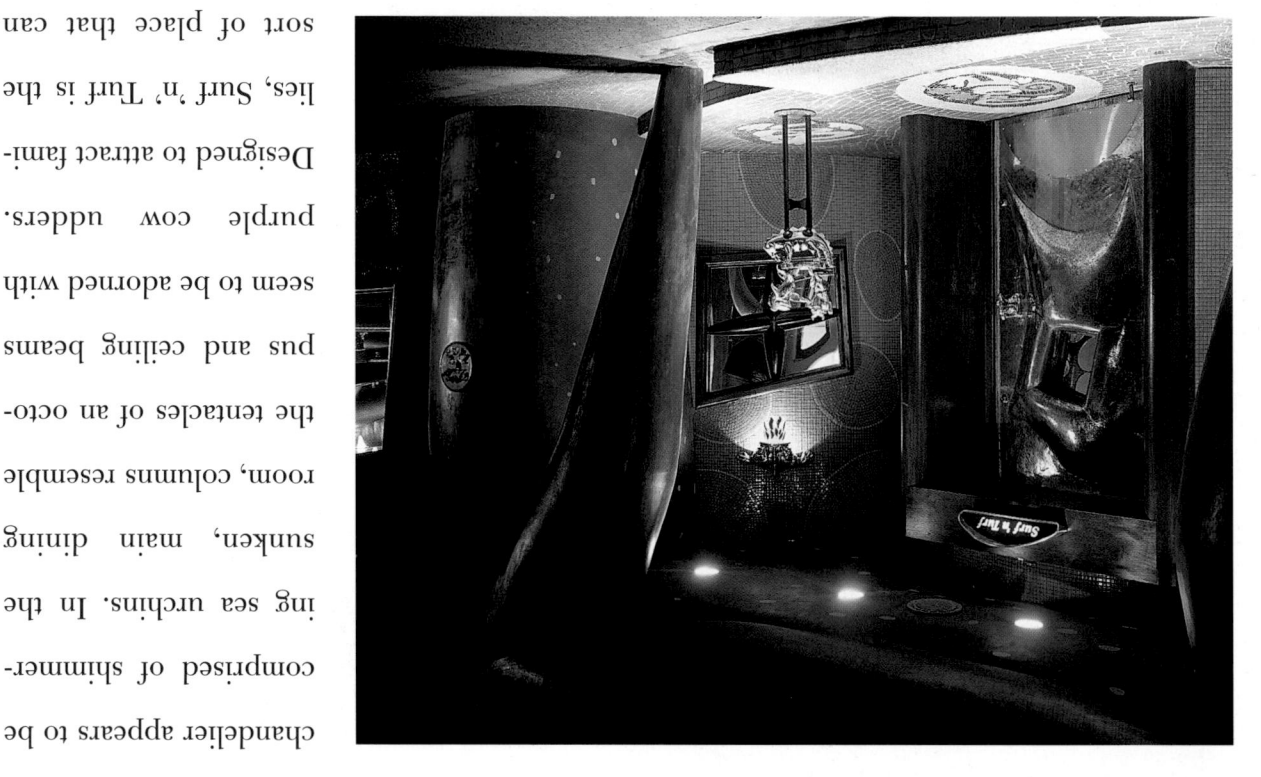

restaurant's entry, where the doorknob is a hand that customers must shake in order to get inside; exiting requires a "high-five." Chairs and stools have feet sculpted in wood, the backs of the booths are undulated, and the chandelier appears to be comprised of shimmering sea urchins. In the sunken, main dining room, columns resemble the tentacles of an octopus and ceiling beams seem to be adorned with purple cow udders. Designed to attract families, Surf 'n' Turf is the sort of place that can turn even the stodgiest diner into a kid—at least for the evening.

ABOVE At the entryway, cast bronze statues of a dancing fish and cow symbolize "surf" and "turf." OPPOSITE Soft curves lend animation to these purple columns, which resemble octopus tentacles.

ABOVE *This airbrushed, lacquered column extends like a wave from the segmented, tile floor.* RIGHT *At the dining platform, copper cactii shimmer beneath a sea urchin chandelier.*

location **Matsuyama, Japan**

architect and interior designer **Jordan Mozer & Associates, Ltd.**

photography **Take Ichi**

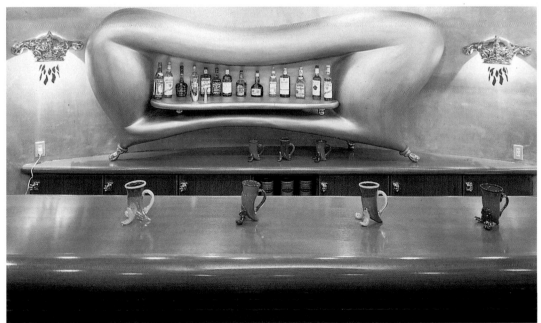

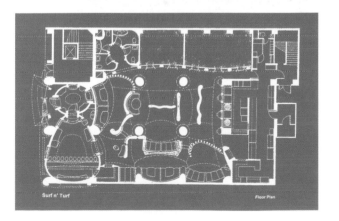

TOP *Ceiling fixtures in the form of cow udders illuminate the dining room.* ABOVE *Bronze and slumped-glass "Godzilla" sconces flank the rounded bar display.*

year designed **1993**

square feet **6,000**

budget **$720,000 $120/sq. ft.**

seats **150**

Sullivan's Steakhouse

location **Austin, Texas**

architect and interior designer **Aumiller Youngquist, P.C.**

photography **Eric Futran, The Futran Studio**

A traditional, masculine atmosphere perfectly complements the pugilistic theme of Sullivan's, a 1940s-style steakhouse that was named after a bare-knuckle boxing champion. Art-Deco inspiration is revealed in the curves of the 6,850-square-foot eatery's wooden bar and the design of the dining room's matching booths. An open kitchen provides drama that is the culinary equivalent of a heavy-weight bout, and mirrors on the ceiling add a sense of depth. Behind glass, a wine room stores

130 different varieties, and martinis are served in glasses that are etched with the restaurant's logo. A private dining room, partly walled in glass, looks down on the main seating area and manages to be discreet without losing out on the overall ambience of Sullivan's. Wood paneling throughout the restaurant creates a warm, clubby atmosphere that is accented by vintage political cartoons culled from the files of a local newspaper.

OPPOSITE *Sullivan's Steakhouse features a private dining area with sliding, beveled-glass doors.* RIGHT *A statue of John L. Sullivan, the last bare-knuckle world heavyweight champion, oversees the main dining room.*

year designed **1996**
square feet **6,830**
seats **200**
check average **US $40**

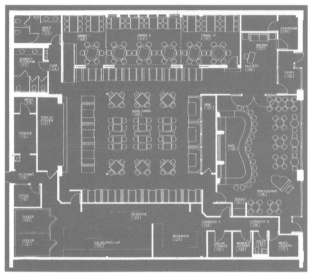

ABOVE *One section of the dining area evokes the comfortable sophistication of a library.* LEFT *The streamlined bar in Art Deco-style features a mahogany counter.*

Oceana

Oceana has been redesigned to resemble a 1930s-era ocean-liner—an elegantly accomplished task at a budget of $250,000. A bar, lounge, and holding area for waiting diners have all been added to the restaurant through repositioning, refinishing, and redecorating of the interior. What remains intact, partly due to budgetary constraints, is the existing architecture. Wood has been faux-finished to a rich, teak color, and a second-floor, paneled ceiling incorporates recessed lighting and decorative pendants of brushed stainless. All are original materials which combine to evoke the period. The custom carpet is in a pattern reminiscent of the great oceanliner ballrooms, 1930s-style sconces accent the pilasters, and

LEFT *A wood-paneled, atrium-style ceiling and mirrored étagère add a sense of authenticity to the oceanliner theme.*
ABOVE *An existing floral mural was replaced with a Mediterranean mural that depicts the sea on this side of the dining room and a harbor on the other.*

OPPOSITE *A wine rack with a rolling ladder structures the back bar.*

the removal of two interior columns presently allow for increasingly flexible seating arrangements. Strip and track lighting along with low-voltage pin-spots emphasize artwork (including original 1930s oceanliner posters) while providing illumination for side-seated diners. For anybody questioning the freshness of Oceana's fish, a shucking station has been installed to provide seafood on the half-shell and emphasize the high quality of all offerings on the menu.

location **New York, New York**

architect and interior designer **Morris Nathanson and Blase Gallo, Morris Nathanson Design, Inc.**

photography **Warren Jagger Photography**

year designed **1995**

square feet **4,500**

budget **$250,000**

seats **120**

check average **US $60**

daily covers **350**

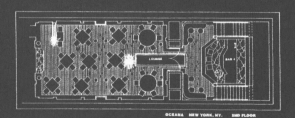

OCEANA NEW YORK, NY. 2ND FLOOR

ABOVE *1930s-style sconces complement billboard posters of the era.* RIGHT *Barstools are in the bentwood style with black, faux-leather upholstery.*

SOUTH by SOUTH SOu

Zest Cantina

Far East meets American West in this Tex-Mex themed restaurant that is situated in Japan. Zest Cantina splendidly serves as an idealized version of an eating/drinking establishment that you'd find on the range of your dreams. The color scheme is chili-pepper red and saddle-bag tan with all manners of distressed woods and Native-American patterns adorning the restaurant. Lighting comes courtesy of iron chandeliers and craftsman-style pendants that convey an air of authenticity. Tables are butcher block, chairs are in a classic barrel-style, and bar stools are covered in cowhide. Western artifacts—including a Native-American headdress and a wood-carved eagle—are everywhere while video monitors augment a state-of-the-art sound system. Casual, earthy, and inexpensive, the restaurant with its string-tied, cowboy-vest

RIGHT *Wood fixtures combined with Native-American crafts maintain an air of authenticity throughout the restaurant.*

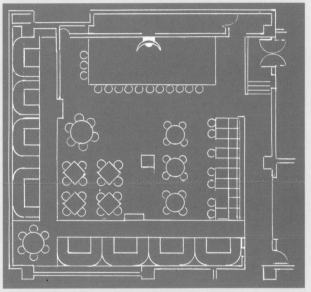

wearing waiters, attracts a broad crowd of businessmen, families, and kids. They all want to experience their version of the American-Western dream.

location **Tokyo Shibuya, Japan**

architect and interior designer **O'Brien & Associates Design Inc.**

photography **Mayumi Chiba**

RIGHT *A Native-American headdress and copper- and steel-inlaid eagles adorn the bar dais.*

year designed **1995**

seats **100**

Airstreams Roadside Cafe

LEFT *A three-dimensional billboard and yellow passing markers on the entryway floor begin the Airstreams' journey.* **BELOW** *The dining tour continues in a room resembling a train car. Railroad tracks are installed into the ceiling.*

Travel to tourist destinations around the United States without leaving your table at the restaurant! This is the idea behind Airstreams Roadside Cafe, a restaurant with five discreet dining rooms that depict Cape Cod, Napa Valley, Sun Valley, a Grand Central Station bar, and a 1960s motel. The interior of this 4,500-square-foot space has been lauded for its ability to assault the senses with a variety of props that underscore the theme. Specialized elements include a sun-shaped light fixture mounted over a seating area that resembles a wine vat, a chair lift (complete with a mannequin passenger) that rides above diners, an upside-down fishing boat that's been fashioned from a former coffer, and train tracks that are laid in what had once been a lighting recess. The restaurant is loaded with more than $100,000 worth of props and artifacts, creating an environment that immerses diners in broad-reaching themes.

location **Avon, Connecticut**

architect and interior designer **Judd Brown Design, Inc.**

photography **Warren Jagger Photography Inc.**

year designed **1991**

square feet **4,500**

budget **$300,000**

seats **150**

LEFT *The flannel-shirted skier rides above the table in the Sun Valley Room, where a golden sun hangs from the blue-sky ceiling.* **BELOW LEFT** *The entire ceiling of the Cape Cod room is shaped to accommodate the bottom of a boat.*

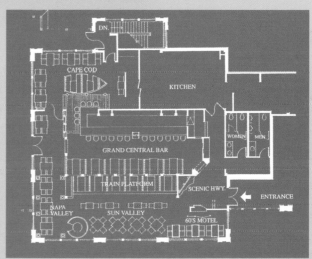

Tapika

Created with a Southwestern theme, Tapika has been redecorated from the old Symphony Café with two separate aesthetics: one for the interior and another for the exterior. This 2,400-square-foot restaurant offers a design approach with heavily wood-paneled walls that are sectionally obrey-plastered in shadings of desert clay. The remaining wood treatment, made of ash, was bleached, stained, and wire-brushed to lighten and empha-size its textures. The exterior perimeter uses a fence motif that incorporates hand-painted draperies and shields patrons from the garish lights flashing on nearby Eighth Avenue. A seating platform divides the main dining area

ABOVE *The bar repeats Tapika's cowboy motif, complemented by rawhide barstools.*

year designed **1995**

square feet **2,400**

seats **130**

daily covers **250**

into thirds. The added wainscotting was treat-
ed to match the walls and has been branded
with genuine branding irons obtained from a
ranch in Texas.

location **New York, New York**

architect and interior designer **Rockwell Group**

photography **©Paul Warchol**

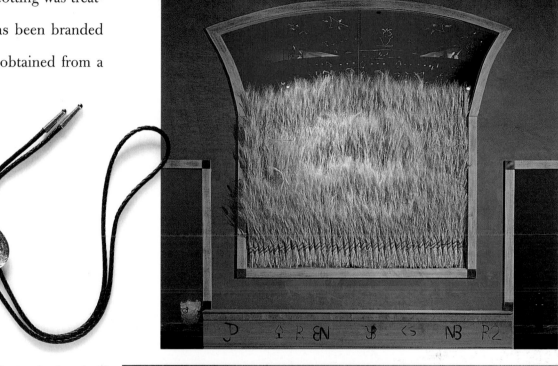

ABOVE RIGHT *A three-dimensional artwork, adorned with*
bundles of wheat, lends a tactile element to the Southwestern
theme. **RIGHT** *The dining area is visible through cowboys*
who have been cut out of the interior wall.

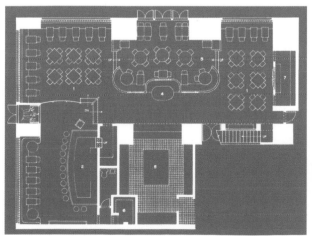

King Crab Lounge

Located several blocks from the Pacific Ocean, King Crab Lounge is an extension of an existing seafood restaurant next door. In an effort to make the King Crab casual and inviting, the 1,500-square-foot interior is loaded with vintage Coca-Cola ads, hand-painted signs, and shellacked jazz album covers.

Though it's a relatively new enterprise, the restaurant has the feel of a longstanding eatery that has stood the test of time. There is an enormous bar, an oyster-shucking station, and a loungey environment that permeates the atmosphere. The

ABOVE *Chrome and vinyl chairs, and vintage signs add to the "good-old-days" appeal of the dining area.* **LEFT** *The open facade and signage evinces American roadhouse style.*

identity of the restaurant—which is built in a space that had previously served as an office—is established on its exterior where a neon sign depicts a king riding a crab. The walls are painted a nostalgic shade of greenish blue and the floors are covered in glossy linoleum. Decorative lighting—a combination of bare bulb pendants with exposed filament, green-glass, grape-cluster sconces, and neon sig-nage—combined with a lively soundtrack of jazz, blues, and zydeco (pumped through a Bose sound system) contribute to the restaurant's post-war ambience.

location **Long Beach, California**

architect and interior designer **Hatch Design Group**

photography **Scott Rothwall Photography**

year designed **1995**

square feet **1,500**

seats **100**

check average **US $16**

daily covers **250**

RIGHT *A stand-up oyster bar is reminiscent of that in a Southern, seaside roadhouse.*

The Double A

Simultaneously vast and intimate, dramatic in scale, the Double A aims to serve as a timeless template for a great Western dining room. The 6,000-square-foot restaurant presents an image of the West that is modern, elegant, and refined. Its design is subdued— thus allowing for an uncluttered visual experience—and the space is constructed largely from metal, wood, stone, and plaster. Paying homage to the historical building that houses The Double A, these materials are prematurely-weathered and col-

ored in tan, burgundy, ash, and mahogany. All details are illuminated with theatrical spots, soft lighting at the tables, and lamps are outfitted with rawhide shades for a campfire effect. Bar stools are designed to resemble saddles, leather upholstery abounds, and the dining tables are topped with two inches of pure ash. Decorative

ABOVE *A hand-cut stone structure marks the entrance, which is highlighted by a sconce displaying the restaurant's logo.* OPPOSITE *Natural tones of the booths are complemented by the tabletop decor—a prairie-grass centerpiece, rawhide lamp, and a display of vintage fishing tackle.*

details tend to be quirky and ironic: vintage cowboy novels, antique-Western toys, and rusted, roadside objects that are elevated to works of art in museum-quality display cases. Western iconography extends to the graphics of Double A, which received the 1996 James Beard Restaurant Design Award for best graphics.

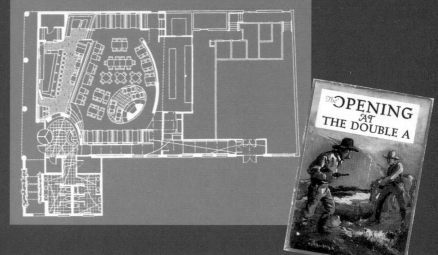

location   **Santa Fe, New Mexico**

architect and interior designer   **Cheryl Brantner, Fernando Bracer, Wayne Schlock: Brantner Design Associates**

photography   **Douglas Hill and Tim Street-Porter**

year designed **1995**
square feet **6,000**
budget **$3 million**
seats **125**
check average **US $47**
daily covers **100**

OPPOSITE *Dining seating is reminiscent of old court-house furnishings. "Campfire" lamps and 25-foot-high ceilings create an open-air environment.* ABOVE LEFT *The bar combines a grand painting of a horse, "buzzard" lamps, and an elk-horn ceiling sculpture. The rear wall recreates a log cabin.* ABOVE RIGHT *Natural materials are displayed with theatrical spotlights.*

Road Trip

Six regions of the United States are represented—both geographically and gastronomically—within the walls of this restaurant that boasts a proudly exposed, chrome-fronted kitchen. The long and narrow space is designed to give customers the feeling of an actual highway experience. Illumination comes courtesy of glaring "headlight" fixtures painted neon yellow (intentionally bright, so as to emphasize a busy road's confusion). A 145-foot mural runs the length of the restaurant with dividing columns that were reconfig-

ABOVE *Designers took advantage of the long and narrow space to serve the Road Trip theme, adding "headlight" sconces to the wall panels.* LEFT *The front door is ornamented with a metal cutout depicting cars in motion.*

location **Boston, Massachusetts**

architect and interior designer **Darlow Christ Architects Inc.**

photography **Anton Grassl Photography**

ured to serve as road markers. The travel theme continues into the bar, where small-scale map elements—such as roads, rivers, and topographic lines—are cut into metal boxes that are emphasized by backdrops of color lighting. The overall effect of the restaurant's design is one of elegant fun, with coasters, specialty menus, and signage playing off of the theme while the furnishings are kept simple. Topping off its travel theme, Road Trip houses a gift shop and makes sure that all diners leave the restaurant with at least one souvenir: a complimentary postcard.

ABOVE *A sculpted sail imparts a sense of dimension upon the seashore "region" of Road Trip's 145-foot-long mural.*

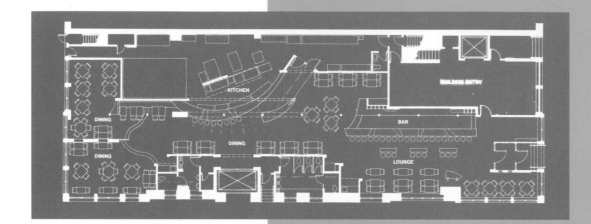

year designed **1995**
square feet **5,400**
budget **$500,000**
seats **150**
check average **US $35**

RIGHT *The mural artfully depicts a pseudo "road trip."*

LEFT *At the bar, a wine rack is constructed on a strong diagonal which recreates the perspective of a receding road.*

Chimayo Grill

Designed to invoke the spirit of New Mexico, Chimayo Grill is resplendent with hues and textures of the Southwest. Occupying an existing restaurant within a large, upscale shopping center, the interior space was enlarged and enhanced by extending the original storefront. This alteration increased the capacity of the restaurant and allowed for the creation of two patio dining areas, a lounge, and a main dining room. All spaces exude the simple beauty of New Mexican architecture while remaining unique to Chimayo. This is achieved through

ABOVE An exterior storefront was enlarged to make Chimayo stand out from its shopping-center surroundings. RIGHT Natural wood ceiling beams, and hand-plastered walls which surround a fireplace evoke the rustic craftsmanship of the Southwest.

RIGHT *Artwork and natural materials are highlighted with low-voltage halogen downlights in the dining room.*

the use of design elements that include natural wood beams, hand-plastered walls, and warm colors (amber, terra-cotta, dusty red) that are accented with metal details of bronze and copper. Lighting emphasizes artwork and creates a

warm, inviting atmosphere. Chimayo's unique, dynamic approach to Southwestern restaurant design successfully blends simplicity with style.

location   **Newport Beach, California**

interior designer   **Hatch Design Group**

photography   **Dennis Anderson Photography**

ABOVE   *A floating lighting soffit mimics the curvature of the bar.*

year designed **1995**
square feet **5,500**
seats **165**
budget **$1 million**
check average **US $25**
daily covers **400**

The bold signage and neon logo of Route 66 recall the roadside billboards of the early days of the automobile.

look of a garage interior. Variations on traditional design elements—banquettes that are reminiscent of roadhouse booths and a maitre d' stand that resembles a mechanic's tool chest—complement the atmosphere of fun. Illumination comes courtesy of fixtures fashioned from hubcaps and

the industrial-style lights that one would find in an auto-repair bay. All of this was incorporated at the relatively low renovation cost of $225,000. The budget necessitated the implementation of simple industrial finishes and materials, with no exterior renovations except for a new facade. Fittingly, it is decked out with a corrugated-steel billboard that is visible from the adjacent highway.

location   **Merrick, New York**

architect and interior designer   **Pentagram Architecture**

photography   **©Peter Mauss/Esto**

Route 66

The classic American open road looms within the walls of Route 66. Named after the mother of all interstates, it simultaneously conveys the experience of traveling along Route 66 and the ambience of a dining establishment that might have once been located there. The main room of this 2,000-square-foot restaurant (located in a former garage that dates back to the 1920s) is bound by a wooden billboard map of Route 66 and an erector-set-inspired bar that retains the

ABOVE *Vintage postcards double as suitably atmospheric wallpaper.*

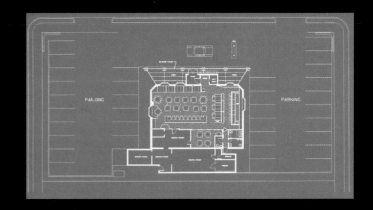

LEFT *The cowboy cut-out in the wall of the dining room is the only overt representation of the West.* **ABOVE** *The open bar is trellised by a metal frame hung with lights and rolling TVs, and backed by a sheet of corrugated steel.*

year designed **1994**

square feet **2,060**

budget **$225,000**

seats **135**

check average **US $21**

happy

hour

Alcatraz Brewing Company

Raw-steel bars, metal railings, and twisted lengths of chain-link fencing set the incarceration motif that defines Alcatraz's theme. This contemporary brewery celebrates the San Francisco Bay with design elements that recall the legendary Alcatraz—quarry tile and concrete flooring, bare-bulb table lights, and exposed ductwork. Other lighting touches include institutional pendant lamps (hanging from a grid) and copper-gelled lighting that makes the 8,200-square-foot restaurant's stainless-steel brew tanks appear richer in color. Traditional looking zinc table-tops, industrial-inspired chairs, and pub booths are offset by prison-style railroad nails that double as coat hooks. While the "international orange" that bedecks the Golden Gate Bridge dominates the color scheme, reds, greens, and warm, amber tones are prominently used as well. A freestanding, painted steel drink rail is modeled after Art-Deco supports of the Golden Gate Bridge, and glass tiles made from reconstituted beer bottles (and lit from within) accent the bar.

location **Indianapolis, Indiana**

architect and interior designers **Engstrom Design Group, Sady S. Hayashida, To Design**

photography **Greg Murphey Studio**

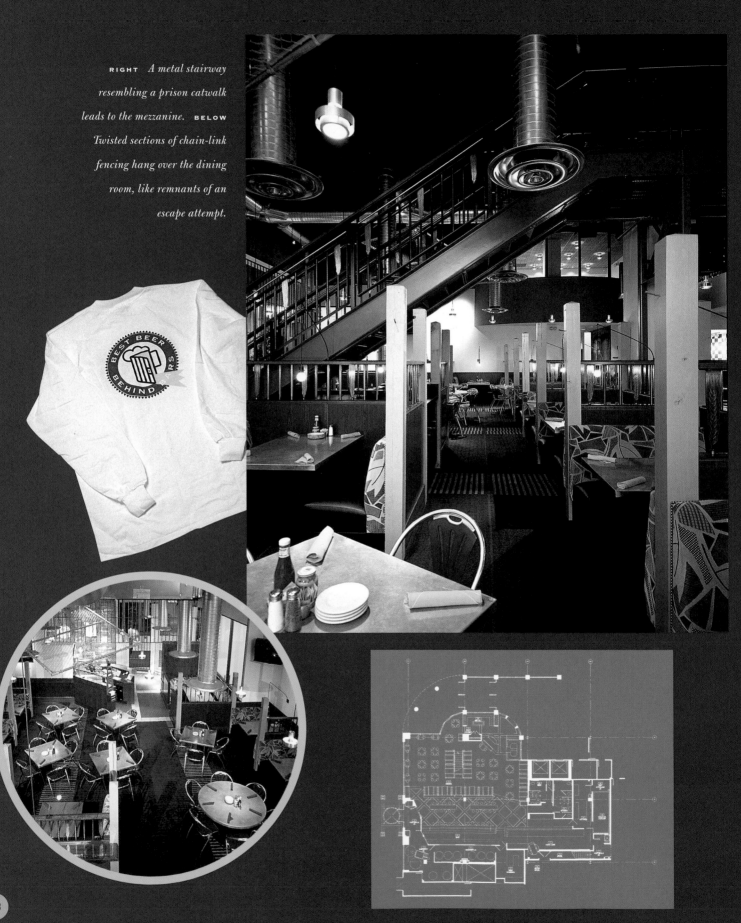

RIGHT *A metal stairway resembling a prison catwalk leads to the mezzanine.* BELOW *Twisted sections of chain-link fencing hang over the dining room, like remnants of an escape attempt.*

BEST BEER BEHIND BARS

BELOW *Fully operational, stainless-steel brewing tanks provide the backdrop for private parties and overflow customers on the mezzanine level.*

year designed **1995**
square feet **8,200**
budget **$2.5 million**
seats **200**
check average **US $15**

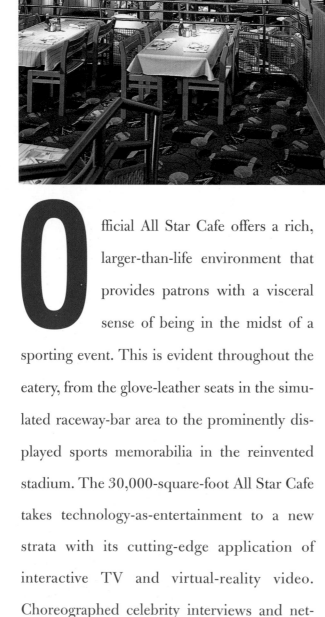

LEFT *From a perch on the restaurant's upper deck, all sports collide, from game-themed carpeting to the panorama of video screens.* OPPOSITE *State-of-the-art monitors surround the casual dining area, where old-fashioned wooden chairs contrast against hard-edged technology.*

Official All Star Cafe offers a rich, larger-than-life environment that provides patrons with a visceral sense of being in the midst of a sporting event. This is evident throughout the eatery, from the glove-leather seats in the simulated raceway-bar area to the prominently displayed sports memorabilia in the reinvented stadium. The 30,000-square-foot All Star Cafe takes technology-as-entertainment to a new strata with its cutting-edge application of interactive TV and virtual-reality video. Choreographed celebrity interviews and net-work sports segments provide sports fans with dining entertainment. Myriad monitors create an illusion of live action in this restaurant, where time-outs seem to be nonexistent.

location **New York, New York**

architect and interior designer **Rockwell Group**

photography **Norman McGrath, courtesy of Official All Star Cafe**

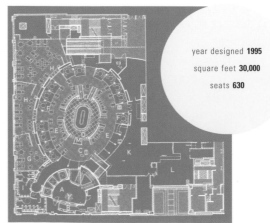

year designed **1995**

square feet **30,000**

seats **630**

Heartland Brewery

Heartland Brewery epitomizes the American brewpub by providing a casual, warm environment for lovers of freshly made beer. It is located in a historic, high-ceilinged building that offers an ideal space for an establishment that exudes comfort and encourages camaraderie. The main level's design centers around a 40-foot-long mahogany bar. Scenes from America's heartland are depicted on a mural that stretches from the exposed brick walls to a rear drinking area. A gas fireplace warms the 6,200-square-foot Heartland's seating area, which is

ABOVE *Heartland Brewery's two-story, metal and glass exterior in industrial style conveys the working operation of the brewery inside.* **RIGHT** *Exposed brick and a weathered logo give the impression of a long-standing establishment to Heartland.*

located away from the bustle of activity. Dark, warmly shaded woods and natural materials serve to heighten the comfortable, cozy feel of the restaurant.

year designed **1995**
square feet **6,200**
seats **250**
budget **$750,000**
check average **US $17**
daily covers **600**

location **New York, New York**

architect and interior designer **Morris Nathanson Design, Inc.**

photography **Warren Jagger Photography, Inc.**

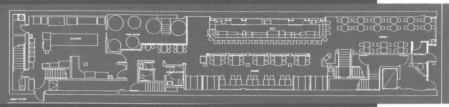

LEFT *The brewhouse is visible from the dining area and bar through a glass enclosure.*

Brew Moon

Sometimes beer is more than just a drink. At Brew Moon, where brewing tanks serve as part of the sleek decor, it's a theme that drives the restaurant. The walls themselves serve as architectural expressions of various beer types, and a custom-made frieze graphically illustrates the making of handcrafted beer. Custom-designed cylindrical forms are pierced with bands of backlit, cast glass, which serve to express the translucent qualities of the product. The restaurant is colored in warm tones (reflecting the flowing qualities of beer) and cool blues (creating a modern backdrop for the processing area). Custom, hanging light fixtures reinforce the phases of the moon and wall-mounted lights portray the technological aspects of the brewing process. Quilted, bird's-eye maple is used for table and bar tops, accented with hammered copper and sandblasted steel, which combine to express the more textured quality of beer. The setting encourages patrons to think about what they experience as they sip their amber liquids.

location **Saugus, Massachusetts**
architect and interior designer **Darlow Christ Architects**
photography **William T. Smith/Architectural Photography,**
Tony Rinaldo Photography

LEFT *Dining chairs emphasize the lunar form with a moon-shaped back.* BELOW LEFT *This custom frieze graphically illustrates the brewing process.*

year designed **1995**

square feet **10,000**

seats **260**

check average **US $12**

1 FUNCTION ROOM
2 DINING ROOM
3 LOUNGE
4 BAR
5 BREW HOUSE
6 FERMENTATION ROOM
7 BEER COOLER
8 MILL ROOM
9 KITCHEN
10 MEN'S RESTROOM
11 WOMEN'S RESTROOM
12 AUXILIARY SPACES

S martly combining the themes of a microbrewery with a Thai restaurant, Typhoon Brewery matches industrial-looking elements of the beer manufacturing process with simplistic lines and shapes that are reminiscent of the Far East. Building the restaurant necessitated a gut renovation of a two-story, turn-of-the-century town house; additional space comes courtesy of a ground-floor section that's built into a 45-story

Typhoon Brewery

high-rise. The color scheme is minimal and based on an Asiatic palette, whimsical lighting is designed to create a sense of drama, and furniture is elegantly hard-cdgcd. Scating is arranged in a manner that exposes diners to the open kitchen's theatricality. Brew tanks are prominently displayed to diners as well as pedestrians, and a glass-and-steel canopy (suspended over an entryway of muted, galvanized metal) signals entry into a contemporary space that is anchored by the tradition of brewing.

location **New York, New York**
architect **CORE**
photography **©Michael Moran**

year designed **1995**

square feet **12,000**

seats **130**

check average **US $45**

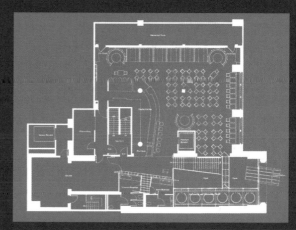

OPPOSITE *A wall of glass encloses brew tanks, allowing a dining-room view into the beer-making process.* LEFT *Circular banquettes repeat the curved design of the brew tanks.* BELOW *A sleek, L-shaped exhibition kitchen adds visual drama to the second-floor dining room.*

Mickey Mantle's

theme: Mickey Mantle. This 5,000-square-foot monument to the baseball great features multiple televisions, strategically placed around the restaurant for unobtrusive viewing of all sporting events. Its collection of museum-quality memorabilia—from players who include Joe DiMaggio, Billy Martin, Lou Gehrig,

Upon entering the restaurant and noticing members of the staff wearing Yankee jerseys adorned with "sevens" on back, you instantly realize the

year designed **1988**
square feet **5,000**
budget **$25,000**
seats **210**
check average **US $25**
daily covers **300–600**

and Mantle himself—draws patrons in from the sidewalks of posh, Central Park South. Additionally, the dining room offers sport-oriented artwork and photographs for purchase. Also available is a wide range of souvenirs such as T-shirts, autographed caps, and key rings, all of which boast Mantle's signature and the Yankee Stadium-inspired white picket fence. The allure of Mickey Mantle's is evident in its popularity as a sight for book parties and special radio broadcasts.

location **New York, New York**
architect and interior designer **Hirsch-Bedner Associates**
photography **courtesy of William Liederman, Mickey Mantle's**

A 1950s-era paint store provided unlikely inspiration for the people behind Star Bar, a drinking establishment that occupies the former retail space. A glass-curtain wall at the street-side facade offers an inviting view of the cozy interior, and the addition of a new sidewalk patio/seating area addresses the urban nature of the location. Muted colors lend a subtle shimmer to the space, while neon cove lighting

LEFT *Point lights sparkle near this custom-designed wine rack which displays bottles as if they were sculptural elements.*

in custom-designed, star-shaped fixtures accentuates the bar's structure. Additional illumination is provided by low-voltage point-lights which offer a sparkle effect. Furnishings are simple and clean, underscoring the uncluttered design and allowing the star patterns—evident in the front and back bar—to stand out. The scale of the interior is intimate, with low, soothingly blue ceilings, cozy banquette seating, and indirect lighting. A copper faux-finish paint treatment at the rear wall provides a subtle glow, which is echoed in the copper screen shades that cover some of the lights. Beyond the bar, a custom-made wine rack flanks an open assembly kitchen which serves Caribbean-style sandwiches and light hors d'oeuvres.

year designed **1995**
square feet **2,165**
seats **90**

OPPOSITE ABOVE *The glass wall allows a view inside Star Bar, where a lowered ceiling soffit and mirrored rear wall repeat the zigzag form of the "star bar" itself.* OPPOSITE BELOW *The playfully overscaled sign is an assemblage of curved and perforated metal and neon.*

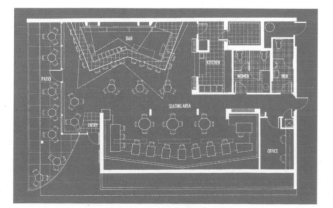

location **Austin, Texas**

architect and interior designer **Dick Clark Architecture**

photography **©Paul Bardagjy Photography**

The Bungalow

D esigned to be a friendly, casual, intimate retreat, The Bungalow emphasizes the drinking of martinis and the smoking of cigars via a lower-level dining area that opens onto an outside patio. Evident in the two-level restaurant is the inspiration of the Arts and Crafts movement, which focuses on creating warmth through architecture that emphasizes handcrafted materials and objects. The entire upper dining space is divided into two areas by square and tapering mahogany columns. These project from a wide, low mahogany wall, suggesting strength and stability as a structural art

form. These same columns support a massive beam under highly detailed rafters. Pendant lanterns, filled with colored glass and small overhanging roofs, are suspended over craftsman-

LEFT *A large Anne Fields mural makes the entire wall come to life with its playful Arts and Crafts-inspired imagery that emphasizes cigars and camaraderie.*

year designed **1996**

square feet **3,800**

budget **$400,000**

seats **128**

check average **US $55**

daily covers **180**

LEFT Rich wood paneling and furnishing suggest strength and stability as a structural art form. BELOW LEFT The bar is dark-stained mahogany with decorative battens and a hand-crafted iron foot rail.

detailed tables. Upstairs and down, inside and out, The Bungalow represents a return to the old school—in terms of its craftsmanship and its encouragement of the raffish camaraderie that comes from drinking martinis and smoking cigars with good friends.

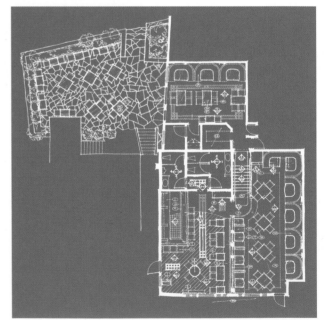

location **Corona del Mar, California**

architect and interior designer **Hatch Design Group**

photography **Scott Rothwall Photography**

OPPOSITE High-backed booths, upholstered in deep burgundy mohair, create intimate spaces that are perfect for quiet conversations.

**d
naTUre**

Rainforest Cafe

Remi

The Cheesecake Factory

Torre di Pisa

Monsoon Cafe

Americas

Yellow Giraffe

El Divino

Osteria del Circo

Rainforest Cafe

ituated in Walt Disney World's Village Marketplace, this 30,000-square-foot restaurant uses a combination of live and animated animals, simulated volcanoes, show lighting, and three sound systems to create the experience of dining inside a tropical rain forest. Live birds soar over cascading waterfalls, steam clouds rise in the air, and the ground shakes with the

ABOVE *Show lighting imparts a dramatic air to the theme-park inspired restaurant.* RIGHT *Talking trees complement the tables and chairs, supported by wood that is designed to resemble bamboo.*

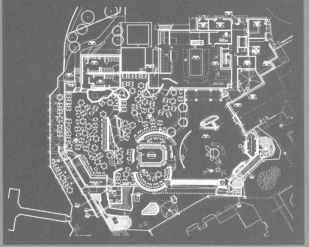

ABOVE *Special effects of steam clouds reinvent the sensory experience of the tropics.*

simulated stampeding of elephants. Hand-painted bar stools, shaped and colored like animal figures, have a fitting backdrop of rain-forest green. The authenticity of the experience is completed through simulated rainstorms, an erupting volcano, and a ventilation system that emits a specially designed rain-

forest floral aroma. Staff members dress in safari attire, the cuisine is eclectic, and an adjoining retail store sells a wide range of memorabilia (featuring Rainforest items from around the world with eight proprietary animals). Free entertainment, reasonable prices, and generous portions all contribute to elevating the perceived dining value of a meal at Rainforest Cafe.

location **Lake Buena Vista, Florida**

architects **Tod Elkins, Kevin Thade; Cuningham Group**

interior designer **Jon Greenberg Associates**

photography **Dana Wheelock Photography**

year designed **1995**
square feet **30,000**
seats **550**

LEFT *Stools around the bar are hand painted to resemble animal figures.*

LEFT *The lighted "porthole" of the mahogany bar's back wall displays Tihany's collection of antique Murano glass.* OPPOSITE *Architectural elements downscale the immense proportions of the dining room, with its ceiling height of 27 feet.*

bridges that cross Venice's canals; and nautical influences are evident in the interior's striped, cherry and maple floors (designed to resemble the deck of a luxury yacht) as well as in the blue and white striped upholstery. Further touches of Italian influences can be seen in the lighting, which comes courtesy of Venetian glass chandeliers and custom-designed sconces in murano glass. The restaurant's 3,000-square-foot dining room, monikered *Canal Grande*, is designed to accommodate as many as 160 diners; additional seating can be found in the glass-roofed Atrium Garden outdoor cafe. Wherever patrons decide to enjoy their meals, however, they all seem to finish in true Italian fashion by sidling up to the grappa bar for a postprandial drink.

location **New York, New York**

interior designer **Adam D. Tihany International**

photography **Peter Paige**

Remi

n terms of cuisine and theme, Remi takes its diners on memorable trips to Venice. Even the restaurant's name is reflective of the romantic city: Remi means "oars" in Italian. A 120-foot mural of Venice, resembling a restored Renaissance fresco, adorns the dining room wall; flying buttress archways echo the

year designed **1990**
square feet **3,000**
seats **160**
check average **US $50**

OPPOSITE *The 120 foot-long mural of Venice in the dining room creates the illusion of cruising through a Venetian canal.* RIGHT *Catering to the take-out crowd, Remi-To Go provides a grand assortment of gourmet dishes direct from the restaurant kitchen.*

E stablishing instant brand awareness was a chief goal for designer Jordan Mozer and restaurateur, David Overton when the two teamed up to design Chicago's interpretation of chain-restaurant success, Cheesecake Factory. The design challenge presented by a below-street-level entrance within the concourse of the John Hancock Tower, compelled Mozer to create a unique and somewhat radical exterior presence.

A dramatic restaurant facade marked with large copper awnings that resemble enormous, undulating flames stand in contrast to the austere, angular steel forms of the prestigious office building on Michigan Avenue. Signature hues of burnished orange and gold (the colors of baked goods)

ABOVE *Jordan Mozer's unique interpretation for Chicago's Cheesecake factory is marked by an overscaled awning in copper and sheet-metal finish.* RIGHT *The plaster ceiling is multileveled in the form of cheesecake filling.*

130

radiate warmth and transport diners into a cheesecake fantasy. Traditional decor of the Cheesecake Factory concept is upgraded through richness of detail and materials; evident in the intricately etched mirrors and glass lights, cast-aluminum railings, terrazzo floor mural, columns, and plaster ceilings. The restaurant/bakery seats 450 people on two levels with a display kitchen on the lower level which delivers a theatrical center stage within a gastronomically entertaining wonderland.

location **Chicago, Illinois**

architect and interior designer **Jordan Mozer & Associates, Ltd.**

photography **David Clifton**

year designed **1995**
square feet **16,500**
seats **450**

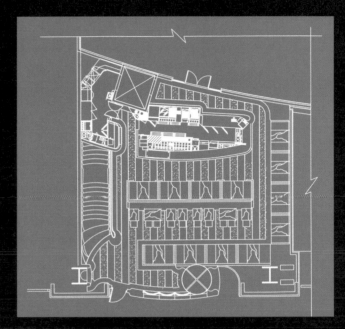

OPPOSITE *Intricately detailed, aluminum railings along the stairwell are interpreted from garden vegetation.* **LEFT** *Lotus-shaped columns complement the flame motif, which is repeated throughout the restaurant.*

Torre di Pisa

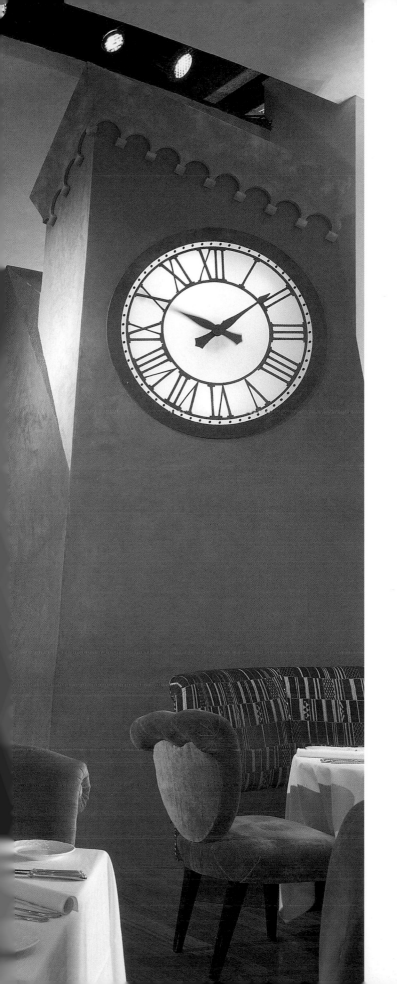

The authenticity of this Milanese-themed restaurant is insured by the pedigree of its proprietors, a father and son team who already own a prized restaurant by the same name in Italy. The 4,383-square-foot outpost in New York focuses on the history of Milan, makes imaginative use of space, and offers lighting that manages to illuminate without casting glare. The interior is loaded with imagery derived from Tuscany. Chairs are custom designed by The Pace Collection, and feature ebony wood legs and crushed velvet. The fabric is created in gold for the dining room and a deep, eggplant color for the restaurant's Cigar Room. Luxurious and playful, the Cigar Room offers a club-like atmosphere, state-of-the-art ventilation system, and custom-built humidor. An

LEFT *Dusty colors and soft angles combine to convey the approximation of a surrealistic town square.*

antique, four-foot-long, silver wall sconce, found in a Milan antique shop near the original Torre di Pisa, provides subtle lighting and a dramatic visual element. The Cigar Room is a perfect place for post-meal nightcaps and relaxing smokes.

location **New York, New York**
architect and interior designer **Rockwell Group**
photography **©Paul Warchol**

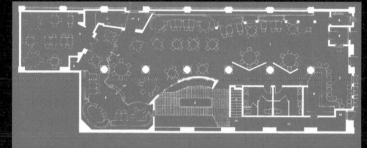

OPPOSITE British plates appear to be suspended a few inches from the tilting wall.
ABOVE The angled screens of leather latticework allude to the famed tilting tower.
LEFT The dining room features the Marcia Chair—the first Rockwell Group design to be included in the Pace Collection.

137

Torre di Pisa

year designed **1995**
square feet **4,383**
budget **$1.35 million**
seats **150**

RIGHT *The antique wood bar and stools are reminiscent of old-world cafes in Milan.* **BELOW** *Dark-blue walls are decorated by original oil paintings, including one that was offered in lieu of lira at the conclusion of a meal in Milan.* **OPPOSITE** *The Love Letter Bar wall collage, created by David Rockwell, is fabricated of actual love letters and authentic Italian momentos.*

Monsoon Cafe

Several Asian cultural influences whip themselves into a single culinary storm within the spartan, tropically themed walls of Monsoon. From every seat in the restaurant, diners harmoniously experience the interior (bold-red ceilings with silver ornaments; walls that are adorned with brightly colored fabrics, paintings, and artifacts) and exterior (open terraces, skylights, a lily pond) in equal measures.

Lighting comes through fixtures that have been fashioned from cast bronze, dragon heads, pearls, jewels, and brilliant cuts of glass. Less conspicuous is the sound system, which features hidden speakers that fill the restaurant with Asian melodies. One challenge in the design of this restaurant was to have a single,

ABOVE *A lily pond adjoins Monsoon's dining area, where seating is arranged as in an outdoor terrace.* **OPPOSITE** *Exotic light fixtures provide contrast against the naturalistic, bamboo ceiling.*

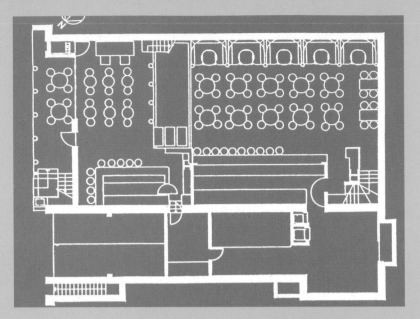

resented at Monsoon is the style of dress provided for the wait staff: men wear drawstring pants, band-collared shirts, and button-down cotton jackets; the women wear traditional batik, sarong-like dresses. The end result is a multicultural dining experience—in terms of food as well as ambience.

location **Tokyo, Japan**

architect **APS Design Office**

interior designer **Margaret O'Brien; O'Brien & Associates Design, Inc.**

photography **Mayumi Chiba**

open kitchen servicing the entire 8,500-square-foot enterprise. It was resolved through the implementation of a complex dumbwaiter system and prep stations situated on each floor. Universal among the many Asian cultures rep-

BELOW *Teak chairs and tables were purchased in Bali and carved by hand.*

ABOVE *Asian artifacts carry tradition throughout the elegant, yet earthy restaurant design.* **LEFT** *Exterior seating is available on multiple levels.*

year designed **1995**
square feet **8,500**
budget **$3.5 million**
seats **300**
check average **US $25**

143

A40-foot-high, woven wall emanates the powerful, tactile imagery of weaving as it flows through Americas; a creative endeavor inspired by the synthesis of South, Central, and North-American cultures with a Pre-Colombian influence. The ancient mysticism of Mayan, Aztec, and Incan cultures which predominated these lands is conceptualized throughout the 8,700-square-foot space, where arches, doorways, and sacred niches formed by moss-covered, sculpted rocks greet the dining adventurer. The journey through the terrain of the Americas progresses from the Tapas Bar, where tables resembling huge, entangled branches correlate imaginatively with the rain-forest fantasy above. Accessed by an open steel staircase, the 200-seat dining

ABOVE   *Primary colors add to the visual orchestration of rain-forest imagery.*

room creates a fantastic balance between jungle imagery and architectural intervention. Structural columns and pilasters transformed into fluid shapes and covered in mosaic tiles form "trees," while "leaves" of oxidized copper branch out from the tree's main arms. Ruby and emerald detailing, gold-leafed sculptural skylights, and embellished bronze door handles weave elements of traditional craftsmanship into the modern dining experience of Americas.

location **Houston, Texas**

architect/interior designer **Jordan Mozer & Associates, Ltd.**

photography **David Clifton**

ABOVE *A woven wall based at the first-floor Tapas bar extends upward and carries the theme into the dining room.* LEFT *Rope bridges found in the jungle served as inspiration for the open, steel staircase.*

year designed **1994**

square feet **8,700**

budget **$650,000**

seats **240**

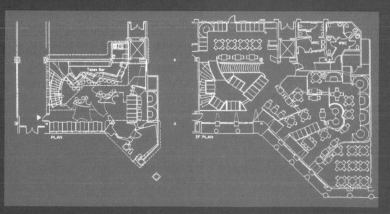

n the ecologically themed Yellow Giraffe, the quiet, rich beauty of the Brazilian rain forest meets the contemporary efficiency of a fast-food eatery. Walls are painted in a prehistoric cave-drawing style, while chairs are designed to resemble the elongated neck of a giraffe. Natural materials predominate and a mirror near the restaurant's entrance reflects trees from the front of the building. Water imagery is created by the use of shimmering, blue mosaic tile, and the lighting system is designed to enhance the illusion of natural illumination. Electronically controlled sun filters

ABOVE *The entry is lined with mirrors to expand the sense of space, and the blue, mosaic floor is constructed of a glass-paste tile made locally in Brazil.* OPPOSITE *The naturalistic ambience is completed by skylights, which illuminate stucco-treated walls.*

are employed during the day; at night there is intentional chromaticity via fixtures that give off intense light along with closed and spot foci. The resulting restaurant manages to be stylish, primitive, and alluring.

location **São Paulo, Brazil**

architect **Arthur de Mattos Casas**

photography **Tuca Reinés**

year designed **1993**
square feet **1,000**
seats **90**

ABOVE *Photographs of animals in their Kenyan habitats are placed above banquette seating in the second-floor dining room.* **RIGHT** *A metal stairwell lends a contemporary edge to the jungle theme.*

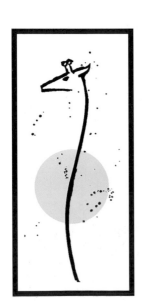

ABOVE *Free-standing light*
fixtures accentuate tables of
ivory wood and metal.

El Divino

Dali, Gaudí, and Miró, masters of Catalan art, are paid tribute in this neo-Gothic residence transformed into a chic restaurant. Located on the *Avenida de la Reforma*, the most celebrated thoroughfare in Mexico City, El Divino entertains a lively bar crowd of up to 500 and seats 240 within its six dining rooms. Intensive restoration of the dilapidated structure (it had been abandoned for 25 years) included the removal of walls, the installation of air-conditioning ducts, and new wooden floors. Interiors display a sophisticated restoration of the building's traditional grandeur while recreating a surrealistic atmosphere, with stained-glass windows imparting a cathedral-like drama to the stone walls of the castle structure. The

ABOVE *A 50-foot mural pays homage to Dali in the dining room, where chairs and tables are the only contemporary element in this turn-of-the-century structure.*

LEFT *The vaulted, neo-Gothic entryway gives the illusion of a canopy, tent-like and suspended from a bundled mast.*

selection of decorative elements was based on respect for the building's tradition and heritage, using velvet draperies that recall the rich colors of Catalan banners. Gigantic mirrors, huge draperies, and snake-shaped, brass door-pulls underscore the use of ornamentation in the works of the Spanish Surrealists. El Divino's masterful interpretation in restaurant design has earned accolades in the design field, including the Best of Competition Award bestowed by the IIDA in 1995.

location **Mexico City, Mexico**

architect and interior designer **Carlos and Gerard Pascal; Pascal Arquitectos**

photography **Victor Benitez**

ABOVE *The castle-like house possesses structural elements similar to a cathedral, in which stained-glass windows emit a radiant, blue light.*

OPPOSITE *The building was restored to reveal the light hues of the original stone structure.* RIGHT *A wrought-iron dragon recreated from Gaudí's Casa Guell in Barcelona embellishes the entrance.* BELOW *Illumination which highlights art in the style of Catalan painters creates a surrealistic atmosphere.*

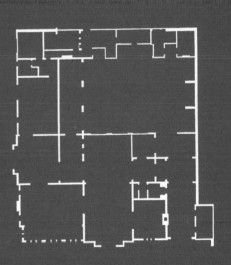

year designed **1994**
square feet **16,500**
seats **240**
design budget **$2 million**

153

Whimsical design, eccentric details, and bright colors combine to create the atmosphere of a European circus in this appropriately named Italian eatery. Osteria Del Circo is a spacious, 4,200-square-foot restaurant with a large bar area, two dining rooms, open kitchen, and take-out facility. Circus elements, which proliferate throughout the space, are most evident in a ring-patterned car-

pet, harlequin-themed bar front, and star-reflected lighting. All of the restaurant's joyful design touches are enhanced by innovative illumination. Behind the parachute material of an imaginary tent, special-effect lighting creates the illusion of characters in motion. Brightly colored stains on high quality woods—burgundy

ABOVE *High ceilings, embellished with parachute fabric in bright hues, convey the sense of being under the "big top."*

on mahogany and golden orange on sycamore—add to the festive ambience. An exhibition kitchen, clad in vibrant tiles, cool steel, and warm wood emphasizes that the preparation of food is a performance in and of itself. And for those who like to be at the center of the culinary action, Osteria Del Circo offers an unusual dining feature; a private glass-enclosed dining room in the kitchen which is known as *Gabbia del Leone,* Italian for "The Lion's Cage."

location **New York, New York**

interior designer **Adam D. Tihany International**

photography **Peter Paige**

ABOVE *The world of the "saltimbanco," or devilish clown is highlighted by theatrical spots on clown etchings.* **LEFT** *The blue canopy of the exhibition kitchen recalls the proscenium arch where circus performers make their grand entrances.* **RIGHT** *The shadow of a revolving monkey "pours" champagne into this sculpted creature's glass.*

year designed **1995**

square feet **4,200**

seats **200**

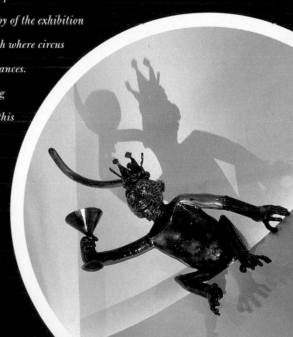

h

for holly

Planet Hollywood

Jekyll & Hyde Club

Sullivan's

The Night Gallery Cafe

RaV

ood

Planet Hollywood

When Planet Hollywood was launched in New York in 1991, it was the world's only dining experience inspired by the worlds of film and television. Jointly owned by four celebrity principals—Arnold Schwarzenegger, Sylvester Stallone, Bruce Willis, and Demi Moore—the restaurant today is a spectacular landmark in cities throughout the world. Storefronts are converted into dramatic cinematic presences, through which patrons feel as if they are making their own Hollywood entrance. Adorned with movie memorabilia including Dorothy's dress from *The Wizard of Oz*, and the Batman suit from *Batman Forever*, Planet Hollywood is paradise for the movie buff. As lighting is of primary importance in Hollywood production, illumination approximates theatrical display in the restaurants when used to create a spaceship observation deck or to introduce a light show. Video screens and dioramas are choreographed to movie clips with soundtrack backgrounds, creating a dramatic amphitheater of sight and sound. Through its multitude of international locations, Planet Hollywood brings the glamour and the thrill of Hollywood cinema to the starry-eyed diner.

ABOVE RIGHT *The earth-like, exterior sphere rises 110 feet above a body of water and is accessed by an escalator.* **LEFT** *A model train launches the dining experience, beginning at the blue-tiled bar which recreates an undersea adventure.*

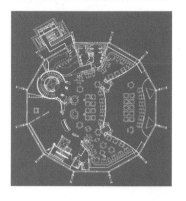

RIGHT *Merchandise is displayed in a structure that creates the image of a spacecraft observation deck.* BELOW *The multileveled dining room is decorated with intriguing movie artifacts suspended from the ceiling.*

ABOVE *The trademark mural of the Hollywood hills showcases a plethora of movie-star faces.*

ABOVE *The dining area resembles a narrow, submarine portal which leads to an observation room.* **LEFT** *A life-sized statue of "The Terminator" surveys dining tables.*

ABOVE *The facade in Hong Kong combines the trademark earth with a dragon sculpture.* **RIGHT** *Movie memorabilia are exhibited in museum-style display cases.*

LONDON

ABOVE *In London, the spectacular show-lights of the signage create a striking contrast with the old-world-style structure.* RIGHT *A model of Star Trek's U.S.S. Enterprise and a lunar module are suspended from the ceiling.*

FAR LEFT *A mannequin of Sylvester Stallone in* Demolition Man *floats above the mural wall's video screen.* LEFT *The dragon facade brings sci-fi adventure to San Diego.*

SAN DIEGO

RENO

BELOW *Beside gambling tables, a wall illuminated by pink neon resembles a movie star's sunglasses.* RIGHT *Dining tables are surrounded by glass-enclosed movie artifacts.*

BELOW *Banquette seating and palm trees are reminiscent of Hollywood movie-star glamour.* RIGHT *A video porthole is framed by life-sized Batman and Robin figures in glass enclosures.*

CHICAGO

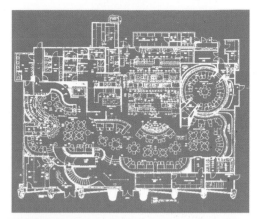

SANTA ANA

WASHINGTON, D.C.

ABOVE LEFT *Santa Ana's exterior resembles a spectacular Hollywood-style, movie marquee.* **ABOVE RIGHT** *An alien sculpture from the film, Aliens, is perched on a ledge above the dramatic curvature of the bar and dining area.*

location **Santa Ana**

architect **James Whaley Architect**

interior designer **Hatch Design**

photography **©Norman McGrath**

celebrity photography **©Planet Hollywood Corp.**

LEFT *A wall panel displaying continents evokes Planet Hollywood's global appeal.*

Bizarre and unusual, theatrical effects of the Jekyll and Hyde Clubs in upper and lower Manhattan produce a phantasmagoric haunt through history. The flagship restaurant's facade displays ruins, fallen icons, skeletons, and incorporates transparent glass and a talking head of Ramses to engage passersby. A classic, English gentleman's club decor sets the theme—a ghost-like aura which is carried upstairs with materials such as mahogany, limestone, wrought iron, elaborate moldings, and sumptuous fabrics. Guests may take part in a séance in the grand, turn-of-the-century-style, second-floor library, or sit beside the horrible remains of experiments gone bad in the Victorian doctor's laboratory recreated on the third floor. The fourth-floor mausoleum, complete with a gruesome collection of crypts and coffins, leads to the observatory; an astronomic perch which houses a stage that is raised and lowered so that patrons on various floors can be intimately entertained. The smaller, sister location downtown extends this macabre conviviality within a pub atmosphere.

location   **Upper Manhattan and Greenwich Village; New York City**
architect   **Rosenberg Kolb Architects, PC**
architect and interior designer   **Rosenberg Kolb Architects, P.C.
with Eerie Entertainment**
photography   **Bob Krasner and Nathan Sayers**

LEFT *At the upper Manhattan location,
the exterior is constructed from custom-
cast GFRC panels.*

Jekyll and Hyde Club

location **Upper Manhattan**
year designed **1994**
square feet **13,000**
seats **230**

LEFT *A talking statue of Zeus, "living" portraits, and an organ-player corpse animate the five-story space.*

LEFT *Tables lined with banquette seating are illuminated by sconces in the form of skulls and theatrical spots.*

RIGHT *Animatronic monstrosities, in a setting of wrought-iron railings and a spiral staircase, create a Gothic atmosphere.*

LEFT Interactive special effects, such as this body that falls through a trap door, are operated from a behind-the-scenes control room. BELOW The Jekyll and Hyde Club in lower Manhattan provides outdoor seating, with an awning that welcomes explorers and mad scientists.

location **Greenwich Village**
year designed **1993**
square feet **2,500**
seats **150**

LEFT In the dining area horrific images collide, from Frankenstein's monster to a bullet-riddled biplane.

167

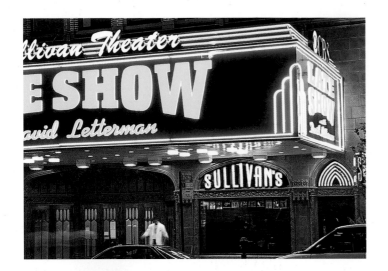

Sullivan's

and quieter conversations are likely to be in order. To maintain a nostalgic sensibility, sprinkler pipes are exposed and the HVAC is hidden behind ornamental wooden grilles.

The days of early television are alive and well at Sullivan's Restaurant and Broadcast Lounge. This 1950s-era bar/restaurant, named after Ed Sullivan, is located downstairs from David Letterman's soundstage (sight of the original "Ed Sullivan Show"). Paying homage to the golden age of television, neon signage on the exterior approximates the original sign, and a dark mahogany bar is reminiscent of the Irish bar that once occupied this 5,200-square-foot space. Televisions frame the upstairs bar, goldfish swim in a fishbowl that resembles a TV, and half-round banquettes dominate the second floor. Acoustics are designed to be reflective in the downstairs bar, and more subdued upstairs where dinner

ABOVE LEFT *The restaurant is located within the landmark Ed Sullivan Theater, currently the home of* The Late Show with David Letterman. **ABOVE** *Snapshots of great moments in the history of television add to the nostalgic setting.* **OPPOSITE** *The bar's mirror, framed with a reproduction of the curtain from the Ed Sullivan theater, is 25 feet high and 50 feet wide.*

Decorative elements include a reproduction of
Ed Sullivan's original red curtain, vintage music
stands, and an interior marquee. The theatricality of food and design is especially fitting in
light of Sullivan's location.

location   **New York, New York**

architect and interior designer   **James Biber, AIA; Pentagram Architecture**

photography   **Peter Margonelli, ©Peter Mauss/Esto**

ABOVE *The upper floor is lined with "Hollywoods," classic half-round banquettes.*

LEFT *The grand staircase ascends to the balcony, which is lined with the best seats and tables in the house.*

BELOW *Lighting is designed to mimic the aura of a stage.*

year designed **1996**
square feet **5,200**
seats **125**
check average **US $21.50**

The Night Gallery Cafe

The Night Gallery Cafe is based on the scary television show, "The Night Gallery," that used a horrific painting to introduce each episode. Maintaining the spirit of its namesake, this eatery creates the atmosphere of a television studio set with gruesome paintings and sculptures situated throughout the space. The restaurant's 100-foot frontage completely folds away, thus creating outdoor dining as well as an interior that beckons to pedestrians. This was especially important since the restaurant needed to avoid being overshadowed by the three-story health club upstairs. Inside the cafe, the space is organized around a race-track-shaped bar with seating for 50. A prodigious array of audio/video equipment includes a nine-screen video wall and 24 individual monitors. An open kitchen is located

ABOVE *Theatrical spots highlight the bar which is overseen by statues of horrific characters.* LEFT *The Night Gallery Cafe's exterior unfolds to accommodate outdoor seating.*

on the southern end of the space, new ducts
and wiring are exposed below the ceiling slab,
and theater lighting hangs from a steel pipe
grid. The overall effect is spooky, otherworldly,
and hair-raisingly fun.

year designed **1995**
square feet **5,400**
seats **225**

location **New York, New York**
architect **Rosenberg Kolb Architects, P.C.**
interior designer **Rosenberg Kolb
Architects, P.C. with Eerie Entertainment**
photography **Bob Krasner and
Nathan Sayers**

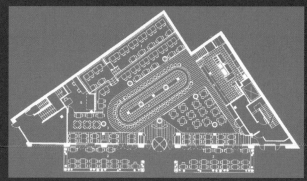

BELOW *Cadaverous faces lend a ghastly
dimension to famous paintings.*

Directory

RESTAURANTS

Airstreams Roadside Cafe
51 East Main Street
Avon, Connecticut 06001
Tel: (203) 677-9026

Alcatraz Brewing Company
Circle Centre
49 West Maryland Street
Indianapolis, Indiana 46225
Tel: (317) 464-1430

Americas
Saks Fifth Avenue Pavillion
1800 Post Oak Boulevard
Houston, Texas 77056
Tel: (713) 961-1492

Annette's Diner
Disney World Paris
France
Tel: 011-33-16-030-6030

Brew Moon
114 Broadway, Route One North
Saugus, Massachussets 01906
Tel: (617) 941-BREW

The Bungalow
2441 Coast Highway
Corona del Mar, California
Tel: (714) 673-6585

Café Centro
200 Park Avenue
New York, New York 10036
Tel: (212) 972-7000

Cheesecake Factory
John Hancock Building
875 North Michigan Avenue
Chicago, Illinois 60611
Tel: (312) 337-1101

Chimayo Grill
327 Newport Center Drive
Newport Beach, California 92660
Tel: (714) 640-2700

Country Star
1000 Universal Center Drive
Universal City, California 91608
Tel: (818) 762-3939

Dive! Las Vegas
Fashion Show Mall
3200 Las Vegas Boulevard South
Las Vegas, Nevada 89109
Tel: (702) 369-3483

Dive! Los Angeles
Century City Shopping
Center & Marketplace
10250 Santa Monica Boulevard
Los Angeles, California 90067
Tel: (310) 788-DIVE

The Double A
331 Sandoval Street
Sante Fe, New Mexico 87501
Tel: (505) 982-8999

El Divino
Paseo De La Reforma 483
Col. Chauhtemoc tbd
Mexico City 06500, Mexico
Tel: 011-52-5-286-0066

Hang Town Grill
9828 Great Hills Trail
Austin, Texas 78759
Tel: (512) 349-9944

Harley Davidson Cafe
1370 Avenue of the Americas
New York, New York 10019
Tel: (212) 245-6000

Heartland Brewery
35 Union Square West
New York, New York 10003
Tel: (212) 645-3400

Hi-Life Restaurant & Lounge
1340 First Avenue
New York, New York 10021
Tel: (212) 249-3600

Jekyll & Hyde Club
1409 Avenue of the Americas
New York, New York 10019
Tel: (212) 541-9517

Jekyll & Hyde Pub
91 Seventh Avenue South
New York, New York 10014
Tel: (212) 989-7701

Joe's American Bar & Grill
North Shore Shopping Center
Route 128 and 114
Peabody, Massachussets
Tel: (508) 532-9500

King Crab Lounge
100 West Broadway
Long Beach, California 90802
Tel: (310) 432-7463

Mediterraneo
366 Greenwich Avenue
Greenwich, Connecticut 06830
Tel: (203) 629-4747

Mickey Mantle's
42 Central Park South
New York, New York 10019
Tel: (212) 688-7777

Monsoon Cafe
Tokyo
Japan
Tel: 011-81-3-5467-5221

Monte's
164 Sloane Street
London SW1X 9QB
England
Tel: 011-171-44-245-0896/7

Motown Cafe
104 West 57th Street
New York, New York 10019
Tel: (212) 581-8030

The Night Gallery Cafe
117 Seventh Avenue South
New York, New York 10014
Tel: (212) 675-5244

Oceana
55 East 54th Street
New York, New York 10022
Tel: (212) 759-5941

Official All Star Cafe
1540 Broadway
New York, New York 10036
Tel: (212) 840-TEAM

Osteria del Circo
120 West 55th Street
New York, New York 10019
Tel: (212) 265-3636

Pete & Martys
Corporate Office
24 Duncan Street, Suite 500
Toronto, Ontario M5V 2B8
Canada
Tel: (416) 977-2670

Planet Hollywood, Beverly Hills
9560 Wilshire Boulevard
Beverly Hills, California 90212
Tel: (310) 275-7828

Planet Hollywood, Chicago
633 North Wells Street
Chicago, Illinois 60610
Tel: (312) 266-7827

Planet Hollywood, Hong Kong
3 Canton Road Harbour City
Tsim Sha Tsui, Hong Kong
Tel: 011-852-2377-7888

Planet Hollywood, Lake Tahoe
Caesar's Lake Tahoe
55 Highway 50
Stateline, Nevada 89449
Tel: (702) 588-7828

Planet Hollywood, London
13 Coventry Street
London W1V 7FE
England
Tel: 011-171-44-287-1000

Planet Hollywood, New York
140 West 57th Street
New York, New York 10019
Tel: (212) 333-7827

Planet Hollywood, Orlando
1506 East Buena Vista Drive
Lake Buena Vista, Florida 32830
Tel: (407) 827-7827

Planet Hollywood, Reno
206 North Virginia Street
Reno, Nevada 89501
Tel: (702) 323-7837

Planet Hollywood, San Diego
197 Horton Plaza
San Diego, California 92101
Tel: (619) 702-7827

Planet Hollywood, Santa Ana
1641 West Sunflower Road
Santa Ana, California 92704
Tel: (714) 668-7585

Planet Hollywood, Washington, D.C.
1101 Pennsylvania Avenue, N.W.
Washington, D.C. 20004
Tel: (202) 783-7827

Rainforest Cafe
The Disney Village Marketplace
Walt Disney World Resort
Lake Buena Vista, Florida 32830
Tel: (407) 827-8500

Remi
145 West 53rd Street
New York, New York 10019
Tel: (212) 581-4242

Road Trip
54A Canal Street
Boston, Massachussets 02114
Tel: (617) 720-2889

Route 66
33 West Sunrise Highway
Merrick, New York 11566
Tel: (516) 477-8550

Star Bar
660 West 6th Street
Austin, Texas 78701
Tel: (512) 477-8550

Surf 'n' Turf
Shikoku Island
Matsuyama
Japan

Sullivan's Restaurant and Broadcast Lounge
1697 Broadway
New York, New York 10019
Tel: (212) 541-1697

Sullivan's Steakhouse
300 Colorado Street
Austin, Texas 78701
Tel: (512) 495-6504

Tapika
950 Eighth Avenue
New York, New York 10019
Tel: (212) 597-3737

Torre di Pisa
19 West 44th Street
New York, New York 10036
Tel: (212) 398-4400

Typhoon Brewery
22 East 54th Street
New York, New York 10022
Tel: (212) 754-9006

Yellow Giraffe
Praca Vilaboim, 73
Higienopolis
São Paulo, CEP 01415-000
Brazil
Tel: 011-55-11-66-9633

Zest Cantina
Campari Building 6
2F 1-6-8 Jinnan
Shibuya-ku, Tokyo
Japan
Tel: 011-81-3-5489-3332

ARCHITECTS & DESIGNERS

Adam D. Tihany International
57 East 11th Street
New York, New York 10003
Tel: (212) 505-2360
Fax: (212) 529-3578

Andrew Young & Company, Inc.
33 West 67th Street
New York, New York 10023
Tel: (212) 580-1422
Fax: (212) 580-1012

APS Design Office
154 1-39-16 Remonnoki, #1F
Shimouma Setagayaku
Tokyo
Japan
Tel: 011-81-3-5430-3131
Fax: 011-81-3-5430-3160

Aumiller Youngquist, P.C.
Bill Aumiller
111 East Busse Avenue, Suite 603
Mt. Prospect, Illinois 60056
Tel: (847) 253-3761
Fax: (847) 394-8320

Back Bay Restaurant Group
Michael McKay
284 Newbury Street
Boston, Massachussets 02115
Tel: (617) 425-5204
Fax: (617) 425-5222

Brantner Design Associates
Cheryl Brantner
2940 Nebraska Avenue
Santa Monica, California 90404
Tel: (310) 264-5450
Fax: (310) 264-5452

CORE
Peter F. Hapstak III, AIA
Ghassan Abukurah
Jeff Barber
Dale Stewart
Dom Vokic
1010 Wisconsin Avenue NW, #405
Washington, D.C. 20007
Tel: (202) 466-6116
Fax: (202) 466-6235

Cuningham Group
Tod Elkins
Kevin Thode
201 Main Street SE, Suite 325
Minneapolis, MN 55414
Tel: (612) 379-3400
Fax: (612) 379-4400

Darlow Christ Architects Inc.
Peter G. Darlow
Catherine A. Christ
Paul Michael Scanlon
Mary Jo Verde
2326 Massachusetts Avenue
Cambridge, Massachusetts 02140
Tel: (617) 497-9191
Fax: (617) 497-9090

Dick Clark Architecture
Dick Clark
Jay Corder
Heidi Goebel
Patrick Ousey
207 West 4th Street
Austin, Texas 78701
Tel: (512) 472-4980
Fax: (512) 472-4991

DiLeonardo International, Inc.
Robert J. DiLeonardo
2350 Post Road, Suite 1
Warwick, Rhode Island 02886
Tel: (401) 732-2900
Fax: (401) 732-5315

Eerie Entertainment
D.R. Finley
91 Seventh Avenue South
New York, New York 10014
Tel: (212) 989-3743
Fax: (212) 989-9060

Engstrom Design Group
1414 Fourth Street, Suite 200
San Rafael, California 94901
Tel: (415) 454-2277

Frank Gehry & Associates, Inc.
1520B Culver Field Boulevard
Santa Monica, California 90404
Tel: (310) 828-6088

Frederick Brush Design Associates
53 East Avenue
Norwalk, Connecticut 06851
Tel: (203) 846-0828
Fax: (203) 846-2570

Hatch Design Group
Jeffrey D. Hatch
198-D Airport Loop Drive
Costa Mesa, California 92626
Tel: (714) 979-8385
Fax: (714) 979-6430

**Haverson Architecture and
Design, P.C.**
Jay M. Haverson
289 Greenwich Avenue
Greenwich, Connecticut 06830
Tel: (203) 629-8300
Fax: (203) 629-8399

**Haverson/Rockwell Architecture,
P.C.**
*(see Haverson Architecture and Design,
P.C. and Rockwell Group)*

Hirsch-Bedner Associates
Michael Bedner
3216 Nebraska Avenue
Santa Monica, California 90404
Tel: (310) 829-9087
Fax: (310) 453-1182

James Whaley Architect
3198-D Airport Loop Drive
Costa Mesa, California 92626
Tel: (714) 662-2474
Fax: (714) 979-6430

Jon Greenberg Associates
29355 Northwestern Highway
Southfield, Michigan 48034
Tel: (810) 355-0890

Jordan Mozer & Associates, Ltd.
320 West Ohio Street 7th floor
Chicago, Illinois 60610
Tel: (312) 397-1133
Fax: (312) 397-1233

Judd Brown Design, Inc.
Michael Gillespie
Steven McMahon
Mark Palazio
Lisa Simeone
647 Jefferson Boulevard
Warwick, Rhode Island 02886
Tel: (401) 738-8624
Fax: (410) 732-4730

Lawrence Berkley & Associates
137 North Wabash Avenue
Chicago, Illinois 60602
Tel: (312) 332-1823

Meisel Associates, Ltd.
Joe A. Meisel III
800 North Clark
Chicago, Illinois 60610
Tel: (312) 664-4814
Fax: (312) 664-1861

Morris Nathanson Design Inc.
Morris Nathanson
Blase Gallo
163 Exchange Street
Pawtucket, Rhode Island 02860
Tel: (401) 723-3800
Fax: (401) 723-3813

O'Brien & Associates Design, Inc.
Margaret O'Brien
222 Washington Avenue #12
Santa Monica, California 90403
Tel: (310) 458-9177
Fax: (310) 451-0812

Pascal Arquitectos
Carlos Pascal
Gerard Pascal
Atcaltunco 99, Tecamachalco
EDO, Mexico, C.P. 53970, Mexico
Tel: 011-525-294-2371

Pentagram Architecture
James Biber, AIA
Michael Zweck-Bronner
204 Fifth Avenue
New York, New York 10010
Tel: (212) 683-7000
Fax: (212) 532-0181

Rockwell Group
David Rockwell
5 Union Square West
New York, New York 10003
Tel: (212) 463-0334
Fax: (212) 463-0335

Rosenberg Kolb Architects
Eric Rosenberg
Michele Kolb
164 East 91 Street
New York, New York 10128
Tel: (212) 996-3099
Fax: (212) 996-3097

Sady S. Hayashida
Sady S. Hayashida
Jeff Ellis
832 Bancroft Way
Berkeley, California 94710
Tel: (510) 644-2491

Saubot Et Jullien Architecture
12 Avenue Jean Jaures
Montrouge 92120
France

**Studio Arthur de Mattos Casas
Arquitetura Design**
Arthur de Mattos Casas
Alameda Ministro Rocha
Azevedo 1052
São Paulo, 01410002
Brazil
Tel: 011-55-11-2826311
Fax: 011-55-11-2826608

To Design
Barbara Hofling
424 Marine Street
Point Richmond, California 94801
Tel: (510) 236-5717

Tony Chi & Associates
Tony Chi
Noel Bernardo
215 Park Avenue South, Suite 702
New York, New York 10003
Tel: (212) 353-8860
Fax: (212) 673-1454

Wimberly Allison Tong & Goo
2nd Floor, Waldron House
57 Old Church Street
London SW3 5BS
England
Tel: 011-171-376-3260
Fax: 011-171-376-3193

GRAPHIC DESIGNERS

Adrienne Weiss Corporation
12100 Wilshire Boulevard,
Suite 1450
Los Angeles, California 90025
Tel: (310) 979-4800
Fax: (310) 979-4803

i Level
Mike Fink
100 North Fourth Street
Clarksville, Tennessee 37040
Tel: (615) 551-3355
Fax: (615) 553-8977

Oak
Jonathan Baird
31 St. James Avenue
Boston, Massachussetts 02116
Tel: (617) 426-5090
Fax: (617) 338-2273

On The Edge
Jeff Gasper
505 30th Street, Suite 211
Newport Beach, California 92663
Tel: (714) 723-4330
Fax: (714) 673-2263

Patricia Spencer Design
205 East 78th Street
New York, New York 10021
Tel: (212) 517-2029
Fax: (212) 561-7556

Pentagram Design
Michael Bierut
Emily Hayes
204 Fifth Avenue
New York, New York 10010
Tel: (212) 683-7000
Fax: (212) 532-0181

plus designs inc.
Anita Meyer
25 Dry Dock Avenue
Boston, Massachussets 02210
Tel: (617) 478-2470
Fax: (617) 478-2471

PHOTOGRAPHERS

Anton Grassl Photography
259 A Street, Suite 27
Boston, Massachussets 02210
Tel: (617) 261-7678

Architectural Photography
William T. Smith
40 Dudley Street
Reading, Massachussets 01867
Tel: (617) 944-5841

Victor Benitez
Guanajuato 130
Col. Roma D.F. 06700
Mexico
Tel: 011-525-574-8032
Fax: 011-525-584-7571

Cameron Carothers Photography
1340 Glenwood Road #8
Glendale, California 91201
Tel: (818) 246-1057

Mayumi Chiba
202-7-9-17 Ebaha Shinagawaka
Tokyo
Japan
Tel: 011-81-35-702-2145

David Clifton
2637 West Winnemac Avenue
Chicago, Illinois 60625
Tel: (312) 334-4346
Fax: (312) 275-4175

Dana Wheelock Photography
800 Washington Avenue North
Minneapolis, Minnesota 55414
Tel: (612) 333-5110
Fax: (612) 646-0023

Dennis Anderson Photography
48 Lucky Drive
Grenbrae, California 94904
Tel: (415) 927-3530
Fax: (415) 927-2659

Doug Snower Photography
2711 West Fulton Street
Chicago, Illinois 60612
Tel: (773) 265-1500

Douglas Hill Photography
2324 Moreno Drive
Los Angeles, California 90039
Tel: (213) 660-0681

Esto Photographics
Peter Mauss
222 Valley Place
Mamaroneck, New York 10543
Tel: (914) 927-3530
Fax: (914) 927-2659

The Futran Studio
Eric Futran
3454 North Bell Avenue
Chicago, Illinois 60618
Tel: (312) 525-5020
Fax: (312) 525-1305

Greg Murphey Studio
RR2 Box 191
Trafalgar, Indiana 46181
Tel: (812) 597-0113

Karl Herrmann
5870 Green Valley Circle, #306
Culver City, California 90230
Tel: (310) 337-9809

Jud Haggard Photography
4620 Holt Street
Bellaire, Texas 77401
Tel: (713) 667-0092

Bob Krasner
Eerie Entertainment
91 Seventh Avenue South
New York, New York 10014
Tel: (212) 989-3743
Fax: (212) 989-9060

Peter Margonelli
524 Broadway, #603
New York, New York 10012
Tel: (212) 941-0380
Fax: (212) 941-8997

Michael Moran Photography
Michael Moran
245 Mulberry Street, #14
New York, New York 10012
Tel: (212) 226-2596
Fax: (212) 219-1566

Norman McGrath
164 West 79th Street
New York, new York 10024
Tel: (212) 799-6422

Paul Bardagjy Photography
4111B Marathon Boulevard
Austin, Texas 78756
Tel: (512) 452-9636
Fax: (512) 452-6425

Paul Warchol Photography
133 Mulberry Street
New York, New York 10013
Tel: (212) 431-3461
Fax: (212) 274-1953

Peter Paige Photography
269 Parkside Avenue
Harrington Park, New Jersey 07640
Tel: (201) 767-3150

Reinés Studio
Tuca Reinés
Rua Emanuel Kant 58
São Paulo
Brazil
Tel: 011-55-11-3061-9127

Tony Rinaldo Photography
33 Riverdale Avenue
Cambridge, Massachussets 02140
Tel: (617) 576-3001
Fax: (617) 757-3115

Roy Wright Photography
55 Van Dam Street
New York, New York 10013
Tel: (212) 645-4558

Nathan Sayers
93 Eagle Street
Brooklyn, New York 11222
Tel: (718) 349-1911

Scott Rothwall Photography
25 Fremont Street
Newport Beach, California 92663
Tel: (714) 673-3023
Fax: (714) 673-3025

Tim Street-Porter
2074 Watsonia Terrace
Los Angeles, California 90068
Tel: (213) 876-8030
Fax: (213) 876-8795

Tim Lee Photography
2 Zachary Lane
New Milford, Connecticut 06776
Tel: (860) 355-4661
Fax: (860) 350-3526

Warren Jagger Photography
150 Chestnut Street
Providence, Rhode Island 02903
Tel: (401) 351-7366
Fax: (401) 421-7567

YUM Incorporated
Ron Manville Photography
202 Park Avenue
Cranston, Rhode Island 02905
Tel: (401) 785-3030

Index